The evolving role of nation-building in US foreign policy

MANCHESTER
1824

Manchester University Press

The evolving role of nation-building in US foreign policy

Lessons learned, lessons lost

Thomas R. Seitz

Manchester University Press

Published by Manchester University Press
Altrincham Street, Manchester M1 7JA, UK
www.manchesteruniversitypress.co.uk

British Library Cataloguing-in-Publication Data is available

Library of Congress Cataloging-in-Publication Data is available

ISBN 978 1 7849 9113 5 *paperback*

First published by Manchester University Press in hardback 2012

This paperback edition first published 2015

The publisher has no responsibility for the persistence or accuracy of URLs for any external or third-party internet websites referred to in this book, and does not guarantee that any content on such websites is, or will remain, accurate or appropriate.

Printed by Lightning Source

For Stephanie, who has given me so much.

Contents

List of abbreviations

1290-d	NSC Action ordered in December 1954 to strengthen developing societies against communist subversion. Redesignated as OISP in 1957.
ANZUS	Australia – New Zealand – United States
CI	Counterinsurgency
CIA	Central Intelligence Agency
CIDG	Citizens' Irregular Defense Group
CoCom	Coordinating Committee for Multilateral Export Controls
CORDS	Civil Operations Revolutionary (later, 'Rural') Development Support
CPSU	Communist Party of the Soviet Union
DLF	Development Loan Fund
ECA	Economic Cooperation Administration
ECA	Economic Cooperation Act of 1948, *also known as* the Marshall Plan
ECA	Economic Cooperation Agency
EPU	European Payments Union
ERP	European Recovery Act
ESF	Economic Support Funds
FMF	Foreign Military Financing
FMS	Foreign Military Sales cash and credit programs
FOA	Foreign Operations Administration
IBRD	International Bank for Reconstruction and Development, *also known as* the World Bank
ICA	International Cooperation Administration
IDAB	International Development Advisory Board
IDF	International Development Fund
IMAF	International Military Assistance Force
IMET	International Military Education and Training
IMF	International Monetary Fund
JCS	Joint Chiefs of Staff
MAP	Military Assistance Program
MDAA	Mutual Defense Assistance Act of 1949
MSA	Mutual Security Act of 1951
MSA	Mutual Security Agency

MSAP	Mutual Security Assistance Pact of 1954
MSOP	Mutual Security Operations Plan
NATO	North Atlantic Treaty Organization
NIE	National Intelligence Estimate
NLF	National Liberation Front, *also known as* Viet Cong, the communist insurgency in South Vietnam
NSAM	National Security Action Memorandum
NSC	National Security Council
NSZ	National Security Zone
OCB	Operations Coordinating Board of the NSC
OISP	Overseas Internal Security Program
OSANSA	Office of the Special Assistant for National Security Affairs
PKI	Communist Party of Indonesia
PPC	Policy Planning Council
PPS	Policy Planning Staff, US State Department, *also known as* Policy Planning Council
PRC	People's Republic of China
PRT	Provincial Reconstruction Team
SEATO	South East Asia Treaty Organization
SSA	Security Supporting Assistance
STEM	Special Technical and Economic Missions Program
SUNFED	Special United Nations Fund for Economic Development
USAID	US Agency for International Development
USIA	United States Information Agency
USOIDP	United States Overseas Internal Defense Program
USSOCOM	US Special Operations Command
USSR	Union of Soviet Socialist Republics, *also known as* Soviet Union

Acknowledgements

This book would not have been possible without the help of a great number of people and institutions I would like to acknowledge and thank.

Professor Michael K. MccGwire, fellow at Clare Hall, Cambridge and a wise and patient Ph.D. supervisor, provided me with incisive critiques during my time at Cambridge and with superb insights and helpful advice on many occasions since then. Professor Andrew J. Williams has been a friend as well as a wise and gracious mentor since my first postgraduate course, and has commented on this project at various points in its development. Steve Ropp, Julie Reeves, Stephen Chan, Steve and Tammy Biddle, Chester Pach, Bud Moore, George Oliver, Steve Courtney and many other friends and colleagues contributed comments, criticisms and insights throughout the development of this book, and I am grateful to you all.

I would also like to thank Silvana Dean and Joan Brownell for their valuable help and advice. Regina Greenwell at the Lyndon B. Johnson Presidential Library and particularly David Haight at the Dwight D. Eisenhower Presidential Library were extremely patient and helpful in my quest for the documents that underpin much of this study. Additionally, I would like to express my appreciation to the editors and staff of Manchester University Press for their patience and assistance in seeing this project to its conclusion.

Numerous individuals kindly agreed to grant the interviews that have so enriched this project. Among these, the late Townsend Hoopes, Herbert Brownell, Walt W. Rostow and William Colby were extremely helpful to a young researcher, and expressed genuine interest in this project. I am eternally grateful for their insights and their advice. I am especially grateful for the advice of the late C. Douglas Dillon, who concluded an interview by warning me that it may have still been a bit too early for an exploration of this still sensitive subject. That interview was in 1994, and a great deal has happened since then to underscore the importance of exploring this topic.

I was fortunate to receive valuable support for my research from a range of institutions. I would like to thank Emmanuel College, Cambridge as well as the Cambridge Overseas Trust for their support in the early phases of this research. I am grateful to the Institute for International Legal Studies at the University of the Philippines for granting me a research fellowship, and to Dr. Alex Calata of the Philippine Fulbright Programme for making that research possible. Finally, I gratefully acknowledge the support I received from the Institute for the Study of World Politics and the Lyndon Baines Johnson Foundation.

I am grateful to my daughters, Madeleine and Chloe for gracefully enduring the stresses and strains generated by their father's work and time away at various archives. Most of all, I would like to thank my wife, Stephanie Anderson, for her immeasurable love and support, for our endless discussions on security policy and IR theory, and her comments, advice and exhortations at all stages of this work. She is the ideal wife and colleague rolled into one, and I could not have produced this book without her.

1

Introduction

At the cost of a great deal of treasure and no small amount of blood, the United States of America implemented nation-building and other internal security programmes – that is, programmes designed to strengthen a recipient state's control over its territory, enhance its popular legitimacy and generally improve its stability and viability – in dozens of developing countries at the height of the Cold War. A generation after these policies peaked in scope and intensity, representing what Townsend Hoopes called the 'tidal high water mark' of America's intervention in the internal politics of developing countries, the USA has embarked on similar projects in a range of countries, the most ambitious being in Iraq and Afghanistan.[1]

However, recent studies of America's experience with nation-building neglect these Cold War-era experiences in the developing world, instead looking to the post-Second World War democratization projects that transformed Nazi Germany and Imperial Japan for lessons that might inform today's efforts. Where are the lessons of these other, more relevant cases – costly lessons from efforts by which the USA attempted to build functioning, cohesive and legitimate state institutions in less developed contexts, including new states emerging from the decolonization process? Have these lessons been learned, or have they been lost?

A substantial body of scholarship has argued that American foreign policy-makers have long exacerbated or even created problems of instability and militarism in the Third World through shortsighted 'security assistance' programmes. One central problem such scholars perceive is a tendency on Washington's part to analyse events in the Third World through a Realist lens and formulate its policy responses in accordance with the dictates of the Realist framework of analysis. Security assistance has often been reduced to a policy of 'bolstering dictators' with weaponry or otherwise throwing American support behind leaders whose legitimacy in their own societies is either presumed or considered irrelevant in the greater scheme of East–West power politics. In their blinkered focus on securing recipient states against external threats, American policy-makers ignored the domestic challenges to the security of Third World states and the societies within them. This neglect of their recipients' internal sources of insecurity has left a legacy of regional arms races, militarized dictatorships and entrenched authoritarianism in the developing countries.[2]

Such arguments suffer from their incomplete assessment and analysis of American policies in the developing world. These arguments paint a more accurate portrait of Washington's security assistance approach from the Nixon era onward, but they hardly do justice to the more complex, interventionist approach of presidents Johnson, Kennedy, Eisenhower and even Truman. Contrary to the assertions of some scholars, the USA and other actors were promoting state-building and nation-building efforts in developing countries long before the end of the Cold War.[3] The first two decades of the Cold War embodied an American approach to Third World security that was qualitatively different from policies implemented after 1969. During those early decades, Washington pursued the political development of recipient states as an indispensable element of efforts to contain communism. In America's pursuit of these 'nation-building' and similar political development objectives the primary instrument was foreign aid, non-military as well as military.

This study explores Washington's use of foreign aid as an instrument of security policy in the Cold War. Specifically, it explores the central place of nation-building objectives in Washington's containment efforts in the developing world in the period 1953–68, a period in which American policy-makers came to perceive a clear link between security and stability in the developing world and security at home. The ensuing chapters will illuminate the ways in which the USA constantly pressed aid into service as a weapon, especially during the early decades of the Cold War when the nation was embarked on a broad political development project in the developing regions of the globe.

The purpose of this study is threefold. First, it explores a largely unexplored aspect of US foreign policy – how development assistance became a key element of US security policy. Second, it provides a comprehensive, descriptive analysis of America's evolving Cold War security assistance policies using newly available source materials, evaluating these US policies in terms of their intended aims and critiquing these in terms of their side effects. Third, it challenges Critical Security School scholarship that attributes the failure of US policy-making in this area to its reliance on Realism for its theoretical underpinnings. In this manner, this study illuminates lessons applicable to current policies intended to promote security at home by promoting development and/or stability abroad.

In the process of challenging criticisms focusing on the presumably Realist nature of US policy approaches, this study offers its own criticism of US policy, namely, a critical exploration of the 'universalist' nature of US security assistance policies, the presumed applicability as well as desirability of American ideas, institutions and government ethos in every political, social, cultural and economic context of the developing world. As subsequent chapters will show, just as elements of America's own political culture shaped the conceptualization and formulation of these policies, these same elements effectively undermined their implementation.

The study also demonstrates that Washington's analysis of developing world politics was more sophisticated than is often assumed in retrospective studies. Further, Realist analyses of the Cold War in the developing world and, more importantly, analyses that presume American decision-makers operated within a narrow, Realist framework fail to address three key characteristics of US containment policies. First, aside from helping to secure basing and transit rights for US forces, security assistance was not primarily designed for power projection in the developing world, nor to create 'proxy forces'. Second, Realist analysis fails to address the importance of domestic politics in US decision-making: not only the role of US domestic politics in the foreign policy decision-making process but also the importance of the recipient's internal political situation in American decision-making. Washington did not necessarily view recipients as unified actors. Finally, US policy in the developing world reflected strong ideological motivations that often belied the presumption of rationality so basic to Realist analysis.

The geographic focus of this study is on Southeast Asia, the region to which America's foreign aid policy focus shifted after the Korean War, and the region in which most of Washington's nation-building approaches were developed and tested. While these nation-building efforts were often most intense in Indochina, this study views the Indochina Conflict in the context of regional political developments. As will be shown, Washington devised these programmes on a region-wide, even worldwide basis, and American actions in Indochina were often responses to events transpiring elsewhere in East and Southeast Asia. Vietnam was but one of the dozens of countries in which the USA implemented these measures, but it was the case wherein these efforts went most terribly awry.

The time frame for the study spans the Eisenhower, Kennedy and Johnson presidencies, allowing us to examine the evolution and development of Cold War policy in the context of massive structural change, namely the emergence of dozens of new states from what were colonial possessions of the West. After setting the stage through a theoretical discussion and brief examination of Truman-era policy development, the study begins its in-depth exploration with the launch of the National Security Council (NSC)'s Action 1290-d̲ programme, the Eisenhower administration's attempt at a coordinated, multi-agency institution-building effort designed to meet the communist threat of 'piecemeal conquest' through political aggression. This exploration concludes with Johnson's spring 1968 decision against further escalation of the war in Vietnam, the turning point representing what Townsend Hoopes called the 'tidal high water mark' of US political and military intervention in the developing world.[4] While Johnson's successors continued with nation-building efforts in Indochina during the 1969–75 period, these efforts represent America's efforts to extricate itself from the conflict there, part of Nixon's 'Vietnamization' policy. The Guam Declaration of 1969, or 'Nixon Doctrine', signaled a retreat from the deeply involved, interventionist policies of the 1950s and 1960s. The broad, region-wide, hands-on institution-building approach to containment had given way to the more distant approach that reflected Nixon's analysis of world trends as well as America's broader disillusionment with such interventions. Nixon's approach prevailed, for the most part, until the events and aftermath of 11 September 2001, when American policy-makers seemed to discover anew the conceptual link between security at home and development abroad.

Nation-building was a fundamental, if understated, element of containment from the earliest years of the Cold War and indeed, through most of the twentieth century.[5] As eventually codified in the text of NSC 68 in 1950, American victory in the Cold War would require the building-up of the economic and political strength of the 'free world' to the point where its success would overwhelm the communist bloc economically and undermine it politically through the power of its compelling example. However, in light of the presumed aggressive nature of world communism, these building-up processes would require 'an adequate military shield under which they could develop.'[6]

Beneath the umbrella of American military power and beneath a system of military alliances and 'Mutual Security' pacts, Washington instituted nation-building programmes in dozens of developing countries. During the time covered by this study – roughly from 1948 to 1968 – foreign aid programmes and policies sought to promote economic and political stability in recipient countries, especially those new states emerging from what had been the empires of the great powers. These aid programmes made up the 'internal security' or 'internal defence' element of US policy, representing a relatively small but crucial element of containment overall. However, these programmes, with their interweaving political, economic and military efforts, formed the central project of containment in developing areas.

As the Cold War progressed, American policy-makers recognized that, in the long term, containment in the developing world hinged on the success of these broad, internal defence programmes, for as internal upheaval offered opportunities for communist exploitation, internal stability was essential to protecting societies from communist subversion. As George Kennan had said, communism was like a 'malignant parasite' that fed on 'diseased tissue'.[7] Although a strong sense of universalism certainly permeated containment policies, this was not the driving force behind the internal defence effort. Instead, a sense of urgency drove these nation-building programmes, a sense that the Cold War was not going well, and that time was not on the side of the free world when it came to securing developing regions.

These nation-building and other internal defence programmes addressed what Averell Harriman called the 'politics of despair'.[8] Washington acknowledged the link between the deprivations suffered by a society and its potential for radicalization, and presumed that the communist bloc stood ready and willing to exploit actively and capitalize on such popular radicalism.

The USA was keenly aware of the strategic importance of Western Europe in the event of any East–West conflict and of its vulnerability to communist subversion in its shattered post-war condition. Consequently, American efforts to secure this area from communism featured massive programmes of economic and technical assistance to ease such deprivations while US military commitments and security assistance helped to fend-off aggression and keep domestic communist movements under control. These efforts proved quite successful; the European Recovery Program had a fixed time limit of only a few years and, in the end, finished its work ahead of schedule.

The situation in the developing world was far more challenging. In the early years of the Cold War, the US relied on the European powers to secure their own colonial possessions from presumed communist aggression. However, structural change in the international system was already underway, change that would threaten containment in less developed regions of the periphery. To base containment in developing areas on a presumption that the imperial powers could retain control of their remote possessions was, in effect, to build on sand. The decolonization process, like an incoming tide, shifted the sand and rocked the foundations of containment in the periphery. Washington now had to strike up alliances and security agreements with the governments of these new states in order to secure their regions from communism.

Establishing and maintaining such pacts confronted Washington with a complex set of challenges. The entire Mutual Security concept could be undermined by the endemic economic and political instability that characterized many of these new allies, as security agreements were only as stable as the governments with which they were made. The decolonization process created an ever-broadening array of new states with a range of internal problems qualitatively different from those addressed by the European Recovery Program. In developing areas, the task at hand was not so much one of rebuilding shattered economic and political institutions; but rather one of building them virtually from scratch, or from the remnants of the previous, colonial state. To compound Washington's problems, many elites in these new states did not share the American view of the communist threat; in fact, communism, with its example of speedy industrialization, held broad appeal among many groups in the less developed world.

To secure these areas, the USA found it necessary not only to deter the communist bloc from acts of outright military aggression but also, more fundamentally, to combat the communist *idea* as well, all the while trying to stabilize 'the internal political and economic situations of aid recipients, consolidate the authority of their new governments, build functioning internal institutions and promote the legitimacy of regimes. The South East Asian Treaty Organization (SEATO) and similar security agreements could provide for US military intervention in the event of external attack, but truly securing these areas from communism required stability-building programmes, programmes to address the political and economic upheaval and despair that undermined regime legitimacy and lent credibility to communist appeals. At the same time, these programmes would require an internal 'military shield' to protect development processes and developing institutions from internal threats, generally identified as communist insurgents, subversives and 'fellow travellers'. Throughout the 1950s and 1960s Washington progressed through ever-deepening stages of involvement in the inner workings of recipient societies. In this context, military and non-military aid programmes served as complementary instruments of America's broader nation-building efforts. However, establishing a proper balance between the stability-building programmes and the 'shield' intended to protect them proved a chronic problem in the nation-building approach to containment, and ultimately undermined political development efforts.

This aforementioned issue of *time* – on whose side it truly was, and of buying time – emerged repeatedly in the formulation and reassessment of US policies towards developing areas. This concern reflects a chronic tendency on Washington's part to intervene, not simply in contexts of severe need and dislocation but more specifically when it perceives what might be called an ideational threat in the context of systemic change or upheaval. In Cold War policy, the ideational threat was communism, and the context was the postwar decolonization process. Arguably, more recent US policy is motivated by the threat of an ill-defined and somewhat amorphous 'extremism' in the context of accelerating globalization. Harriman's 'politics of despair' aside, desperate need and even internal political violence were never enough to move Washington to action. For the USA to intervene, its leaders had to perceive a threatening idea by which such despair could be exploited by the other side. While the triggering idea may vary with time, the challenges of nation-building were and are embodied in the context, and in the situation on the ground. Accordingly, the lessons of these Cold War interventions remain relevant today.

Terminology and categories of aid

Most of the aid programmes dealt with herein can be grouped under the broad rubric of 'security assistance', but these efforts involve much more than just military aid. Military assistance as well as non-military aid instruments, such as technical assistance, economic aid, development assistance and food aid, were all elements of Washington's containment efforts in Southeast Asia and elsewhere, and all of these aid instruments were employed in pursuit of security objectives.

As mentioned at the outset, for the purposes of most academic studies, foreign aid is divided into 'military' and 'non-military' (or 'economic' or 'development') categories, a distinction strictly observed by most scholars. Since US government statements tend to use such categories, it is perhaps understandable that scholars of US foreign aid have taken these at face value. These categorizations facilitate quantitative approaches to analysing aid policies; they make aid relationships easy to code. For example, even while observing that the line dividing military and non-military aid is rarely clear, Steven Hook argues that 'ambiguities regarding donor motivation' inhibit attempts to understand development aid as an instrument of policy. Security assistance, he maintains, is by contrast designed to serve 'explicit foreign policy interests and is thus less open to interpretation'.[9] In addition to Hook's fine comparative analysis of foreign aid policies, post-Cold War scholarship has produced a host of statistical analyses testing linkages between US aid flows and recipient behaviour – mostly in the area of human rights performance – which use these rigid aid categories.[10]

However, the government's distinction between aid categories is far more a product of the appropriations process in Washington than a reflection of policy objectives. Thus the empirical rigidity of these categorizations is not what it seems.

This study therefore considers aid programmes primarily in terms of their objectives rather than the category through which they were funded, and will demonstrate that during the early decades of the Cold War virtually all categories of foreign aid were employed as instruments of US security policy in the developing world. Removing the purely bureaucratic distinction between differing types of aid enhances the analysis in two ways.

First, this approach tracks the shifting of aid programmes between categories for political purposes. The most notable example of this is what is now known as Economic Support Funds, or ESF.[11] Now the largest category of foreign economic aid, the ESF concept was born in the Mutual Security Act of 1951 as Defense Support, and was intended to help protect recipient economies from the often crippling burden of maintaining military establishments. Although under Truman and Eisenhower Defense Support had been administered as part of the Military Assistance Program (MAP), in Kennedy's first year as President, much of the sizeable Defense Support budget was removed from the MAP, renamed Security Supporting Assistance (SSA), and transferred to the Official Development Assistance category to be administered by the newly established US Agency for International Development (USAID). In this transfer process, the character and objectives of aid programmes funded under SSA changed little, but the move was politically important and is erroneously viewed by many today as evidence of Kennedy's emphasis on development aid in contrast to Eisenhower's emphasis on military assistance.

The second advantage to categorizing aid by objective is that it allows for analysis of various aid programmes as discrete contributions to broader US foreign policy efforts. We can view aid programmes as tools in a tool bag, to be selected as appropriate for specific tasks in a greater project. In this way the study will demonstrate, for example, that USAID was directed to employ its development resources in support of military and counterinsurgency efforts.

'Mutual Security Assistance', 'security assistance' and similar terms came in and out of use not only with the changing of the political guard, as in the above example, but also as Washington tried to develop and implement a unified, coordinated approach to foreign aid. In the course of these efforts the Economic Cooperation Agency gave way to the Mutual Security Agency, which gave way to the Foreign Operations Administration, which gave way to the International Cooperation Agency, which was replaced by USAID. This study examines the development and testing of these successive approaches, and strives to keep the terminology in order. The important thing to bear in mind is that 'security assistance' represents a broad range of economic, political and military efforts designed to promote US security objectives using a variety of aid instruments.

Overview of US security assistance approach

Washington rested its approach to containment in developing areas on two sets of nested assumptions. Specifically, within a cluster of one or more *doctrinal* assumptions is nested a *fundamental* assumption. For our purposes, fundamental assumptions are relatively discrete elements of an ideology, reflecting one or more of the unchallenged, core beliefs upon which that ideology is based. In contrast, doctrinal assumptions are the most basic prescriptive formulations derived from fundamental assumptions in the face of perceived threats to those core beliefs.

The first such fundamental assumption held that the Western path to development, featuring Western-style socio-political institutions and market-driven economies, was viable, embodied the 'state of the art' and would naturally be followed by new states. The doctrinal assumption proceeding from that foundation held that the way to promote development in these new states was simply to protect these 'natural' processes from interference.

A second fundamental assumption was one of communist aggressiveness. Herein resided the perceived ideational threat that world communism had embarked on an unrelenting expansionist drive. The proceeding doctrinal assumption here was that, should one means of expansion be blocked, the communists would shift tactics to continue expansion by other means. Thus if US and allied military power could halt communist expansion through overt military attack, the bloc would shift to other means, such as political subversion.

Traditional forms of security assistance, particularly military aid, were of little use against the subversive threat. In the late 1940s and early 1950s Washington intended that military aid to most developing recipients would bolster their defences against external aggression. At the same time, Truman's security advisors knew that even with American military hardware, most of the Third World had little military capability, and as a consequence military aid was provided primarily for its psychological effect, to bolster recipients' *will* if not their ability to resist aggression, and to foster free-world cohesion in the face of the communist threat.[12]

By the mid-1950s the NSC recognized that, at least in the developing areas, the communist threat had shifted from one of overt aggression to one with more political, subversive tactics. However, Washington faced substantial political obstacles should aid be redirected to meet this non-military threat. Resistance to such changes would come from the US Congress as well as from the aid recipients themselves.

With respect to the recipients, there were two primary concerns. The most basic was the fear that any significant shifts in either the nature or the volume of aid flows might be interpreted as a weakening of US support, and thereby cause a loss of recipients' resolve to maintain a firm, anti-communist stand and to stay firmly within the free-world camp.

Additionally, security assistance had become a 'gravy train' for certain recipients, especially for their military elites, and any substantial shift in aid emphasis would prove a very delicate issue in Washington's relations with these regimes. The NSC and the Defense Department observed that recipients were very comfortable with the considerable political prestige as well as material benefits they derived from American military assistance. In this context, American security planners understood that, if they were to secure the local military's cooperation in efforts to meet the new communist threat, any sudden shifts or reductions in military assistance were out of the question.

Meanwhile, the US Congress tended to be sceptical of foreign aid in general, but was most amenable to aid programmes that had a clear link to US security interests. Aid programmes and packages had a fighting chance of making it through the appropriations process if they were couched in security terms, but the security rationale behind many of the stability assistance programmes needed to blunt the subversive threat appeared too oblique for the fiscally conservative Congress of the early 1950s. While radical redeployment of existing aid allocations would generate resistance from recipients, any significant expansion of foreign aid efforts would entail a bitter fight with Congress.

The nation-building, internal security programmes offered more politically acceptable means of providing for internal security in new states. These programmes began as attempts by Washington to counter the emerging subversive threat while simultaneously weaning recipients off military aid. The USA intended that recipient military establishments could gradually be reoriented towards internal security missions such as counterinsurgency, leading to reduced transfers of 'prestige' weapons systems such as fighter aircraft, ships and units of heavy armour. Additionally, through these programmes' efforts to create civil police forces separate from the military, Washington intended that the military units already filling a police role in various countries would be made redundant and phased out, resulting in significant reductions in flows of military aid. Finally, the new internal security programmes seemed particularly well suited to new states that the NSC deemed to be of only moderate strategic importance, as the programmes gave Washington a hand in controlling the threat of subversion in these countries without incurring new military aid obligations and defence commitments.

Initially, the internal security programmes were relatively inexpensive; they did not involve significant amounts of public sector development aid. In the beginning, these programmes concentrated on the establishment of new, Western-style institutions such as civil police and a functioning judiciary, while striving to consolidate regime authority and promote its legitimacy. At this point in time, Washington's 'Trade, Not Aid' approach to development maintained that the private sector would supply the capital needed to promote growth and economic stability in the periphery. The internal security programmes focused on controlling communist interference and fostering a stable investment climate, which would allow new states to pursue their own development in accordance with the Western example.

However, by the late 1950s Washington learned that the communist *example* seemed most compelling in many emerging new states, and that this example, not the subversive agitator or 'fellow traveller', posed the greatest threat to containment in the developing world.

Presuming the universal applicability of their own institutions and development philosophy, as well as seeing an opportunity to prevent encirclement by allies of the West, the Soviets began actively promoting their own model of rapid industrial and economic development. Moscow offered trade and aid without tying recipients to specific security treaties and commitments, as Washington often did. These Soviet initiatives lent increased credibility and prestige to communist parties and other leftist organizations throughout the developing world, strengthening their positions in the ongoing political struggles that attended the decolonization process.

The US leadership reacted to these Soviet initiatives with alarm, perceiving yet another tactical shift to what Eisenhower called the 'economic phase of the Cold War'. Washington was unable to see the communist challenge as legitimate competition, and argued that the developing world was being misled by apparent Soviet (and later, Chinese) accomplishments with the communist model. As Eisenhower's Secretary of State put it, Third World elites did not see the 'cruel and terrible methods' by which communism attained such success, from the daily sacrifices in the quality of life to the widespread use of slave labour.[13]

Still, the communists were scoring considerable political gains with their new trade and aid initiatives, and the USA was forced to enter into competition with the bloc for influencing the paths to development taken by emerging new states. The success of these Soviet initiatives drove the USA to institute its first large-scale programmes of public sector development aid. In the course of this competition the USA strove to develop and promote 'showpieces', successful examples of countries that chose the non-communist path. These examples (most early US efforts focused on India) would outshine the accomplishments of the Union of Soviet Socialist

Republics (USSR) and the People's Republic of China (PRC), and through this approach Washington hoped to discredit the communist idea and undermine the widely held belief that communism was the wave of the future in Asia.

However, this competition involved far more than a simple 'beauty contest' between economic development models. Washington did not presume that recipient states represented solidly unified actors. Leaving aside local communist parties, which Washington viewed as proxies or instruments of Soviet foreign policy, the USA recognized the struggles between more or less legitimate factions underway in many of these new states, and used foreign aid to actively intervene in these struggles.

Internal defence programmes, as part of the broader Mutual Security effort in the developing world, were designed to work as a coordinated effort functioning at three levels. The first level was prevention of armed overthrow or seizure of the recipient government. Measures employed at this level included aid programmes to develop counterinsurgency capabilities in the armed forces or creating paramilitary constabularies as in Iran and the Philippines.

The second level involved the fundamentals of state building, measures aimed at consolidating the recipient regime's authority throughout its entire territory. Programmes at this level included the funding and training of civil police forces as well as projects to expand communications and transport infrastructures.

The third level featured the nation-building programmes, which strove to promote the legitimacy of the government and its institutions, as well as crystallize nationalist sentiment around that government. These efforts ranged from propaganda campaigns, designed to bolster the prestige of the central government and its institutions, to aid for funding basic societal reforms, such as land reform projects. Other initiatives sought to build a sense of common identity among disparate ethnic groups with the central government. Still others threw economic assistance behind the economic programmes of selected local leaders to boost their popular support and undermine the appeals of their more radical opponents.

Inadequacy of the critique of Realism

In providing a detailed, descriptive analysis of US security assistance policy during the 1953–68 period, this study also challenges those criticisms of US policy in the developing world which attribute the failures of that policy to its being founded on and informed by Realist theory. Whatever the failings of such policy, Realism was not the problem during the Eisenhower, Kennedy and Johnson administrations.

Discourse on international relations theory has long included calls to broaden conceptions of security beyond the constraints of the long dominant framework of analysis, namely Realism. Realist analysis, with its focus on state actors to the virtual exclusion of all others, tends to view states as unitary actors, internally cohesive entities interacting in an 'anarchic' international system comprised of other states. Fred Halliday refers to this concept as Realism's 'national-territorial totality', embodying 'a notion of the state as a unified, self-identifying and ordered society which is solely focused on external threats to territoriality and sovereignty'.[14]

Realism's obsession with external, military threats and dismissal of other dimensions of security has long been a principal target for its critics, especially those focusing on security challenges in developing areas. With the passing of the Cold War, an impressive array of international relations scholars has stepped forward to assert that now is the time for a departure from analysis as well as policy predicated upon Realist conceptions of security. More to the point, many of these scholars lend urgency to this agenda by attributing much of the developing world's present 'security predicament' to the powerful influence of Realism in shaping the doctrines and policies of the superpowers – particularly the USA – with regard to Cold War security.[15] This may be an important criticism of the Cold War in general terms, but in respect to Washington's security assistance policy it is largely unjustified.

While efforts to move beyond the constraints of Realist analysis are laudable, and a re-examination and broadening of the concept of security in the Third World is certainly welcome, there are worrisome reductionist tendencies at work here in respect to analysis of US policies. Reducing a broad and diverse range of Cold War-era security approaches to a simplified, orthodox version of Realism and relegating them as such to the dustbin of history would be hasty and irresponsible; before doing so we must sift through the history of this period and retrieve the valuable lessons contained therein. Before moving on to a 'post-Realist' era of security studies we must re-examine the early decades of the Cold War, a period when US security assistance policies reflected a broader conception of what 'security' meant to newly emerging states in the developing world. Examining the development of these policies over time, along with the circumstances and events leading to their virtual abandonment, offers insights that remain relevant not only to present-day policy-makers but equally so to historians studying the origins of some of the current security predicaments in developing regions.

US containment policies in the developing world, especially the foreign aid component thereof, were never coldly rational in the Realist sense. While in retrospect these policies may seem to fit the Realist framework, they did not appear that way to the leading Realist scholars of the time. To these scholars, making political and economic development a goal of US foreign policy deviated from the cold, cost-benefit analysis so central to Realist behaviour. Hans Morgenthau, for example, argued that any efforts to actually develop nations were foolhardy and dangerous, as with economic development came increased war-making potential. Morgenthau reminded policy-makers that the Soviet Union was not considered a military threat while it was underdeveloped; 'it became such a threat at the very moment its economic development transformed it into a modern industrial power.'[16]

What little utility Realists saw in foreign aid was encapsulated in what Edward Banfield referred to as the 'doctrine of direct interest'.[17] From this perspective, aid was used by one state to bribe another, with a specific policy outcome in mind. This 'direct interest' approach to aid is akin to what Krause would later describe as 'bargaining power' in aid relationships.[18]

The opposite approach to foreign aid policy-making, using aid for 'indirect interest', was being actively promoted by economists and development specialists from the influential research centres at Harvard and Yale Universities, and the Massachusetts Institute of Technology. These individuals included Lincoln Gordon, Lucien Pye, Walt Rostow, Max Millikan and others. Their approach, involving measures for fostering self-sustaining growth in recipient states, growth that would promote stability and the establishment of viable democratic institutions, had been steadily gaining influence in Washington since 1954. When President Kennedy, who favoured this approach, took his planned development programmes to the American people to gain their support, Realist intellectuals railed against them.

Like many in Congress, Realists maintained that such aid amounted to throwing money away. Morgenthau and others argued that the proposed aid programmes would fail because they did not address the need for the 'intellectual transformation' that less-developed states needed to undergo in order to progress. Washington's approach to development had stressed the provision of technical know-how and, to a lesser degree, materials, but Morgenthau maintained that the real problem took the form of

> human deficiencies which preclude economic development. As there are individuals whose qualities of character and level of intelligence make it impossible for them to take advantage of economic opportunities, so are there nations similarly handicapped. To put it bluntly; as there are bums and beggars, so are there bum and beggar nations.[19]

Additionally, attempts at economic development would be disruptive of the 'social fabric' of society, the 'social nexus of family, village and tribe'.[20] Persons so dislocated could readily become thoroughly disaffected, and thus make easily radicalized targets for subversion. When combined with efforts to raise literacy levels, this dislocation would produce an explosive mixture. Banfield argued that literacy made subversive literature suddenly accessible and further eroded tradition and other forms of authority. In this way, development could actually be incompatible with freedom and democracy.[21] Morgenthau even suggested that democracy and development might be *inversely* related, pointing out that the totalitarian style of the Soviet government was largely responsible for the rapid industrialization of the USSR.[22]

Finally, Morgenthau argued that even if such aid did promote some degree of economic and political stability, this would in itself prove counter-productive. In Morgenthau's view, which foreshadowed T. R. Gurr's theory of 'progressive deprivation', the 'bum and beggar' nations were incapable of attaining self-sustaining growth, or in the economist Rostow's terms, 'take-off', so no amount of aid injected into these societies would result in actual development. Any levels of aid provided would ultimately fall short of the continuously rising levels of expectations, but the provision of aid would have raised those expectations so much that the levels of frustration and violence present in the inevitable upheaval would be far greater than if the society had been left alone. In any event, Morgenthau argued, any changes development aid might bring about would disturb the status quo in developing regions 'whose continuing stability remains our main interest.'[23]

In fact, Washington had abandoned any hope of preserving such a 'status quo' by the mid-1950s. In the developing world, events were already moving too rapidly to resemble any semblance of a 'status quo' such as Morgenthau described. In most of these new states the traditional 'social fabric' had already been rent by the processes of colonization itself. The nexus of 'family, village and tribe' had long since collided with the nexus of waged labour, cash transactions and foreign markets. Traditional authority had been either done away with or co-opted into the new, colonial administration's authority structure, which was normally centralized. While trappings of traditional society remained in most cases, traditional structures had long since broken down. Now colonial structures and authority were either being packed up by the withdrawing imperial powers or swept away by rebellion. In either case what remained in the newly independent states was a rising tide of expectations regarding what changes independence should bring.

As new governments' abilities to meet these expectations lagged, the rising tide became one of radicalism, calling for a departure from the political and economic philosophies of the West. Radical intellectuals within these societies promoted communism as an 'off-the-shelf' alternative to Western development strategies and continued subjection to the whims and instabilities of Western market practices. Washington had observed communism's ever-growing appeal as a development model, and how this appeal greatly increased when the USSR initiated its Third World trade and aid 'offensive' in late 1955. As Third World communist parties and leftist organizations gained a champion and benefactor in the Soviet Union, so did they gain credibility and prestige locally. From Washington's perspectives, Moscow was positioning itself to reap tremendous political gains from the political upheaval this rising tide of radicalism was bound to produce. Doing nothing, as Morgenthau, Banfield and like-minded Realist scholars advocated, hardly seemed a viable option. Third World politics were steadily boiling down to the 'politics of despair', and in their despair, many among the elites of these new states advocated turning to communism. In Washington's eyes, once these countries did so, they would be lost.

Rebuttals to Realism in US security assistance policy

Keith Krause argued that, during the Cold War, the West imposed its own externally oriented security concept on Third World states.[24] Through a combination of policies based upon the exercise of 'bargaining power', essentially bribes designed to effect certain recipient policy behaviour, and 'hegemonic power', a transfer to recipients' of the donor's world view and concepts of the 'rules of the game',[25] the West, and especially the USA, have initiated Third World arms races in various regions. While such arms races might be destabilizing in terms of what Robert Jervis called the 'security dilemma',[26] Krause maintains that the greater dangers are to the militarized state and society itself.

Krause and others argue that in concentrating on the external dimensions of security the USA instituted policies that ultimately undermined and continue to threaten the security of recipient states in the developing world. David Shafer criticizes Washington's tendency to base Cold War security policies on the 'presumption' that recipient regimes were legitimate authorities and representatives of societies' interests.[27] Mohammed Ayoob argues that through the course of the Cold War the internal security concerns of Third World states were ignored by the superpowers in their blinkered fixation on external threats. The insecurity of Third World states and regimes was enhanced because their internal security requirements 'seemed to have virtually no impact on the global security agenda fashioned by the Cold War concerns of the superpowers and their major allies.'[28] Similarly, Krause himself asserts that as a result of Washington's obsession with external security, US security assistance has built up powerful military establishments in recipient states in the Third World, and that these establishments are themselves the principal threat to society and to the viability of the states in question.[29]

The assumption evident in these analyses, that the USA applied Halliday's 'national-territorial totality' to its analyses of events in the developing world, is highly problematical. During the period under study here, US security policies in the developing world ran contrary to the Realist paradigm and its prescriptions in three important ways.

First, aside from its role in securing basing and transit rights for US forces, security assistance was not primarily designed for power projection in the developing world nor to create 'proxy forces'. Indeed, Washington knew by the mid-1950s that US military aid did little to build real military capability in third world recipients, and subsequently the USA began a process of trying to re-orient such aid toward bolstering *internal defence* capabilities as attention focused on the domestic challenges facing these new regimes. From the earliest years of the Cold War military aid to developing countries was designed primarily for its psychological and political impact, rather than as an adjunct to the US defence establishment.

Second, efforts to force US policies into the Realist mould also fail to address the importance of domestic politics in US decision-making: not only the role of US domestic politics in the foreign policy decision-making process, but also the importance of the recipient's internal political situation in American decision-making. Realist discourse regarding the role of 'bribery' and 'bargaining power' presume a stable, or at least consolidated recipient regime. Washington did not view recipients as unified actors and could not presume the viability, much less the legitimacy, of recipient states in developing areas. As mentioned above, at one level the task at hand was state building in recipient countries, the extension and consolidation of regime authority. However, to enhance long-term viability the USA sought to foster not only economic stability but also political cohesion in these new states. This task involved intervening in the country's interethnic relations as well as the contests between contending political factions. From the 'Marshall Plan' onwards US foreign aid programmes were instruments of intervention in the internal, factional struggles underway in many recipient states, the outcomes of which would determine those states' foreign policy orientations. Aid was intended to strengthen the position and promote the *legitimacy* of favoured factions and their political and economic programmes while undermining the positions of others. I return to this theoretical debate in the concluding chapter.

Finally, US policy in the developing world reflected strong ideological motivations that often contradicted the presumption of rationality so central to Realist analysis. While American decision-makers' analysis of third world politics was more sophisticated than they are often given credit for, it was distorted by this normative lens. The USA could not accept local communist movements as either legitimate or even indigenous. Even in the face of substantial evidence to the contrary, Washington presumed that all communist activity was inspired by, if not directed from, one of the centres of communist power, Moscow or Peking. The US perceived the communist states not simply as competing powers but as 'dark' or 'evil' or 'fanatic' forces bent on enslaving other countries and, ultimately, on dominating the world. As a result, the US never fully grasped the appeal of communism to many peoples of the Third World. This normative-based, 'evangelical crusade' element of American foreign policy also meant that, once engaged in a struggle with communism in any part of the world, Washington was loath to cut its losses and withdraw. In such situations, more than a 'balance of power' was at stake. Melvyn Leffler looks back on Washington's commitment to peripheral areas, concluding that policy-makers attributed 'excessive value' to the Third World.[30]

From a cold, rational perspective Leffler is quite right. However, from Washington's perspective, communism was on the march in the world, especially in East and Southeast Asia. American policy-makers believed they were in a contest throughout the developing world, a contest that went beyond traditional 'balance of power' calculations. To secure the developing regions Washington felt compelled to debunk the seemingly ubiquitous notion that communism was Asia's 'wave of the future'. To do so, the

USA engaged in what it perceived to be a 'test of wills and intentions' with the USSR and, later, with China, the outcome of which would determine whether new states in Asia and elsewhere in the developing world would choose to align themselves with communism or continue to resist it with the rest of the 'free world'.[31]

A central theme of this study is that Washington attempted to promote the development of American-style institutions and governments in new states as a way of promoting the security of those states, of their regions, and of the USA itself; again, development abroad promotes security at home. In this sense, the importance of recipient stability and legitimacy in US security assistance policy has been rooted not only in perceived links between poverty and frustration and radicalism but also in 'universalist' belief in the 'rightness' of American, democratic and economic institutions for all the world.[32]

In the years following the Cold War, the debate over superpower conduct in the Third World moved beyond the 'orthodox' versus 'revisionist accounts among historians ('Realist' and 'Critical', structuralist accounts among international relations analysts), and beyond the polarized 'dialogue of the deaf' resulting from the conflicting assumptions underpinning each of these positions. A significant body of scholarship remains rooted in assumptions that US policy is ever in pursuit of empire and economic hegemony.[33] These assumptions have in turn carried over into the debate over the merits and of development aid, a debate that has intensified over roughly the last decade.[34] In this same time frame, a new crop of historians has explored US policy in the Third World in terms of the ideas, motives and political culture elements that shaped and underpinned such policy. Their works, such as Michael Latham's *Modernization as Ideology* and David Ekbladh's *The Great American Mission*, demonstrate that many of the policies characterizing American conduct in the Third World are rooted in ideas dating back to the nineteenth century. These ideas, including America's exceptionalist view of itself and its role in the world, were shaped but hardly generated by the Cold War.[35] As Henry Fielding observed centuries ago, 'it is very uncommon, I believe, for men to ascribe the benefactions they receive to pure charity, when they can possibly impute them to any other motive.'[36] Washington's desire to promote its version of democracy and development has been based not on pure altruism, but on a varying mix of idealism, moralism and practical security concerns. The latter motive represents the focus of this book.

America's nation-building projects abroad have always reflected a need to strengthen recipients against communist takeover on the one hand, and a belief that democratic governments would naturally exist in harmony on the other.[37] However, in translating this goal into security assistance policy, the USA resorted to attempts to transfer or graft-on US-style political and social institutions to recipient societies. This approach revealed policy-makers' beliefs that not only were these out-of-the-box institutions universally appropriate for, and applicable to, new states, but also recipients would naturally prefer these to communist economic and political models. Upon becoming aware that communism was setting an appealing example among the peoples of developing countries, Washington found itself drawn ever deeper into 'ideological competition', attempting to promote its own political development agenda while suppressing the (equally universalist) development models of communism.

Organization

In its re-examination of the first two decades of the Cold War, this study draws upon many thousands of pages of newly declassified US government documents.[38] To assess the impact and effectiveness of American foreign aid policies in the developing world one must first have a clear picture of the actual objectives behind those policies. With this in mind, the project begins with the highest levels of decision-making in the US government, scrutinizing the discussions of the President with his cabinet officers and the discussions and deliberations of the NSC.[39] Relevant directives and action memoranda are then followed down through the bureaucratic levels of the implementing agencies. Due attention is given to field reports, intelligence assessments, contemporary news reports and other inputs to the decision-making processes. In this way the study attempts to place the formulation of these nation-building and other security assistance policies in the context of the events and perceptions of their time. In addition, this archival research has been supplemented by interviews with individuals involved in the making and implementation of security assistance policies, from cabinet officers to field operatives. Analysis of the actual implementation and impact of these policies in the developing world completes the 'triangulation' approach.

The organization of the book allows us to study the development and evolution of security policies in the developing world over time, assessing the impact of changes in political leadership in Washington as well as the impact of events in the developing world. The chapters are organized as follows.

Chapter 2 studies the evolution of Washington's perception of the communist threat as well as its own role during the early years of the Cold War, and examines the place of the developing world in US security policy, particularly that of Southeast Asia. The chapter also explores the origins of security assistance and the Truman-era programmes.

Chapter 3 examines the Eisenhower administration's perception of the communist threat, particularly the perceived tactical shift away from overt communist aggression and toward subversion, and Washington's efforts to re-orient security assistance programmes in developing countries toward internal security missions. The chapter goes on to trace the development of the internal defence concept for developing areas, as embodied in the Overseas Internal Security Program (OISP).

Chapter 4 focuses on Eisenhower's conviction that the communist threat was shifting more into the economic sphere, in what he called the 'economic phase of the Cold War.' After exploring the Soviet initiatives in question, the chapter goes on to examine how the US re-assessed its approach to security assistance and related programmes, particularly how the Soviet initiatives drove Washington to initiate significant public-sector development assistance programmes. The White House intended such aid to further US security objectives through its impact on competition between Western and Communist development models, as well as between factions within target states. Finally, the chapter describes the administration's re-examination of security assistance, the problems highlighted regarding the balance between military and non-military aid instruments.

Chapter 5 examines the Kennedy 'difference', the Kennedy administration's tendency to view the threat in Maoist terms, as opposed to the previous administration's tendency to see a more Leninist threat. Adjustment to meet this Maoist threat resulted in the Kennedy administration's emphasis on counterinsurgency, and the grass-roots-oriented 'hearts and minds' approach. The chapter also studies the Johnson administration's efforts to implement the Kennedy initiatives in the face of an increasingly volatile situation in Southeast Asia. A series of challenges in Indochina, Indonesia and elsewhere drove Johnson to resort with increasing frequency to military measures in security assistance, usually at the expense of nation-building efforts. (Indonesia and Indochina will be contrasted in this chapter.) The argument in each of the three presidential chapters (3–5) follows the same basic structure.

The concluding chapter looks back over the development of US internal security efforts, critiques this approach in terms of its effectiveness and side effects, and considers the legacy of such US efforts in developing countries. In this present foreign policy climate, reviewing Washington's earlier democratization and nation-building projects, and making comparisons with current operations in Afghanistan, Iraq and elsewhere, may provide some valuable lessons for today's strategies for promoting democratization, 'good governance', improved performance in the area of human rights and the pursuit of similar political development objectives.

Notes

1 Townsend Hoopes, *The Limits of Intervention* (New York: W. W. Norton & Co., 1987).
2 See, for example, David Shafer, *Deadly Paradigms: The Failure of US Counter-insurgency Policy* (Leicester: Leicester University Press, 1988); Mohammed Ayoob, *The Third World Security Predicament* (Boulder, CO: Lynne Rienner Publishers, 1995); Keith Krause, 'Military Statecraft: Power and Influence in Soviet and American Arms Transfer Relationships,' *International Studies Quarterly*, 35 (1991): 313–336; Michael Cox, 'Why Did We Get the End of the Cold War Wrong?', *British Journal of Politics and International Relations*, 11,

2 (May 2009): 161–176.

3 See, for example, David Chandler, *International Statebuilding: The Rise of Post-Liberal Governance* (New York: Routledge, 2010), pp. 2–3.

4 Hoopes, *Limits of Intervention*.

5 For background on earlier initiatives, see David Ekbladh, *The Great American Mission*. Also, Andrew J. Williams, *Failed Imaginations: New World Orders of the Twentieth Century* (Manchester: Manchester University Press, 1998).

6 United States Objectives and Programs for National Security, NSC 68. *FRUS*, 1950, vol. 1, pp. 234–292.

7 Moscow Embassy Telegram no. 511, 'The Long Telegram', 22 February 1946, in Etzold and Gaddis, *Containment: Documents on American Policy and Strategy, 1945–1950* (New York: Columbia University Press, 1978), p. 62.

8 Chester J. Pach, *Arming the Free World: The Origins of US Military Assistance Programs 1945–1960* (Chapel Hill, NC: University of North Carolina Press, 1991), pp. 204–205.

9 Steven W. Hook, *National Interest and Foreign Aid* (Boulder, CO: Lynne Rienner, 1995), p. xv.

10 See, for example, Steven C. Poe, 'Human Rights and US Foreign Aid: A Review of Quantitative Studies and Suggestions for Future Research', in *Human Rights Quarterly*, 12 (1990): 499–512; Katarina Tomasevsky, *Development Aid and Human Rights* (New York: St. Martin's Press, 1989), D. Carleton and M. Stohl, 'The Foreign Policy of Human Rights: Rhetoric and Reality from Jimmy Carter to Ronald Reagan', in *Human Rights Quarterly*, 7, 2 (1985): 205–229.

11 Most of this broad interpretation of military assistance legislation took place under the Eisenhower administration, under the heading of 'Defense Support', later known as 'Security Supporting Assistance'. With the Foreign Assistance Act of 1961, this category of aid was transferred from military aid to developmental assistance (DA) where it remains as of this writing under the name 'Economic Support Fund' (ESF).

12 Chester J. Pach, *Arming the Free World*.

13 John Foster Dulles quoted from *FRUS*, 1955–57, vol. 10, p. 182.

14 Fred Halliday, *Rethinking International Relations* (Basingstoke: Macmillan, 1994), p. 78.

15 Ayoob, *Third World Security Predicament*, chs 1 and 2.

16 Hans Morgenthau, 'Preface to a political theory of foreign aid', in Robert A. Goldwin (ed.), *Why Foreign Aid?* (Chicago, IL: Rand McNally, 1963), p. 85.

17 Morgenthau, 'Preface', pp. 87–88, citing Banfield.

18 Krause, 'Military Statecraft'.

19 Morgenthau, 'Preface', p. 79.

20 *Ibid,* p. 82.

21 Edward C. Banfield, *American Foreign Aid Doctrines* (Washington, DC: American Enterprise Institute for Public Policy Research, 1963), p. 15.

22 Morgenthau, 'Preface', pp. 84–85.

23 *Ibid.,* pp. 83–84.

24 Keith Krause, 'Insecurity and State Formation in the Global Military Order: The Middle Eastern Case'. Paper presented at annual meeting of the International Studies Association (ISA), Chicago, IL, February 1995 (Photocopy).

25 Krause, 'Military Statecraft'.

26 In this dilemma each state's attempts to advance its own national security,

usually through the accrual of military capabilities, create and perpetuate an order of decreased relative security for that state as well as for its neighbours. See Robert Jervis, 'Security Regimes', *International Organization,* 36 (Spring 1982): 357–378.

27 D. Shafer, *Deadly Paradigms: The Failure of US Counterinsurgency Policy* (Leicester: Leicester University Press, 1988).

28 Ayoob, *Third World Security Predicament,* p. 98.

29 Krause, 'The Middle Eastern Case'.

30 Melvyn Leffler, *A Preponderance of Power: National Security, The Truman Administration, and the Cold War* (Stanford, CA: Stanford University Press, 1992), p. 506.

31 National Intelligence Estimate 50–61, 28 March 1961. NSF, National Intelligence Estimates, box 6–7 (LBJ Library).

32 For a discussion of such Wilsonianism in Washington's broader foreign policy, see Tony Smith, *America's Mission: The US and the Worldwide Struggle for Democracy in the Twentieth Century* (Princeton, NJ: Princeton University Press, 1995).

33 See, for example, Gabriel Kolko, *Confronting the Third World* (New York: Pantheon Books, 1988); also, David Chandler, *Empire in Denial: The Politics of State Building* (London: Pluto Press, 2006).

34 Chandler, *Empire in Denial*; also his *International Statebuilding: The Rise of Post-Liberal Governance* (New York: Routledge, 2010). Also, Mark Duffield, *Global Governance and the New Wars: The Merging of Development and Security* (London, Zed, Books, 2001).

35 Michael E. Latham, *Modernization as Ideology: American Social Science and 'Nation Building' in the Kennedy Era* (Chapel Hill, NC: University of North Carolina Press, 2000); David Ekbladh, *The Great American Mission: Modernization and the Construction of an American World Order* (Princeton, NJ: Princeton University Press, 2009).

36 Henry Fielding, *The History of Tom Jones, a Foundling,* book 8, ch. 7.

37 The 'democratic peace' argument, although rooted in the middle ages, has recently enjoyed a renaissance in international relations discourse, particularly in the works of Bruce Russett, Michael Doyle and others. The idea that 'democracies don't fight each other' has been cited by US President William J. Clinton as 'the closest thing to an empirical fact' in international relations. The Wilsonian vision that informed early Cold War policy-makers – that of a world free of alliances, dictatorships, spheres of influence and economic nationalism – is described in Daniel Yergin, *Shattered Peace: The Origins of the Cold War* (New York: Penguin Books, 1990), pp. 8–11.

38 The bulk of these documents have been declassified upon the author's application over the course of several years.

39 More attention is paid to correspondence within and among the relevant 'Special Groups' in studying the Kennedy administration, given Kennedy's de-emphasis on the NSC as a policy-shaping body.

2

Towards a 'tolerable state of order'

The purpose of this short chapter is to establish how, through its changing perceptions of its own security requirements in the wake of the Second World War, the USA acquired a stake in the security of developing countries in distant parts of the world. This chapter also explores the origins and development of Washington's security assistance concept up to the Korean War. It reveals on one hand how Washington came to view the entire world as what Michael MccGwire calls its 'National Security Zone', while exploring on the other hand the process by which American leaders convinced themselves that they were both capable of and responsible for securing the globe.

The Cold War has often been described and analysed in terms of great power competition, using such concepts as balance of power and spheres of interest. However, the Cold War embodied a very different dimension – at least in US foreign policy – and that was a peculiar, normative dimension. As spelled out in 1950 in NSC 68, as well as its antecedent beliefs and attitudes that Daniel Yergin illuminates in his 'Riga Axioms',[1] the USA came to view as its adversary not a state, but an idea (or, to use de Tracy's useful definition of ideology, a 'science of ideas'), and the state or states that embodied that idea. NSC 68, a foundation document of America's approach to the Cold War, in describing the state in question, declared that the Soviet Union, 'unlike previous aspirants to hegemony, is animated by a new, fanatic faith, antithetical to our own, and seeks to impose its absolute authority over the rest of the world ... The issues that face us are momentous, involving the fulfillment or destruction not only of this Republic but of civilization itself.'[2]

While one might ascribe such hyperbole to popular propaganda, it is worth recalling that this was a Top Secret document that was not declassified until the 1970s. What the authors of NSC 68 describe is not a near peer competitor but the 'dark side'. States in and of themselves are not the problem, to one of such a mindset. States are 'animated by', held 'captive' by and 'lost' to the dark side. Conflict with such an adversary is not a matter of competing interests but a struggle against 'evil'. And when one is struggling against evil, can balance of power be a meaningful concept? What represents an acceptable balance with evil? What part to the globe would one cede to the dark side as a sphere of influence?

Such are not the underpinnings of a rational foreign policy, nor do they allow for effective bargaining in negotiation. Yet these assumptions upon which many American policy-makers constructed their perceptions and analyses of communist politics, parties, leaders and actions had a profound impact on their assessments of the global insecurity environment of the early Cold War.

MccGwire offers a useful concept in his National Security Zone (NSZ), which he defines as 'the area surrounding a state's borders, which it sees as critical to its well-being and security.' He notes that a state's NSZ can change with time, and is 'conditioned by capabilities'.[3] Clearly, in addition to capabilities, there is a cognitive judgment involved in determining what is 'critical', based on a mix that includes experience and assumption. MccGwire's definition of the USA's NSZ is that part of the western hemisphere situated north of the equator.[4] However, while American foreign policy behaviour in the western hemisphere certainly validates MccGwire's definition through the early twentieth century, one might argue that America's concept of its NSZ changed radically during and immediately following the Second World War. This chapter offers a brief overview of the process by which the USA came to regard the entire world as its NSZ. In this process, the USA assumed for itself a leading role in global security, a role which it has yet to relinquish to this day, long after the Cold War passed into history.

Lessons of the war and their influence on policy

The Second World War had taught security planners in Washington a set of sobering lessons regarding the likely conduct of future wars.[5] As Daniel Yergin has pointed out, even before the cessation of hostilities, these policy-makers, planners and analysts were devising new approaches to promoting US security that reflected these new aspects of warfare, forging these into a new, basic theory of 'national security'. However, it was only when the impact of these lessons meshed with the Riga Axioms that this new conception of national security assumed its full meaning.[6]

Three such lessons that proved particularly relevant in the development of security assistance policy were the importance of maintaining a technical edge in military hardware, the absence of mobilization time in future wars, and the truly global nature of war.

Perhaps the most obvious lesson was the importance of maintaining an edge in military technologies. As Yergin observed, the Second World War began with Polish cavalry charges against German armour and ended with the use of nuclear weapons.[7] The state of the art in military technologies had been advancing at a staggering pace, and maintaining a credible defence required that the USA remain at the forefront of these developments. Accordingly, defence research and development could not be allowed to return to prewar levels. Many in Washington believed that technology was changing the nature of armed conflict so rapidly that the next war would be decided with the weapons on hand at the outset.[8]

Such advances in military technologies, particularly in the areas of aviation and rocketry, along with developments such as *blitzkrieg* tactics and the 'sneak attack' on Pearl Harbor, altered Americans' concept of mobilization time. In this new environment war could come very suddenly, allowing little time for the mobilization, equipping and deployment of forces. The lesson offered was the need to maintain a high state of military readiness at all times, including the maintenance of standing forces.[9]

Another lesson was that future wars would be truly global in scale. The Second World War saw US and Allied forces engaged in combat operations throughout the world, in multiple theatres simultaneously. Accordingly, the USA would need to maintain the means to fight such a multi-theatre war in the future. In addition, the war had been brought to America's door. There had been concerns over the vulnerability of the west coast after Pearl Harbor was attacked, with Japanese occupation of US territory in the Aleutian Island chain, and German submarine attacks on the east coast. Although the USA had been spared the devastation suffered by enemies and allies alike during the war, the American homeland was now vulnerable to attack from both Asia and Europe. The belief that North America was protected from such attack by long expanses of ocean, enunciated as late as 1939, was shattered.[10]

The security assistance approach developed during the Truman years reflected these lessons. In terms of maintaining a technical edge, the 'cascading', or transfer of obsolete military hardware to recipients of security assistance, as well as the sale of new equipment to selected recipients, helped to justify keeping US defence industries running at the tempo needed to remain on the forefront of military research and development. One objective of the security assistance programme was to 'augment [US] military potential through improvement of our arms industry'.[11] Whether provided on a commercial sales or a concessional basis, such aid provided consumers for defence industries. New hardware was provided to allies with the justification of furthering the standardization of equipment and thereby improving interoperability among forces. In addition, providing consumers for outdated hardware helped justify new equipment upgrades for US forces and promoted the sale of American military hardware and spare parts.

The US Air Force, for example, was quick to capitalize on this new thinking as the Air Corps moved to eliminate stocks of surplus aircraft in the wake of the Second World War. Recalling how the presence of massive surpluses of aircraft left over from the First World War had caused the domestic aircraft industry to wither away by ninety per cent in the interwar period, Army Air Force Commanding General Henry H. Arnold was determined to keep the same from happening again. Arnold argued forcefully for the disposal of American surplus equipment from the Second World War to friendly nations, pointing out that such a move would not only reduce the glut of aircraft but would also invigorate the US aircraft industry and give defence contractors a 'jump start' in competing for overseas markets.[12] Military assistance programmes provided a means of disposing of such surpluses on a continuing basis.

Similarly, lessons regarding reduced mobilization time and the global nature of future wars led security planners to seek 'defence in depth', the ability to fight future wars as far as possible from the American homeland. This approach required a network of far-flung bases on a distant 'strategic frontier'.

As early as 1943, plans for US security in the postwar era moved America's line of defence far beyond its own frontiers to a new 'strategic frontier', across the Atlantic and Pacific Oceans.[13] This approach involved establishing bases along the distant coasts. In the Pacific a chain of bases was to be established, beginning in the Aleutians and extending south to Japan, Okinawa and the Philippines. This line of outposts was intended to oversee the Asian littoral and prevent the staging of attacks against the western hemisphere from the Asiatic coast. On the Atlantic side the Joint Chiefs of Staff projected a need for bases in Greenland, Iceland, the Azores and/or the Canary Islands and, if possible, in West Africa itself.[14]

Extension of the strategic frontier was motivated not only by the desire to establish defence in depth but also to facilitate power projection. Forward bases were necessary 'in areas well removed from the United States, so as to project our operations, with new weapons or otherwise, nearer the enemy', from which American forces could 'take "timely" offensive action and direct American power at the source of the adversary's capacity and will to wage war.'[15] In the years preceding the introduction of intercontinental bombers and missiles, forward bases were deemed essential for supporting air attacks against targets in an enemy's homeland, as Britain had proved essential for staging attacks into occupied Europe and Germany itself during the Second World War.

Military aid for the Third World

The establishment of this strategic frontier, as well as the maintenance of high-tempo defence production through equipment sales and cascading, demanded an expansion and formalization of Washington's security assistance policies. Early forms of postwar military aid were provided on a quid pro quo basis for securing basing and transit rights for US forces. This category included renegotiated agreements for existing army and naval facilities in Panama, the Philippines and elsewhere, along with a greatly expanded system of air facilities in distant countries. The transfer or ferrying of aircraft to Europe during the war had demonstrated the need for numerous waypoint fields for refuelling stops. The war effort required the carving of new airstrips from remote locales in the frozen north so that tactical aircraft ferrying to Europe need travel no more than a thousand miles per hop. After the war, the range of 1940s-era aircraft remained relatively limited and required that bases be established as close in as possible to potentially hostile shores, with refuelling stops secured at numerous waypoints around the globe. These facilities, along with naval activities and refuelling stations, represent the bulk of what Bruce Cumings calls the 'archipelago of empire'.[16] Additionally, there were electronic listening posts and remote radar warning stations. Even as units of aircraft with mid-air refuelling capabability expanded in the 1950s, reducing the need for refuelling waypoints, forward-deployment bases were established across the world at points from which ships, aircraft and troops could carry the war to the enemy, whoever that enemy might be. Originally, these requirements resulted in a wide array of base agreements with governments around the globe, often secured in return for aid, including military aid. Such programmes were formulated as basic war-fighting requirements to help the USA prosecute wars against any potential enemy. However, by the late 1940s, the USA had begun to concentrate on the USSR as the likely adversary in the next war, and security assistance policies focused increasingly on containing the military power and political expansion of that adversary.[17]

A notable example based on this new perception of threat was Truman's call for support for Greece and Turkey, culminating in passage of the 'Act to Provide Assistance to Greece and Turkey'. Truman's justifications for such aid, centering on the possible 'loss' of Greece and Turkey to leftist insurgents, subsequently became known as the 'Truman Doctrine'. The Truman administration expressed concern that the loss of Greece and Turkey to communism would leave three continents open to Soviet bloc expansion. 'Like apples in a barrel infected by one rotten one,' Dean Acheson told a group of Congressional leaders in 1947,

> the corruption of Greece would infect Iran and all to the East. It would also carry infection to Africa through Asia Minor and Egypt, and to Europe through Italy and France, already threatened by the strongest domestic Communist Parties in Western Europe. The Soviet Union was playing one of the greatest gambles in history with minimal cost.[18]

Under the pressure of an imminent withdrawal of British aid to these countries, Truman asked Congress for 400 million dollars in military and economic aid for the beleaguered regimes in Greece and Turkey. In doing so, he established precedent for providing future aid to 'free peoples' seeking to protect themselves from subjugation through either external pressures or 'armed minorities'.

While the Truman Doctrine was significant, the first truly comprehensive programme of military assistance was the Mutual Defense Assistance Act (MDAA), enacted in 1949. Initially, the MDAA was primarily targeted at Europe and was designed to provide military aid to Western European governments to help them resist possible intimidation by the nearby Red Army. Assistance provided under the MDAA was also intended to help recipient regimes, especially in France and Italy, control their local communist parties and other factions, with the goal of preventing these from interfering in reconstruction programmes established under the European Cooperation Act of 1948, or 'Marshall Plan'. In this respect, the MDAA complemented Marshall Plan aid and was intended to 'shield' European reconstruction from external attack or intimidation as well as from internal disruption. However, the MDAA provided a legislative basis for assistance that went beyond Europe, allowing Truman and successive US presidents to establish military aid programmes for the entire 'free world'.[19]

The MDAA established a military aid programme that comprised several parts. For most of the post-Second World War period military assistance has been administered through three programmes: the Military Assistance Program (MAP), the Foreign Military Sales cash and credit programmes (FMS), and training programmes. FMS authorized the President to provide to eligible recipient countries 'procurement assistance without cost to the United States' for weapons and military equipment.[20] The MAP allowed for the loan or grant of such materiel and/or services, which included military training until this function was removed from MAP and established as the IMET (International Military Education and Training) programme in 1976. In practice much FMS equipment was transferred to recipients on the basis of 'loans' that were subsequently written off by the Executive Branch.

Relationship between military and economic aid

Military assistance provided under the MDAA was largely intended to deny the communists 'early victories' they might obtain by the aggressive use of armed force. In Western Europe, where Washington focused its early military aid efforts, such aid was used to promote and consolidate a regional security organization (NATO) following the signing of the North Atlantic Treaty in the spring of 1949.

However, military aid provided to Europe also bolstered recipient governments against internal threats. Security planners in Washington agreed that economic and social stability was the key to strengthening friendly states against communist takeover. However, a string of recent communist successes, particularly the 1948 coup in Czechoslovakia, had convinced many that the processes which promoted such stability were themselves in need of protection.[21] As a result, a substantial portion of US military aid to Europe served civil police functions aimed at controlling the activities of domestic communist parties, which American decision-makers believed to be well armed.[22]

The State Department was sceptical of military aid to Europe, arguing that it could set back the primary mission of economic reconstruction. The position of the State Department's Policy Planning Staff (PPS), then headed by George Kennan, had long been convinced that any communist takeover of Western Europe would be of a political nature and that the possibility of military attack was remote. In his famous 'Long Telegram', dispatched to Washington from his post in Moscow in 1946, Kennan had stressed the vulnerability to communist takeover of societies in disarray, comparing communism to 'a malignant parasite which feeds only on diseased tissue'.[23] Accordingly, PPS maintained that the primary objective of US assistance was to strengthen recipient resistance to this 'parasite' through rehabilitation of economic and social institutions. Investment in military capabilities in recipient countries would sap resources from the cause of European economic recovery, constituting 'an uneconomic and regrettable diversion of effort.'[24] According to State, European countries' desire for such military alliances resulted from a failure to adequately grasp their situation. 'Their best and most hopeful course of action, if they are to save themselves from communist pressures, remains the struggle for economic recovery and for internal political stability.'[25]

> The Planning Staff recognizes that the communists are exploiting the European crisis and that further communist successes would create serious danger to American security. It considers, however, that American effort in aid to Europe should be directed not to the combating of communism as such but to the restoration of the economic health and vigor of European society. It should aim, in other words, to combat not communism, but the economic maladjustment which makes European society vulnerable to exploitation by any and all totalitarian movements and which Russian communism is now exploiting.[26]

In fact, in the context of postwar European recovery, military assistance provided under the MDAA and economic aid supplied under the ECA emerged as complementary elements of containment. The success of the overall European Recovery Program (ERP) informed and helped shape an approach to containing communism. The ERP's use of military elements to shield processes of economic stabilization and growth was codified in Washington's basic statement of national security objectives in early 1950 in the form of NSC 68.

In outlining a future course for US national security policy, NSC 68 divided the globe into an expansionist 'communist world' and a US-led 'free world' and prescribed:

> a more rapid building up of the political, economic and military strength of the free world than provided for under [current policies and projected programmes] with the purpose of reaching, if possible, a tolerable state of order among nations without war and of preparing to defend ourselves in the event the free world is attacked ... The frustration of the Kremlin design requires the free world to develop a successfully functioning political and economic system and a vigorous political offensive against the Soviet Union. These, in turn, require an adequate military shield under which they can develop.[27]

According to NSC 68 the role of military force was to contain the forces of the 'ideological enemy', deterring this enemy from acts of aggression, while economic, social and political institutions of the 'free world' were being strengthened. Eventually, the compelling example of these free world institutions would overwhelm the communist states ideologically and undermine them politically, shaking even the Soviet grip on the satellites and the people of the USSR itself.[28]

The 'buying time' element is clear. In retrospect NSC 68's prescriptions seem well suited to the postwar European context (where rebuilding under the ERP was already well underway as NSC 68 was being drafted). The task at hand was rebuilding war-devastated economic and political structures that had been thriving a few years earlier. At the same time sufficient military means were deemed necessary to protect this rebuilding process from overt aggression from the nearby Red Army as well as domestic political challenges, or to offset the latent, intimidation value of communist forces. Passage of the Economic Cooperation Act of 1948 provided funding and administration for a massive, direct application of economic assistance, while shortly thereafter the Mutual Defense Assistance Act of 1949 enabled provision of the required military aid. If one presumes that the Soviets had aggressive intentions toward Western Europe, then it is easy to accept the notion that military aid to NATO countries bought time for the rebuilding and recovery of Europe's industry.

The Gordon Gray and Rockefeller Reports: Third World development and Washington's security agenda

While implementing NSC 68's approach in Europe was an enormous task, it was quite finite by comparison with establishing effective social and economic institutions in many former colonial areas. In the less developed areas, functioning economic and social structures and institutions would often require building from scratch. In many cases indigenous structures had long since been disrupted or destroyed by colonialism, and the colonial structures themselves often broke down or collapsed with the withdrawal of imperial administration. There was no Marshall Plan for underdeveloped areas, and American prescriptions for development along Western lines stressed gradual growth and 'local efforts' on the part of developing countries to attract investment.

However, in late 1950 and early 1951, separate studies put before the Truman administration argued that development in these 'backward' areas was an increasingly important *security* matter for the USA. Only long-term development, these reports asserted, could address the dangerous levels of poverty that invited communist exploitation in these less developed areas. These studies – the Gordon Gray and Rockefeller reports – further argued that Washington would have to reconsider its approach to fostering development in the Third World, and that relying on private-sector investment would not meet development needs. As summed-up in the Rockefeller Report, 'Strengthening the economies of the underdeveloped regions and improvement of their living levels must be considered a vital part of our own defence mobilization'.[29]

The link between developing world stability and US security interests had been articulated in a number of specific programmes by 1950. For example, one US objective in Latin America, in the context of the Inter-American Treaty of Reciprocal Assistance, an instrument providing for wartime cooperation in hemispheric defence, stated that US assistance should promote 'the maintenance within each [member] state of political stability and of internal stability to insure the protection of which the delivery of strategic materials depends.'[30]

Aid policies in the Truman era had also included 'emergency' economic programmes in selected developing countries, such as the Special Technical and Economic Missions (STEM) programme. STEM activities were specific to Southeast Asia but focused on supporting immediate defence and political goals. One example of these goals was the easing of local discontent in the context of peasant revolts in the Philippines. These measures were designed primarily to address specific cases leading to political instability, not to effect long-term development.[31]

The Truman administration had been uncommitted and remained sceptical with regard to the prospects for such long-term development in the 'backward' areas. One of the 'points' for action outlined in Truman's 1949 inauguration speech called for the USA to 'assist the people of underdeveloped areas to improve their economic conditions'. The programmes established under the general heading of 'Point Four' stressed that such improvement would take place through the 'sharing of technical knowledge and skills' and 'fostering the flow of capital investment' into these areas.[32] Rather than rely on US government-funded efforts, Point Four stressed the role of private actors, ranging from the capital investment of private corporations to the humanitarian activities of private voluntary organizations.[33] Point Four also determined to concentrate US efforts on those countries that took steps to 'provide conditions under which such technical assistance and capital c[ould] effectively and constructively contribute to raising standards of living, creating new sources of wealth, increasing productivity and expanding purchasing power'.[34] In short, Point Four was primarily concerned with fostering improved investment climates.

The Truman administration took care to ensure that the Point Four approach would not interfere with, or duplicate the efforts of, private enterprise. As a result, Point Four programmes focused on basic infrastructure development, regional trade facilitation and other projects that were good for business.[35] Although it represented a significant step in bringing development assistance onto the US foreign policy agenda, Point Four was funded at a level roughly equal to one tenth of one per cent of Marshall Plan funding.[36] In essence, Point Four was like a promise from the US government to help one build a house, but when such help arrives it consists of a carpenter and a blueprint, but no tools or materials.[37]

Overall, Truman era policy reflected the administration's scepticism regarding the value of economic aid to the developing world. Specifically, the administration was unconvinced that these countries would have the know-how needed to make fruitful use of such aid. Truman's Secretary of State at the time of Point Four, Dean Acheson, later argued that the Marshall Plan was a success precisely because it had been applied to the highly developed nations of Western Europe, which 'could and did make efficient use of the capital made available to them ... capital loans in advance of technical and managerial competence are not only a waste but a disadvantage (through foreign exchange debts) to the borrowing country'.[38]

George Kennan, then head of the State Department's Policy Planning Staff, also remained sceptical of aid's usefulness in less developed areas. In contrast to his position regarding the primacy of economic objectives in Europe, Kennan advised the Secretary of State in early 1950 that economic or military aid to developing countries would only be effective in countries 'where such aid is the only missing component of successful resistance [to communism]. Where other important components are also missing, aid is not only of no use, but often directly strengthening to forces hostile to us'.[39] Kennan maintained that the loss of the less developed parts of Asia, for example, would ultimately prove of little consequence to the USA.[40] Rather, he stressed the importance of a few politically and industrially important 'power centers' in the world, and observed that it would be important to foster in these areas 'political attitudes favorable to our concept of international life'. To foster these positive attitudes in the less developed areas would be 'beyond our power at this time and for many decades to come'.[41]

In the context of such attitudes, the conclusions of the Gordon Gray and Rockefeller reports did little to move the administration to action. What did move policy-makers was the outbreak of war in Korea in the summer of 1950.

The Korean war and a shift of focus

As MccGwire observed, the invasion of South Korea by the North 'trans-formed NSC 68 from a budgetary wish-list into a blueprint for action'.[42] While the militarization of containment is often attributed to NSC 68, it also argued for economic and political programmes as part of strengthening the free world to resist communist aggression. As noted above, part of the 'undermining' and 'overwhelming' of the bloc was to be through positive examples. One of the first such projects was the Republic of Korea itself, where the USA launched a vast programme of nation-building to create an example that would lead Asian peoples away from the idea that communism was Asia's future.[43]

The broader impact of the Korean invasion was to force Washington to reconsider its conceptions of what constituted 'backward', 'peripheral' regions. The idea that communist expansion in Asia would not stop with China was sobering for many in the Truman administration, causing

America and its leaders to look at the less developed regions in a new way. To extend the Mutual Security concept was to provide mechanisms for US intervention in new areas. Accordingly, from June 1950 onward, Truman and his successor Eisenhower worked ceaselessly to extend a network of these Mutual Security organizations around the entire Eurasian periphery of the communist bloc and the world.

After the outbreak of the Korean war in June 1950, economic aid to less developed countries became part of Washington's basic national security approach. Economic aid was intended to 'create situations of political and economic strength in the free world especially in critical areas whose weakness may invite Soviet thrusts'. Such aid was to help recipient governments 'win the confidence and support of their own peoples as a solid foundation for political stability and national independence'.[44]

However, the Truman administration's response to the Korean invasion was primarily military. Presumed to be the outcome of Soviet decision-making, the invasion seemed to validate the threat assessment outlined in NSC 68, that the Kremlin had embarked on a 'drive for world domination'.[45] In terms of Truman era containment policy, the Korean invasion represented a significant, if unexpected, 'leak'.[46] While US and Allied forces were directly involved in the Korean conflict, the 'collective defence' concept was extended from Europe to Asia in the form of bilateral and multilateral 'Mutual Security' agreements: the USA–Japan Treaty (along with a peace treaty), the USA–Philippines Treaty and the Australia–New Zealand–USA (ANZUS) Treaty were all signed in 1951. In its effort to plug Asian leaks in the containment dike the USA began establishing a network of defence agreements committing it to military intervention along virtually the entire periphery of the Eurasian landmass. With these commitments went packages of security assistance for new allies.

The Truman administration had no illusions regarding the military capabilities of its less developed allies, with or without military assistance. In the less developed areas Washington understood that local forces could at best be expected to employ only limited delaying or holding actions in the face of an attack 'of unambiguous nature' by communist forces. However, in such cases analysts believed that military aid lent credibility to the deterrent power of local forces, and strengthened their will to resist aggression.[47] In areas of strategic importance, such holding actions by local forces would, hopefully, provide time for US forces to be brought into play. Again, military aid was intended to deny the communists easy victories, but in the case of less developed recipients, such aid was intended *primarily* to have a psychological effect. 'Hatred and fear alone may inspire, not stubborn and active resistance, but a withdrawal into "neutralism" and a resignation to despair', declared a version of NSC 68 modified after the outbreak of the Korean war. Maintaining allies' will to resist communism depended on their being 'convinced, emotionally and intellectually' that 'the means of accomplishing a successful military defence against Soviet aggression [would] ... shortly be at hand'.[48]

Washington perceived two disturbing trends at the beginning of the 1950s. First, presuming that the invasion of South Korea was directed by Moscow, American analysts deduced that communism was shifting its expansionist drive toward attacks on weak, hitherto peripheral areas. The second trend was a tendency of economically beleaguered European allies to pull back from their prior security responsibilities in threatened areas, as the UK had done in Greece.[49] Suddenly, Washington was worried that France might do the same with respect to Indochina.

In this troubling new environment, Truman called for substantial increases in aid, both military and non-military, to shore up the containment barrier. Having already extended the Truman Doctrine to Asia at the end of 1949,[50] the president requested significant new packages of aid for the Philippines, as the peasant-based 'Huk' rebellion there assumed an increasingly ominous character in light of communism's shift to aggression in East Asia. Similarly, Truman moved to bolster the French position in Indochina. In an effort to keep the French holding on in Southeast Asia Washington provided France with additional security assistance that was intended specifically for Indochina, aid that totalled over 500 million dollars for 1951 alone.[51]

With the establishment of the Mutual Security agreements noted above, the USA attempted to restructure its various aid programmes around the new mutual security concept. Defense Support, economic aid intended to help the recipients of military aid finance the military forces stipulated in mutual security agreements, debuted with the Mutual Security Act of 1951, as did programmes of food aid. The Mutual Security Act also reflected Washington's growing emphasis on non-military elements of security assistance in that it combined military and non-military aid under a single authority for the first time, in the form of the Mutual Security Agency (MSA). At the same time, the MSA introduced a complicating factor in the form of the position of Director of Mutual Security (DMS). In this time of strident claims by Senator Joseph McCarty and his associates that the State Department was thoroughly infiltrated by communists, Congressional Republicans viewed the DMS as a way of administering aid programmes while limiting State's role. However, having evolved from the Marshall Plan and ECA, the DMS and the Mutual Security Agency itself retained a profound bias toward European recipients in designing and implementing programmes that proved hard to shift, even after the outbreak of the Korean war.[52]

Even as the Truman administration worked to extend and fortify its containment barrier through the mutual security network, US containment policy was facing a new set of political challenges that the barrier approach could no longer address. As new, independent states emerged from the developing world, the reliability of the barrier rested upon the stability of their governments; and, in the climate of increasing political upheaval that characterized these new states, that stability was often highly questionable. Yet, the military aspects of containment took precedence during the Truman years, and with his NSC estimating that US military programmes would involve defence spending increases at the rate of 50 billion dollars per year, non-military aid programmes would have to be lean and limited to a highly select list of recipients.[53] In the end, it would be up to a new administration to shape containment in a way that could respond to these new political, rather than military, threats.

Notes

1   Yergin, *Shattered Peace*, ch. 1.
2   NSC 68, 'United States Objectives and Programs for National Security', 14 April 1950. *FRUS, 1950*, vol. 1, pp. 234–292.
3   MccGwire, *Military Objectives in Soviet Foreign Policy*, p. 220.
4   MccGwire, *Perestroika and Soviet National Security*, p. 217.
5   For a variation on this argument, one that employs a larger set of 'lessons', see Yergin, *Shattered Peace*, ch. 8.
6   *Ibid.*, p. 193.
7   Yergin, *Shattered Peace*, p. 200.
8   Institute for Defense Analysis, 'A Study of US Military Assistance Programs in the Underdeveloped Areas', 3 March 1959, pp. 3–4. Draper File, box 12 (DDE Library).
9   Leffler, *Preponderance of Power*, p. 4.
10 Yergin, *Shattered Peace* pp. 196–197.
11 NSC 14/1. This contrasts with NSC 7, which several months earlier had pointed out the necessity of providing precision machining equipment and technical advice to bolster the arms industries of 'selected non-communist states'.
12 Pach, *Arming the Free World*, pp. 15–16.
13 Leffler, *Preponderance of Power*, pp. 3–4.
14 Leffler, *Preponderance of Power*, pp. 5–7.
15 *Ibid.*, quoting JCS 1518, 'Strategic Concept and Plan for the Employment of United States Armed Forces', 19 September 1945, and JWPC 361/5 (Rev), 13 September 1946.
16 Bruce Cumings, *Dominion from Sea to Sea: Pacific Ascendency and American Power* (New Haven, CT: Yale University Press, 2009), ch. 15.
17 For excellent and in-depth studies on the evolution of overall national security policy and threat perception during the Truman years, see Leffler's *Preponderance of Power*. Also see Yergin's *Shattered Peace*.
18 Dean Acheson, *Present at the Creation: My Years at the State Department* (New York: Norton, 1969), p. 219.
19 Pach, *Arming the Free World*, conclusion.
20 R. Grimmett, 'The Role of Security Assistance in Historical Perspective', in E. Graves and S. Hildreth (eds), *US Security Assistance: The Political Process* (Lexington, MA: Lexington Books, 1985), p. 7. Originally such aid was largely war surplus. However, these programmes were also seen as a means of keeping the defence industry running at a higher level than was usual for peacetime.

In addition to improving the standardization of equipment among US allies, military assistance was also seen as a means to 'augment [US] military potential by improvement of our armaments industry', the arms industry requiring 'partial rehabilitation' in order to provide such aid. NSC 14/1, 'The Position of the US with respect to Providing Military Assistance to Nations of the Non-Soviet World', 1 July 1948, in Thomas H. Etzold and John Lewis Gaddis (eds), *Containment: Documents on American Policy and Strategy, 1945–1950* (New York: Columbia University Press), pp. 128–130.

21   Grimmett, 'Role of Security Assistance', p. 8. Grimmett points out that the 1948 communist coup in Czechoslovakia created an air of uneasiness which helped gain passage for the Mutual Defense Assistance Act. It is interesting to note, however, that Kennan had anticipated a Soviet 'clampdown' in Czechoslovakia several months before it happened. Noting the importance of the country in Soviet planning for Eastern Europe, he predicted that the Soviets would take steps to secure Czechoslovakia's orientation in a 'purely defensive' response to European recovery initiatives by the US. See PPS 13, 'Resume of World Situation', 6 November 1947, in Etzold and Gaddis, *Documents*, pp. 90–97.

22   For an example, see Paris Embassy Telegram no. 3049, 21 November 1951. President's Secretary's File, box 155 (3) (Foreign Affairs) (HST Library).

23   Moscow Embassy Telegram no. 511, 'The Long Telegram', 22 February 1946, in Etzold and Gaddis, *Documents*, p. 62.

24   PPS 43, 'Considerations Affecting the Conclusion of a North Atlantic Security Pact', 23 November 1948, in Etzold and Gaddis, *Documents*, p. 155.

25   *Ibid.*, p. 154.

26   *Ibid.*, p. 103.

27   NSC 68, 'United States Objectives and Programs for National Security', 14 April 1950. *FRUS*, 1950, vol. 1, pp. 234–292.

28   Annex 2, NSC 68/3. *FRUS*, 1950, vol. 1, p. 454.

29   For descriptions of these reports, see Baldwin, *Economic Development*, pp. 108–109. Also see Burton I. Kaufman, *Trade and Aid: Eisenhower's Foreign Economic Policy, 1953–1961* (Baltimore, MD: Johns Hopkins University Press, 1982), pp. 5–6.

30   Draft Memorandum for Senior Delegate, US Delegation, Inter-American Defense Board; attachment to NSC 56. *FRUS*, 1950, vol. 1, pp. 605–608.

31   See 'editorial note', *FRUS*, 1950, vol. 1, pp. 852–853.

32   Memorandum, 'Point IV', *FRUS*, 1950, vol. 1, pp. 846–848.

33   *Ibid.*

34   64 Stat. 198, Title IV [AID], section 403(a).

35   Baldwin, *Economic Development*, p. 82.

36   *Ibid.*

37   'Before it even began reaching the field, Point Four aid was co-opted and increasingly diverted from long-term development projects to the type of emergency measures that characterized the STEM programme. Within a year, the programme had become largely ineffective, having 'strangled itself' on the tangle of agencies involved in its execution. Editorial note', *FRUS*, 1950, vol. 1, pp. 852–853. These agencies included the Departments of Agriculture, Commerce, the Interior, Labor, State and the Treasury, as well as the ECA.

38   Acheson, *Present at the Creation*, pp. 265–266.

39   Kennan, Memorandum to Secretary of State, 6 January 1950. *FRUS*, 1950, vol. 1, p. 130.

40 *Ibid.*

41 John Lewis Gaddis, *Strategies of Containment: A Critical Appraisal of Postwar American Security Policy* (New York: Oxford University Press, 1982), p. 30.

42 Michael MccGwire, 'The paradigm that lost its way', *International Affairs*, 77, 4 (2001): 777–803, p. 786.

43 For a fine exploration of US nation-building efforts in South Korea, see Gregg Brazinsky, *Nation Building in South Korea: Koreans, Americans and the Making of a Democracy* (Chapel Hill, NC: University of North Carolina Press, 2007).

44 Annex 2, NSC 68/3. *FRUS*, 1950, vol. 1, p. 441.

45 NSC 68, *FRUS*, 1950, vol. 1, p. 284. Indeed, the massive increases in defence-related spending called for by NSC 68 were approved after the invasion. However, various analysts have pointed out that these were to a great degree mandated by the war effort in Korea rather than primarily by NSC 68's recom-mendations. See Grimmett, 'Role of Security Assistance', p. 8, and Challener, pp. 47–48, both in Graves and Hildreth, *US Security Assistance*.

46 Prior to the 1950 invasion US military planning had allowed for the possi-ble removal of forces from Korea with an eye to transferring these resources to Western Europe, a region of greater strategic concern. Obstacles to such a plan were political, not military. It was thought that such a withdrawal would be detrimental to American prestige after waging 'ideological warfare in direct contact with our opponents' since the end of the Second World War. See JCS 1769/1, Etzold and Gaddis, *Documents*, pp. 77–78.

47 Pach, *Arming the Free World*, p. 5.

48 Annex to NSC 68/3, 8 December 1950. Annex no. 2: The Foreign Military and Economic Assistance Programs. *FRUS*, 1950, vol. 1, pp. 454–455.

49 The Dutch, with US prodding, had already withdrawn from Indonesia.

50 Yergin, *Shattered Peace*, p. 405.

51 Acheson, *Present at the Creation*, p. 673.

52 Memorandum by the Special Assistant for Regional Programs of the Bureau of Far Eastern Affairs (Parelman) to the Deputy Assistant Secretary of State for Far Eastern Affairs (Johnson), 28 November 1952. *FRUS*, 1952–54, vol. 1, pt 1, General: Economic and Political Matters, doc. 156.

53 Annex to NSC 68/3, *FRUS*, 1950, vol. 1, p. 441.

3

Creating a 'climate of victory': Eisenhower and the Overseas Internal Security Program

A note on the two Eisenhower chapters

As codified in NSC 68, the role of military power in containment during the Truman era was to contain the forces of the 'ideological enemy' and deter them from acts of aggression, while economic and social institutions of the 'free world' were being strengthened to the point where their compelling example would overwhelm the communist states ideologically and undermine them politically. The power of this example would be combined with a campaign of psychological warfare 'calculated to encourage defections from Soviet allegiance'.[1] Ultimately, the strength of the free world might lead to changes in the internal politics of the USSR.[2] Subsequent statements of US national security policy argued that maintenance of free-world strength might help dissolve cohesion within the bloc, or lead the communists to modify their conception of international relations and adopt less threatening modes of behaviour.[3] In any case, building the free-world strength necessary to bring about such changes was a process that would take time, and during that time the bloc had to be contained and denied opportunities for further expansion.

The question of *time* – the duration for which containment would be necessary – proved quite vexing for security planners in Washington. Especially after the Korean invasion shifted US attentions to the less developed regions of East and Southeast Asia, policy-makers wondered whether there would be adequate time for these processes to build sufficient fortitude in threatened but underdeveloped countries before similar acts of communist aggression could take place. NSC 68's prescription for building strong societies had proven a fairly straightforward task in Europe where the job was really one of *re*-building. The needs of developing areas were vast, and vastly different, and the resources required to build successful economic and political systems there were enormous as well. Of course, many of these developing areas were far less valued in terms of manpower and industry, or even their strategic position, than were the countries of Western Europe and Japan. As a result, in the early years of containment Washington assigned a relatively low priority to promoting their development. However, by the mid-1950s, Eisenhower and his NSC recognized that these developing areas were emerging as the principal battlefield of the Cold War, and that among many leaders in these areas it was the *communist* example that was the most compelling. Thus ensued a period of ideological conflict in a very real sense, a period of political competition in which Washington made repeated efforts to 'seize the initiative' from communism in dealing with developing countries.

As this chapter and the next will demonstrate, Eisenhower's approach to containment went far beyond 'brinkmanship'. His administration broke new paths and generally prepared the ground for the policies of the Kennedy–Johnson era. For the sake of convenience, these chapters deal with overlapping policy emphases in Eisenhower's security assistance effort; namely, the political and military measures that were intended to form the 'shield', and the economic measures intended to foster development beneath that shield. Over the course of his two terms in office, Eisenhower's perceptions of a changing communist threat in the developing world moved the economic elements of security assistance to centre stage in his foreign policy. While American perceptions of security assistance needs began changing as early as 1955, the impact of these changes on policy became apparent only in 1957. In that year's security assistance budget, the administration requested more aid funds for economic components of security assistance than for military hardware.

This chapter will study the Eisenhower administration's formulation of a broad, internal security concept for developing countries, and the development of the political and military security measures that were to form the 'shield' beneath which development processes were to take place. Chapter 4 will examine the evolution of the Eisenhower administration's economic policies toward developing areas, especially in response to the Soviet Union's own economic initiatives towards new states. Finally, a brief concluding section will contrast the political, military and economic elements of Eisenhower's Mutual Security Assistance policies. Both chapters will explore ways in which the initiatives of the mid- to late 1950s laid the groundwork for subsequent nation-building programmes and changed the emphasis and direction of US security assistance policies.

The majority of the Eisenhower administration's political-military security efforts in the developing world were embodied in Eisenhower's 1290-d programme[4] (redesignated the Overseas Internal Security Program – or OISP – in 1957) and, later, in its successor programme, Kennedy's USOIDP (discussed at length in Chapter 5).

Within Eisenhower's internal security programme, the broadest nation-building objectives were the consolidation of central governmental authority and the extension of the government's presence into remote areas of the target country to foster a sense of national identity among the locals regarding their distant government. An ancillary objective was to observe and control secessionist and irredentist movements, which, Washington believed, could readily ally with, or be co-opted by, communists.

The 1290-<u>d</u> programme also set out to build the image of police and security forces as institutions within the recipient society rather than as instruments for oppressing that society. On one hand, this approach involved steeping recipient military officers in an environment where relations between civilians and the military were appropriate to a democratic society, while on the other hand the goal was improving the image of these forces among the population. Building the prestige of these forces was deemed essential for the recipient regime to secure the public's support and cooperation in the anti-subversion cause. However, this task proved an enormous challenge in much of the developing world, where populations saw many of these security organizations not as an organic part of the local society but as a leftover vestige of the alien colonial state.[5] In various cases, the new state's security forces had been formed from the core of the colonial *gendarmerie* or militia and had inherited their predecessors' place in the hearts and minds of the population.

Along with building prestige, these programmes were intended to establish police-type forces as *separate* institutions from the local military, trained in how to conduct proper relations between police and community, and under the control of a civilian arm of the recipient government. Along similar lines, the 1290-<u>d</u> programme sought to build into recipient societies independent judiciary institutions whose function was to control the activities of these new security forces.

Additionally, these US efforts featured educational programmes delivered through a variety of means ranging from broadcast media to schoolbooks. The principal thrust of these programmes was to erode the appeal of communism and to indoctrinate both the population and its leadership as to its dangers. However, such educational efforts also aimed to develop a sense of national identity centered on the recipient government and to provide American-style civics lessons to prepare its populations 'for the modern, democratic world'.[6]

US perceptions of the global threat

Eisenhower's defence policies reflected his desire for effective containment at minimum cost, a mission driven by his concern over the crippling effect that sustained, high levels of defence spending would have on the US economy, and, ultimately, on the American way of life. Taking office during the Korean war, at a time when federal spending exceeded federal income, the new president made whittling-down the Truman budget a central priority. He set out to accomplish this aim through a restructuring of defence spending.

The Eisenhower administration's first modification of basic US national security policy took the form of NSC 149, 'Basic National Security Policies and Programs in Relations to their Costs', approved in late April 1953. Its central premise is that

> A vital factor in the long-term survival of the free world is the maintenance by the United States of a sound, strong economy. For the United States to continue a high rate of spending in excess of federal income, at a time of heavy taxation, will weaken and might eventually destroy that economy.[7]

NSC 153, which followed roughly six weeks later, was essentially a summary and restatement of Truman era statements of basic national security policy, as modified by NSC 149.[8] Its description of the threat reflected Eisenhower's concerns for the economy:

> There are two principal threats to the survival of fundamental values and institutions of the United States: a) The formidable power and aggressive policy of the communist world led by the USSR; b) the serious weakening of the economy of the United States that may result from the cost of opposing the Soviet threat over a sustained period.[9]

The philosophy codified in NSC 149 led the president and his NSC to chop chunks out of the military budget. Shortly after 149 was approved, Eisenhower invited a group of Congressional leaders to the White House, read the text of 149 to them and announced that his administration's immediate goal was to trim 8.4 billion dollars from Truman's budget for the fiscal year 1954. Certain 'big ticket' items, such as the nuclear aircraft propulsion programme, were cut or deferred.[10]

The bulk of the cuts were directed at conventional forces, primarily the Army's ground forces. While severely cutting the Army's resources, and thereby reducing America's capability for fighting sustained, conventional wars or limited wars, Eisenhower concentrated US defence capabilities in strategic nuclear forces. At the time, this meant long-range bomber forces, which, in turn, meant that the Air Force was as much a beneficiary of Eisenhower's new approach as the Army was a victim. The new approach to defence relied on deterring communist aggression with the credible threat of large-scale nuclear attack, later dubbed 'massive retaliation'. A much smaller, but nonetheless important element of the new defence approach, was the Mutual Security concept.

Mutual Security and the New Look

One of Eisenhower's principal motives in seeking the 1952 Republican nomination for the presidency was a desire to keep the USA from returning to its prewar isolationism, the sort of isolationist position advocated by the leading Republican contender, Robert Taft. Committed to containment, Eisenhower rejected Taft's idea of a 'fortress America', which, in Eisenhower's opinion, reflected Taft's ignorance of world affairs.[11]

What alarmed Eisenhower most about Taft was the latter's lack of commitment to the idea of collective security, as embodied in the system of

Mutual Security organizations such as NATO and ANZUS.[12] Eisenhower himself was dedicated to the mutual security concept, and expanded the network of Mutual Security organizations during his presidency, most notably with the establishment of SEATO. John Foster Dulles, now Eisenhower's Secretary of State, shared this commitment, maintaining that alliances ranked even above nuclear deterrence as the 'cornerstone of security for the free nations'.[13]

As was the case during the Truman years, Mutual Security pacts with less developed countries stemmed from psychological objectives and were designed to bolster the will of recipients to resist powerful, communist neighbours. The actual military capabilities to resist attacks were to be developed over time. Mutual Security Assistance was intended to create a 'strategic reserve' for use in the event of general war with the bloc, and the original force goals set for recipient militaries were formulated in accordance with this eventual goal.

Eisenhower's long-term goal was that such pacts would ultimately serve as frameworks for security cooperation on a regional basis, which, the president hoped, would eventually require ever-decreasing US participation and support. In time, Mutual Security assistance and the promotion of self-sustaining regional defence organizations would represent tremendous savings in US security expenditures. 'Explain it away as you will,' Eisenhower lectured his NSC, 'a foreign soldier costs less to maintain in the field than an American soldier.'[14]

Of course, these security agreements also served as instruments for American intervention in these areas in the event of external aggression against allies. Here lay the vital link between the Mutual Security concept and Eisenhower's restructured security policy, known as the New Look.[15] The states participating in the Mutual Security network became, in effect, a barrier to further expansion of the communist bloc. As a state signed a Mutual Security pact with the US, its border became something of a 'tripwire' that would trigger US intervention and possibly nuclear retaliation if communist forces moved across that border. Accordingly, Washington desired to gird the entire periphery of the communist bloc with its network of Mutual Security organizations.

Truman's experiences had shown that a sustainable mutual security effort required not only direct US military involvement and military assistance but aid designed to promote economic and political stability as well. However, economic aid had been concentrated in Western Europe and Japan. Acheson had maintained that, in the world's less developed areas, the *prerequisites* for growth, stability and development were, for the most part, not yet in place.[16] Whether or not Acheson's assessment was accurate, domestic instability in member states represented potential weak spots in the Mutual Security approach, and, ultimately, in the New Look itself. Security pacts were only as stable as the governments with which they were signed, and if participating states could be subverted and undermined, so too could the

Mutual Security organizations to which they belonged. To undermine the Mutual Security network in this manner was to undermine the containment 'barrier' itself. Accordingly, a major new feature of the New Look was its revised statement of the Soviet threat, which the NSC now described as a combination of the basic Soviet hostility to the US and the non-communist world, Soviet military power and 'Soviet control of the international communist apparatus and other means of subversion and division in the free world'.[17]

Perceptions of threat in the developing world

Even while implementing the New Look, the Eisenhower administration grew increasingly uneasy over the less developed areas and, in particular, those newly independent states emerging from Europe's former colonial possessions. Washington tended to presume, just as it did with respect to its European allies, that these new governments would see alignment with the free world as their only rational choice; they would hardly wish to replace colonial domination with communist domination. At the same time, Eisenhower's security planners understood that these new governments were fragile, and that the upheaval of the Second World War years, the decolonization process, or both, had left economies and political structures in disarray, presenting considerable opportunities for communist penetration. New regimes had not adequately consolidated their authority in many cases and were faced with the daunting task of constructing new social and political institutions from the remnants of the colonial state.

The spectre of the 1948 coup in Czechoslovakia continued to haunt American decision-makers, and both the President and his Secretary of State were keenly aware of how inadequate the 'barrier' approach was in meeting the threat of 'political aggression'.[18] Little in the New Look could address perceived communist efforts to divide and subvert the free world. Neither threats of massive retaliation nor the incorporation of front-line states into collective security organizations could adequately counter the threat of creeping communist 'subversion'. Eisenhower's security policy sought to limit communist expansion by effectively drawing and fortifying a line around the periphery of the communist world and threatening general war should that line be crossed, but this approach provided little or no help in cases where communists might come to power by means short of overt aggression. The President and the NSC agreed among themselves that a communist election victory, for example, would offer the USA little pretext for intervention and could hardly be viewed as a *causus belli*.[19] Yet, to allow more countries to enter the communist orbit by any means was deemed unacceptable.

Eisenhower, Foster Dulles and most, if not all, the Cabinet shared a view of the balance of power as articulated in NSC 68, wherein the balance between the free and communist worlds was already so fine that any further communist gains would be perilous to the USA and its interests.[20] They also shared with the authors of NSC 68 the view that the development of strong economic systems and political institutions in the free world required an adequate 'military shield'. The New Look provided the shield, but the development processes would take a good deal of time, and there was growing uncertainty within the NSC as to whether time was on the side of the USA or the communist bloc.

Buying time

This question of *time* had divided the three task groups participating in Project Solarium in the summer of 1953. Early in his presidency, Eisenhower and his Secretary of State affirmed a need for a substantial reexamination of America's approach to national security. They named the project for the room in which they had devised the plan, the solarium room of the White House. The new administration assembled military and civilian officials in three task groups and convened these experts at the National War College to consider alternative visions of a new security concept for the USA. These three task groups presented their recommendations to the NSC in the summer of 1953. Group A, which advocated a continuation of Truman era containment with certain modifications, and Group B, which recommended drawing a clear boundary line around the bloc and threatening general war should it be crossed, both argued that time was on the side of the USA. As expressed by Task Group A in a memo to the NSC:

> Time can be used to the advantage of the free world; if we can build up and maintain the strength of the free world during a period of years, Soviet power will deteriorate or relatively decline to a point which no longer constitutes a threat to the security of the United States and to world peace.[21]

In contrast, Group C, which saw communism as a more urgent threat, cited a long string of communist victories, and communist successes scored through political rather than military means. In their view, deterrence of Soviet military adventurism did not contain communist expansion; rather, it simply caused the bloc to shift tactics and pursue its expansionist aims through less overt means. Task Group C argued that in the context of these political threats, time worked *against* the USA and called for a more active approach to containment, including measures aimed at 'destroying the communist apparatus in the free world':

> Implied acceptance of the status-quo disqualifies both of those alternatives [A and B] as means to ultimate success. Time has been working against us and still is. We must arrest, reverse this trend by positive action. What is needed is dynamic, offensive political action started now and progressively accelerated.[22]

Shortly after the Solarium Task Groups had presented their reports, CIA Director Allen Dulles reported that the Agency was preparing a 'coordinated estimate' as to whether time was on the side of the USA or the USSR, and he summarized its findings before the NSC. As to the question of the Soviet Union's decline, the outlook was not encouraging:

> While no collapse within the Soviet Bloc can be foreseen, the USSR may lack vitality over the long run. From this point of view time may be on the side of the US, but this factor will not show up critically for 10 or 15 years yet ... If the USSR continues its present policies it will close the economic gap now existing between it and the United States. From this point of view, time is on the side of the USSR.[23]

Time also worked against Washington in relation to the Soviets' own nuclear weapons programme. Much of the New Look's credibility rested upon the threat of massive nuclear retaliation to deter communist aggression. However, the credibility of massive retaliation rested on America's invulnerability to a Soviet nuclear attack, an invulnerability the NSC knew would not last. CIA Director Dulles's assessment noted that while Western military capabilities in areas adjacent to the bloc were increasing, thus improving the relative position of the USA, the USSR would eventually be able to cripple the USA in a nuclear strike. As Soviet nuclear might grew, American willingness to risk general war would lessen, and security planners in Washington predicted that the bloc would grow ever bolder in its subversive endeavours, confident that the USA would not run the risk of general war by intervening in 'peripheral conflicts':

> Aided by their increasing nuclear capabilities, especially as a state of atomic balance with the U.S. is approached, the Communist powers are likely to pursue a strategy of further expansion through subversion, indirect aggression, and the instigation or exploitation of civil wars in free countries, as in Indochina. The advantages of such a strategy, if successful, lie in the continued accretions to Communist strength and prestige and the progressive weakening of the free world coalition, both politically and militarily, while the involvement of the main sources of Communist power is avoided.[24]

The barrier approach as spelled out in NSC 162 was essentially passive, and efforts to counter the subversive threat required more active, 'positive' programmes of action. In the summer of 1954, the NSC's Planning Board drew up NSC 5422, a document that offered guidelines for meeting the growing problem of subversion. This 'Soviet threat of piecemeal conquest' demanded measures not provided for in existing programmes. While the shelter of the American nuclear umbrella and resolve of local armed forces lessened the possibility of outright communist attack upon countries on the periphery, agents of the 'communist apparatus' were still perceived to be at work penetrating, undermining and subverting these countries' domestic institutions, creating the appropriate conditions under which they could disrupt society and seize power at will. What was needed was 'an integrated and flexible combination of political, military, economic and psychological actions participated in by many countries and given determined leadership by the United States'. In particular, the NSC recommended that the USA take political and economic measures to strengthen countries subject to 'indirect aggression'.[25]

During the Solarium discussions, Task Force C had called for expansion and intensification of such 'political warfare' programmes designed to loosen bloc control in communist-controlled countries, even with the understanding that such an active strategy would increase the danger of general war.[26] Opposing this position, Secretary of State Foster Dulles asserted that, should the Americans implement *too* active a campaign of rolling back communism, it would strain and possibly tear apart the Western Alliance itself.[27] Ultimately, such risky measures might well prove unnecessary; Dulles observed what he considered hopeful signs that nationalism in China and the satellites would benefit the Western cause, that increasingly independent attitudes might exert a centrifugal force on states in the Soviet orbit. If this force did not actually detach them, it might well lead to a distribution of power throughout the bloc wherein no individual actor could make a decision that bound all the rest, thus decentralizing, and diffusing the power of, the communist 'monolith'.[28] However, this raised the irksome question of *time* yet again, and the question of just whose side it was on.

In Foster Dulles's view, by the end of 1954, most steps necessary to buy adequate time had been taken. Dulles put great faith in collective defence arrangements, which were, in his view, effectively containing communism in Europe, Latin America, the Pacific Islands and the areas covered by the Manila Pact (SEATO) and ANZUS. The Middle East remained a problem, as did Vietnam, and the situation in Indonesia remained worrisome.[29] Still, he asserted, aside from these gaps, US national security policies were 'pretty generally adequate'. The alliance system, Dulles argued, had 'staked out the vital areas of the world which we propose to hold even at the risk of general war.' Regarding other threatened areas: 'the United States must be very careful never again to let itself get into situations where we do not really plan to defend our interests ... we should withdraw from those positions in the world which we do not propose to defend by military action.'[30]

Eisenhower challenged his Secretary of State on this point, arguing that strategies that drew a line and told the enemy not to cross it automatically ceded the initiative to the enemy to seize everything short of that line, which was entirely unacceptable. While the geostrategic importance of certain specific areas was well established, the president could not agree that others, such as all of South Asia, should simply be abandoned to communism as Dulles and Treasury Secretary Humphrey had suggested.[31]

Dulles clarified his own position on this point, noting that there was 'tenable ground' between committing to a nation's defence and abandoning it. Observing that communist leaders, while 'in essence revolutionary and conspiratorial', were not reckless, he asserted that they would calculate that it was too risky to 'undermine the successful campaign of subversion by indulgence in actions of open brutality'. In Dulles's view, bloc prestige – the image it presented to the world as an innately peaceful entity – could not be reconciled with acts of open aggression. For that reason, if countries threatened by communism could be built-up to the point where they could maintain their own *internal* security, so that they could not be overthrown except by overt aggression, then these countries could resist the Soviet threat on their own. 'Accordingly,' Dulles asserted, 'it would be very much worth our while to provide to these vulnerable nations sufficient military and economic assistance as will enable them to provide for their internal security and for the bettering of their economic health.'[32]

Response: nation-building and the 1290-d programme

The above discussions produced NSC Action 1290-d, which directed the Operations Coordinating Board (OCB) to form a working group to study and report on programmes designed to 'destroy the effectiveness of the Communist apparatus in Free World countries vulnerable to Communist subversion, before it is able to achieve important penetration'.[33]

The initial assessment

At the NSC's direction, the 1290-d Working Group turned in its initial report in February of 1955. In this report, the Working Group, formed of representatives from State, Defense, the FOA and CIA, attempted to define the problem, and described a set of straightforward measures necessary to counter the subversive threat which they defined in broad terms:

> Communist subversion takes forms which range from political penetration to armed insurrection. Communist penetration is directed against every facet of national life; government, labor unions, newspapers, educational institutions and intellectual movements. Local strikes and disturbances are fomented when they will further communist objectives. The principal objective of communist subversion is to build the capability of seizing control of a country without insurrection and at least to reduce the capacity of the local governments to oppose insurrection if the communists resort to it.[34]

The initial approach to countering subversion reflected the basic ideas contained in the NSC 5425 series, namely, the US government's *domestic* anti-communist activities, the internal security policies often associated with the heyday of the House Un-American Activities Committee's activities within the US itself.[35] The prevention and control of subversion, argued the OCB, required for the most part 'preventative, police-type activity including the application of limited force'. This activity included:

a) The detection of communist agents, fellow travelers, front
   organizations and other components of the communist apparatus.
b) The detention of communist personalities or groups.
c) The execution of judicial measures against these persons or groups.[36]

While acknowledging the importance of 'the general political and economic well-being of a country' in countering subversion, as well as the importance of building public support behind the government in target countries, the working group originally recommended that US efforts be limited to improving existing countersubversion forces. The American objective was to develop in these forces the necessary police-type methods and help ensure they had the hardware as well as the software (in the form of popular support) to get the job done. More sweeping changes, the Working Group argued, were simply too impractical to consider.

In addition to making sure countersubversive forces had the necessary arms and equipment, the Working Group argued the need for 'honest and competent administration, more adequate pay, and better training – both basic and technical', as well as the removal of unqualified personnel from police-type forces.[37] A central objective of such reforms was to improve the overall *image* as well as the effectiveness of constabulary forces in recipient countries, to foster a favourable public opinion that would 'lead the citizenry to identify with the local government and security forces in dealing with subversion, and which [would] assist in inducing defections from the communist side'.[38] Such image building would be supported by 'information campaigns' designed to alert the public to the dangers posed by communism, and to 'the advantages of cooperating with the local government in its efforts to eliminate subversion'.[39]

1290-d objectives required some adjustment of the recipient countries' internal politics. The Working Group anticipated a need to 'revise' legislation in target countries 'to permit effective police action', and recommended the 'revision or reorganization of judicial systems which block corrective measures'.[40] Public support for these changes would also be fostered through information programmes.

The OCB recognized that 1290-d required careful programming and fine-tuning to maximize its effectiveness in each target country. With this in mind, they directed the Working Group to prepare a survey instrument to be cabled to US missions in each of the target countries for on-the-spot analysis of the local subversive problem and assessments of what measures the US could take to enhance the local government's countersubversive capabilities.[41] Each Chief of Mission was to assemble his country team to consider the Working Group's recommendations, add their own analysis of the task at hand, and return these in time for the OCB to report the findings to the entire NSC.[42]

Reassessment and broadening of objectives

It was autumn before all of the responses had come back from the field, and the OCB delivered its report to the NSC in November of 1955. This report contained a revised assessment of the task at hand, which no longer paralleled Washington's domestic internal security measures. In less developed countries, the challenge was of a vastly different nature. 'Upon the initiation of this study,' the OCB reported, 'it became clear that U.S.

assistance to countries threatened by communist subversion was a broader matter than simply constabulary forces and could logically embrace the entire spectrum of human endeavor.'[43]

Reports from the field warned of fundamental problems that were beyond the capabilities of even the most professional police forces. As the country surveys were presented one by one to the OCB, a picture emerged wherein the biggest subversive threat in developing regions was not the political agitator or saboteur, but the favourable image of communism itself, and the political influence it wielded in these new states. 'Fellow travelers' were not easily isolated elements in many recipient countries; they were mainstream and were often well represented in government.

The OCB noted a particularly acute threat of subversion in the Far East and Southeast Asia, for two reasons. One was the anticipated psychological impact, the 'defeatism', promoted by the loss of one country upon its neighbours, demonstrated by reactions to the 'surrender' of northern Vietnam to the communists at the Geneva Conference in the summer of 1954. The second was the 'positive attraction' of Communist China, which had emerged as 'the leading political and military power in Asia and self-appointed 'champion of the Asian peoples'.[44] In Southeast Asia and beyond, Moscow's prestige posed similar threats:

> A factor contributing to the internal security problem in many countries, particularly the underdeveloped countries, is the spectacular industrial progress and world-wide prestige of the Soviet Union gained in the last decade, which have deeply impressed such countries and have tended to make certain elements of their population hope that they, too, can achieve similar progress by adopting communism.[45]

The USA found itself losing ground in the 'ideological competition' described in NSC 68. Whereas previous security assistance programmes had concentrated on shielding recipients from military aggression and intimidation, under 1290-d, security assistance was re-oriented to target domestic threats and focused on combating the idea of communism itself, and those who carried and promulgated it.

Washington viewed the main problem in many developing countries as one of political will. After all, argued the NSC, internal security was ultimately up to the threatened peoples and their governments, a function of their 'determination and willingness to take effective action'. The OCB concluded:

> it is in the best interests of the U.S., therefore, to foster development of an understanding of the subversive threat and a 'national will' to oppose it. Until the countries concerned have the determination to control subversive elements, and enact and enforce the necessary security measures or laws, any U.S. assistance to internal security forces will largely be wasted[46]

In many ways, this objective presented an uphill climb for US diplomats. The country surveys noted with alarm that the socialist-dominated ruling coalition in Burma sought to promote friendly relations with communist China, Burma's 'only potential foreign enemy'. The Cambodian government did not 'fully recognize the nature and extent of the communist threat', and 'because of this lack of awareness and because of its avowed neutralist tendencies,' Cambodia was 'disinclined to enter into collective security arrangements, and [was] even suspicious of non-communist neighboring countries.' In Indonesia, a legal communist party was campaigning for upcoming elections 'in the guise of a bona-fide indigenous political force', and was considered well poised to exploit 'nationalist sentiment, basic economic conditions, low income levels, poor housing, foreign domination of business and other usual communist targets'.[47] The US leadership had convinced itself in the early postwar period that in communism it faced a global threat. Now Washington faced the challenge of convincing the developing world as well.

After the NSC accepted the OCB's 23 November report, 1290-d swiftly broadened into a multi-agency effort.[48] While the 1290-d programmes were designed on a country-by-country basis, the broader responsibilities of participating agencies can be described as follows.

The International Cooperation Administration (ICA) had overall authority for the coordination of 1290-d efforts. In addition, the Civil Police branch of ICA was responsible for providing such technical assistance as was necessary in the establishment of civil police organizations, and the recruitment of civil police consultants for service as police advisors in 1290-d countries.

Under 1290-d the Defense Department broadened its Mutual Defense Assistance mission of training and equipping foreign military forces for internal security roles to provide the same to paramilitary and police forces in countries selected for the 1290-d effort. The Defense Department's previous work in creating internal security forces had stressed special police-type forces under military control, such as the Iranian Gendarmerie and Philippine Constabulary.[49] Defense would now help develop new civil police forces that would be under civilian control, and train them in anti-guerrilla and counterintelligence operations. Training of regular military forces expanded to enhance the local military's ability to support the new police establishment.[50]

1290-d directed the United States Information Agency (USIA) to augment its existing information programmes on the dangers of communism and communist subversion, with an added emphasis on persuading recipient *governments* as to the nature of these threats. USIA also developed public relations programmes to enhance the image of, and public support for, recipient countries' internal security forces to foster a degree of public support, as was enjoyed by the FBI, the Royal Canadian Mounted Police and Scotland Yard.[51] USIA designed information programmes to persuade the target populations that police action against communists was different from and more acceptable than police action against other groups.[52] The Agency sometimes coordinated its efforts with the propaganda establishment in the recipient country.[53]

The State Department's primary responsibility was negotiating host country acceptance of the need to implement 1290-d measures. This consisted largely of 'personal diplomacy', which required that the 'Ambassador and his assistants take advantage of every opportunity to persuade foreign officials in 1290-d countries of the necessity and desirability of their countries undertaking [1290-d] activities'.[54] State Department efforts also encouraged participation of SEATO countries in that body's countersubversion committee.

1290-d also tasked State with improving relations between recipient governments and their internal ethnic and tribal groups.[55] 1290-d was intended to bond complex and diverse recipient societies into cohesive state actors within the state system. Eisenhower and his NSC recognized the diverse ethnic communities, secessionist and irredentist movements and also factional competition within most newly emergent states. 1290-d embodied efforts to strengthen and extend the authority of these new states without exacerbating conflict between competing power centres. The programme also exhibited early efforts on the part of Washington to promote a sense of common identity between ethnic groups and their often distant central government. The disaffection of such groups would provide easy opportunities for communist exploitation, as would the upheaval born of factional struggles. In this context, the State Department was directed to facilitate diplomatic contacts at the intrastate level.

CIA responsibilities under 1290-d included aiding recipients in developing their own capabilities to carry out covert operations in coordination with US activities, as well as establishing domestic 'counterintelligence mechanisms'.[56]

The Agency's 1290-d responsibilities reflected its own, expanding covert operation role. In March of 1954, the CIA had been charged with the conduct of covert operations, through NSC 5412. This directive reflected an aggressive, retaliation-in-kind approach to containment, a response to the 'vicious covert activities of the USSR and communist China and the governments, parties and groups dominated by them'.[57] Clearly reflecting the active, aggressive approach to containment recommended by Solarium's Task Group C, the objectives of 5412 often dovetailed rather well with those of 1290-d, and included: creating and exploiting 'troublesome problems' for international communism and disrupting intrabloc relations; discrediting 'the prestige and ideology' of international communism; countering 'any threat of a party or individuals directly or indirectly responsive to communist control to achieve dominant power in a free world country'; and strengthening pro-American orientation by accentuating identity of interest between local peoples and the US and 'by favoring, where appropriate, those groups genuinely advocating or believing in the advancement of such mutual interests'.[58]

No agency was tasked with promoting the modification of laws and establishment of a functioning judiciary system in recipient countries, as was called for by the Working Group in the original 1290-$\underline{d}$ reports.[59] This objective eventually fell by the wayside.[60]

Effectiveness

As the embodiment of the Eisenhower administration's new internal security concept, the 1290-$\underline{d}$ programme and its objectives represented a substantial redirection of US security assistance policy. However, the effectiveness of the various 1290-$\underline{d}$ measures in promoting those objectives was compromised by problems Washington encountered in the areas of recipient resistance, interagency coordination, and the assumptions upon which the 1290-$\underline{d}$ approach ultimately rested.

Recipient resistance

An inherent conflict in the 1290-$\underline{d}$ effort pitted the need to bolster recipients' will to meet the subversive threat against the need to restructure and reorient aid programmes away from external defence and towards internal security, freeing up military aid funds for use in economic aid. The reduction of military assistance programme expenditures by building civil police and constabulary forces remained an unfulfilled objective of the 1290-$\underline{d}$ programme. Once these new forces became operational, the NSC had hoped to achieve significant economies by eventually reducing support of recipient military forces that had been filling internal security roles. However, this objective was in trouble from the start.

The director of the soon to be defunct FOA, Harold Stassen, argued for a major reorientation of the Mutual Security approach. As he saw it, as the communist-free world struggle had shifted to internal subversion, why not reduce military components of security assistance and substitute new guidelines more in line with the current threat? Stassen argued that there was an obvious need to 'indicate clearly that we are shifting to a new form of the long struggle against communist totalitarianism', and on this point, the President agreed.[61]

Getting the allies to agree seemed another matter entirely. It was clearly desirable to reduce foreign force levels to a point where they could be supported by their own economies. Yet, as Foster Dulles observed, many recipients were unwilling to rely on the deterrent power of US military might and wanted visible military forces of their own. Ultimately, Dulles reasoned, it might be possible to disabuse recipients of this notion, 'educate' them to accept the effectiveness of the US deterrent and thereby persuade them to accept reductions in their own forces. However, such change could not be brought about suddenly, lest it strain or break recipients' morale.[62] Further, this education would prove especially problematic since the USA had originally insisted that these existing force levels were the minimum required for maintaining security.[63]

The USA needed greater flexibility in designing security assistance pro-grammes, but given Washington's enduring emphasis on maintaining free world cohesion and combating 'defeatism' among its allies, any changes would have to be cautious and gradual. Washington's programmes to con-vince recipient governments as to the dangers of communism would be undermined by significant reductions in support for their armed forces. At the end of 1955, the Eisenhower administration chose to implement more subtle measures to bring about desired changes in recipients' military estab-lishments. The NSC directed the Department of Defense to 'use its influ-ence' with foreign military personnel to urge awareness of the new, internal subversive threat and of the need to reorganize, and to 'urge reductions in unnecessarily large armed forces'.[64] Washington anticipated that, as 1290-d created effective, civilian internal security forces, regular military units with similar functions would become redundant and be phased out. However, as time passed it became evident that recipient military establishments had little inclination to reduce their forces; they were often less concerned with external threats than with their own power and prestige. 1290-d did little to reduce MAP expenditures and free funds for economic aid programmes; instead it became an added cost to the Mutual Security Program.

Interagency coordination

A chronic problem in implementing 1290-d was inadequate coordination between the agencies involved. 1290-d was designed to be a concerted, multi-agency effort. However, achieving the degree of coordination envisioned by the OCB proved a serious problem, and what interagency cooperation did exist was largely of an ad-hoc nature.[65] On one hand, coordination was impeded by the extreme security surrounding the 1290-d programmes, and the special handling required for highly classified 1290-d documents. Such requirements slowed communications, and kept even those with a clear need-to-know from being adequately informed of their responsibilities under the programme.[66]

The highly compartmentalized nature of information in the counter-subversion effort often resulted in situations wherein participating agencies not only duplicated each other's efforts but directly contradicted and under-mined them. For example, NSC 5412, the covert operations plan, directed that 'in areas dominated *or threatened by* international communism', the CIA would 'develop underground assistance and facilitate covert and guerrilla operations'.[67] This objective fit less comfortably with the broader 1290-d effort; in fact, on this point the CIA and other agencies involved in the 1290-d effort were working at cross purposes. As John Prados observed, these CIA activities ultimately contradicted broader nation-building efforts.[68] While other agencies involved in 1290-d worked to build and extend the recipient government's authority throughout the country, as well as to foster public support for that government, the CIA was organizing resistance movements in the remote areas. NSC 5412 intended that such organizations would provide stay-behind assets in the event their areas came under communist authority, carrying out guerrilla operations and otherwise disrupting communist control.[69] Unfortunately, many such organizations were based on ethnic or tribal groups which were at least as inclined to resist the US-supported central government as they would the communists.

Coordination was also hindered by fallout from the termination of Stassen's FOA and its replacement with the new ICA under the more conservative directorship of John B. Hollister. The accompanying transfer of responsibilities resulted in some ambiguity regarding authority for specific foreign aid programmes, especially those concerned with national security. The Defense and State Departments and the CIA had already been involved in programmes having internal security objectives before the 1290-d programme was launched. However, the country-specific nature of the OCB's recommendations had prescribed leading roles for different agencies in different countries. In light of this, the OCB's Elmer Staats, Foster Dulles and others argued for overall coordination under one authority, in this case the ICA.[70] Eisenhower and the NSC clarified matters with the issue of NSC Action 1486-c, which clearly delineated agency responsibilities in the national security field and reaffirmed, under the President's own hand, that coordinating authority for all 1290-d activities was vested in the ICA.[71]

Even after the issue of NSC Action 1486-c, coordination was patchy at best, both in Washington and at overseas missions implementing 1290-d activities. Various agencies' representatives at US overseas missions aggravated this problem by side-stepping their Chief of Mission and coordinating their activities with their respective agency superiors in Washington. Upon hearing numerous complaints to this effect, Eisenhower directed the State Department to send a telegram in his name to all overseas missions reaffirming that the Chief of Mission was to coordinate all agencies' efforts at the country level in all matters, including those related to Mutual Security.[72] To tighten coordination in Washington, in September of 1956, the OCB re-emphasized ICA's leadership role by making its director responsible for all 1290-d activities *irrespective* of whether these activities and programmes were already part of existing Mutual Security Programs.[73] However, despite chairing a series of high-level coordinating committees drawn from participating agencies, the ICA was never entirely satisfied with the coordination it was able to achieve.

General assumptions and doctrine

In retrospect, the extensive survey the OCB sent to the field in 1955 may represent the OISP's most meaningful contribution to policy-making, as it offered Washington evidence as to the immense and qualitatively different nature of the political processes underway in the developing world. However, decision-makers' basic assumptions regarding events in the developing world so distorted their analysis of these data as to greatly lessen the impact they should have had on security assistance policy.

These assumptions played a decisive role in security assistance policy-making, as the USA continued to presume that threats to the stability of Third World recipients were ultimately *external*, either in the form of subversive agents of the bloc, or in the form of propaganda touting the 'false promise' of the communist development model. Even local Communist Parties were presumed to be neither local nor legitimate, and this presumption led Washington to focus on controlling these presumably foreign agents (subversives, 'fellow travelers' and propaganda) while giving far less attention to conditions within the recipient society that made communism so appealing.

These assumptions also shaped policy through the fundamental if often unspoken belief that US-style institutions were a universally applicable blueprint for nation-building, and that market-based economies were the natural way to prosperity. American decision-makers seemed to believe profoundly that communism was a dead-end, a false path to development, as the economic gains of the communist states were based on slave labour and other oppressive policies rather than the productive labour of 'free men in a free society' as Eisenhower put it.[74] Eisenhower and his NSC believed that, left to their own devices, the peoples of the developing world would *naturally* choose the Western path. For this reason, America's Cold War nation-building programmes in developing countries tended to focus on providing a 'shield', on protecting these societies from ultimately foreign threats and domestic agents thereof, holding these countries together and ensuring that their peoples were left to get on with their own development. Less attention was devoted to ensuring that these peoples had the *means* to build their own societies along Western lines, as substantial public-sector development assistance was still missing from American foreign aid efforts.

The findings of the OCB survey, indicating that the developing world found the communist example more attractive, provided something of a jolt to US policy-makers, but it did not make them look beyond their ideological blinkers. These findings, distorted by Washington's own fundamental aversion to communism and constructed assumptions regarding the magnitude, urgency and *source* of the threat, ensured that institutional transfer to recipients in the developing world would emphasize *security* institutions. Ultimately, 1290-d stressed stability not through any transfer of prosperity but through the establishment of order and control.

Side-effects

The policies derived from and shaped by these flawed assumptions yielded significant and lasting side-effects which made significant impacts on recipient societies. The unchecked ballooning of recipient military establishments along with the serious retardation of political development processes in recipient countries combined to create the most debilitating legacy.

Retarded political development

Ultimately, the 1290-d objectives stressed 'order' as a prerequisite for development. This emphasis was not simply a matter of treating symptoms without addressing the causes of the 'disease'; rather, it reflects the 'trade, not aid' philosophy of the early Eisenhower years, as well as the domestic political resistance within the US Congress that Eisenhower faced on foreign aid issues (see Chapter 4). 1290-d's countersubversion programmes were intended to encourage private investment in developing countries by providing some degree of security for foreign capital, primarily by aiding recipient regimes in quelling armed insurrection and civil disturbances. At the same time, 1290-d's broad brief also targeted radicals in labour unions, the press and intellectual organizations. With the press, the intelligentsia, and labour adequately controlled, recipient regimes with sufficient 'political will' could provide an inviting climate for investment.

The military and police were not the only domestic institutions targeted for help by US programmes, but they were the only sector of society that Washington armed and trained to keep the other sectors under control. Additionally, perceiving a virtually ubiquitous threat of communist subversion and a need to provide a 'shield', Washington saw security institutions as a foundation and as a prerequisite for developing strong, viable societies. American advisors simultaneously taught newly created security forces that proper relations between police and populace were important, and that virtually any means were justified in controlling communists. These measures combined with the ethnic plurality and factional politics of many recipient societies, along with US 'information programmes' that warned of communist penetration of virtually all facets of society, pushed many developing societies toward increasingly violent authoritarianism. Tellingly, the objective of establishing independent judiciaries serving to control the newly-created security forces had fallen by the wayside by the end of 1958.

In this sense, the perceived urgency of the subversive threat, and resulting emphasis on security institutions, tended to undermine the formation of other Western-style institutions, such as independent labour, a free press and the other facets of society cited as likely hotbeds of communist subversion in the 1290-d documentation. The upheaval of the decolonization process was bound to create varying degrees of instability in the new states of Southeast Asia and elsewhere. Fearing that political instability might be exploited by communism, the USA focused on creating local security institutions which, as they grew and consolidated their position within their societies, tended not to protect processes of political and social change but to stifle them.

Bloated recipient military establishments

While acknowledging that the nature of the perceived communist threat had shifted away from overt attack, the Eisenhower administration found it difficult to reduce the levels of military aid within its broader security assistance efforts for political reasons, both domestic (i.e., resistance from

Congress) and foreign (i.e., resistance from recipient governments). By the end of 1954, the NSC estimated that the bloc had shifted from overt aggression to subversive tactics in pursuing expansionist aims. While this shift suggested that a reconsideration of force goals and military aid distribution might have been in order, possible recipient reactions to any substantial revisions severely limited the range of options available to the NSC.

At a meeting in December 1955, at which the OCB's 23 November report was discussed, the NSC considered the future of mutual security programmes as well as the role to be played by 1290-d. Director Hollister and John Ohly of the newly established International Cooperation Administration described the problem as being a matter of priorities. Military assistance and related aid programmes – i.e., Defense Support – were *not* promoting progress towards development by providing a 'shield'; they were in fact promoting oversize military establishments that drained resources from fragile recipient economies. The Defense Support Program, established under the Mutual Security Act of 1951, had been intended to address this problem. Defense Support provided funds for 'direct' as well as 'indirect' support of recipients' militaries, so that their governments would not have to divert funds needed for development in other sectors. However, the militaries in many of these countries grew and grew, with the local US ambassadors joining in the calls for ever greater funding support, while little progress was made in terms of economic development.

Citing Korea as an example of how badly things had gone wrong, Ohly observed that the US had made 'no progress whatsoever in getting the load off its own back and directing Korea in the path of future stability and self-support'. Defense Support funding, especially in the 'indirect support' category, had gone far beyond defence-related expenditures. An ICA status report on the Mutual Security Program described the situation as follows:

> Current force goals necessitate heavy US-financed imports of consumer goods and materials for consumer goods production, required to generate local currency for budgetary support and to cover other defense support activities. Such imports not only maintain consumption at an artificially high level but will make difficult the future increase in savings necessary for economic stabilization and development.[75]

In the Korean case, the US had been injecting resources into the South Korean economy in sums roughly equivalent to that country's entire gross national product.[76] While Korea represented an outstanding case, the problem was common throughout East and Southeast Asia. Vietnam and Pakistan had also become 'black holes' into which aid disappeared without a trace. Unjustifiable force levels in Thailand denied the Thai government funds necessary for the development projects so badly needed to maintain political stability. In Laos, the US was bearing the entire cost of the Laotian armed forces.[77]

In most cases, the US got little 'bang' for its military assistance 'buck'.

Status reports for the Mutual Security Program painted a dismal picture of the actual capabilities of US-supported militaries. Taiwan, for example, was one of the six 'high cost' programmes (which together consumed roughly half of all US foreign aid in the mid-1950s), yet its military's effectiveness seemed doubtful. Semi-annual progress reports by the Joint Chiefs of Staff (JCS) repeatedly cited low combat effectiveness in all of the Republic of China armed services, poor management and planning on the part of Taiwanese forces, and unauthorized diversion of military aid resources. In South Vietnam, the JCS estimated that the local armed forces could not 'retard or delay external aggression without considerable outside assistance.'[78]

The irksome question of time continued to worry US security planners. Instability in developing areas, the ever-present threat of nationalization of assets, and, not least, Congressional resistance to lowering US trade barriers, all contributed to disappointing rates of private investment in the underdeveloped world.[79] 'Trade, not aid' was proving a slow and uncertain means of promoting the growth of strong economies and, in the end, Washington proved unwilling or unable to balance measures designed to promote development in recipient societies with its measures to protect them, like a gardener who devotes all resources to pest and disease control at the expense of fertilizer. When the Eisenhower administration did make its move into significant, public-sector aid to developing countries, it was primarily in response to Soviet initiatives that increased US decision-makers' sense of urgency. Even as Eisenhower and his NSC formulated their response to the bloc's perceived tactical shift towards political subversion as a means of expansion, Moscow was embarking on what Washington would view as an 'economic offensive', what Eisenhower himself called the 'new, economic phase of the Cold War'.[80]

Notes

1   NSC 68, 'United States Objectives and Programs for National Security', 14 April 1950. *FRUS, 1950*, vol. 1, pp. 234–292.

2   Annex 2, attachment to NSC 68/3. *FRUS, 1950*, vol. 1, p. 454.

3   For a discussion of US containment objectives, see John Lewis Gaddis, *The United States and the End of the Cold War* (New York: Oxford University Press, 1992), ch. 2.

4   1290-d was one of a series of actions taken by the NSC (NSC) after its 229th meeting on 21 December 1954. Documents and correspondence subsequently generated in connection with that NSC action continued to carry the 1290-d designation until the overall effort was redesignated the Overseas Internal Security Program (OISP) in 1957.

5   A recent and ambitious examination of the 'colonial state' concept can be found in Crawford Young, *The African Colonial State in Comparative Perspective* (New Haven, CT: Yale University Press, 1994).

6   'United States Overseas Internal Defense Policy', p. 15. NSF, Meetings and Memoranda, box 338, re: National Security Action Memorandum (NSAM)

182 (JFK Library).

7 NSC 149, 'Basic National Security Policies and Programs in Relation to their Costs', 29 April 1953. *FRUS, 1952–54*, vol. 2, pt 1, p. 307.

8 Memorandum from Director, Policy Planning Staff (Bowie), to Secretary of State, 8 June 1953. *FRUS, 1952–54*, vol. 2, pt 1, p. 370.

9 NSC 153, 'Restatement of Basic National Security Policy', 10 June 1953. *FRUS, 1952–54*, vol. 2, pt 1, p. 379.

10 See Discussion at 141st Meeting of NSC, 28 April, 1953. *FRUS, 1952–54*, vol. 2, pt 1, p. 304.

11 Kaufman, *Trade and Aid*, also, Carl M. Brauer, *Presidential Transitions: Eisenhower Through Reagan* (Oxford: Oxford University Press, 1986), p. 49.

12 Kaufman, *Trade and Aid*, p. 13.

13 Gaddis, *Strategies of Containment*, p. 152.

14 Discussion at 229th meeting of NSC, Tuesday 21 December 1954. Whitman File, NSC Series, Meetings and Memoranda, box 6 (DDE Library).

15 The New Look was the name commonly used for the national security policy statement NSC 162/2, approved 30 September 1953. See *FRUS, 1952–54*, vol. 2, pt 1, pp. 491–534.

16 Acheson, *Present at the Creation*, pp. 265–266.

17 NSC 162/2, Basic National Security Policy, 30 October 1953. *FRUS, 1952–54*, vol. 2, National Security Affairs, pt 1, p. 578.

18 Gaddis, *Strategies of Containment*, p. 128. References to the 1948 Czechoslovakia coup are sprinkled throughout the 1290-d and subsequent OISP literature.

19 Discussion at 229th Meeting of NSC, 21 December 1954.

20 Gaddis, *Strategies of Containment*, pp. 130–132. Also reiterated in NSC 5422.

21 Memorandum for NSC: Project Solarium, 22 July 1953. OSANSA, Security Affairs: Records, 1952–61. NSC Series, Subject Subseries, box 9, file: Project Solarium, Report to NSC by Task Force 'A' (DDE Library).

22 Report to NSC by Task Force 'C' of Project Solarium, 16 July 1953. OSANSA, Security Affairs: Records, 1952–61. NSC Series, Subject Subseries, box 9, file: Project Solarium, Report to NSC by Task Force 'C' (DDE Library).

23 Discussion at 157th Meeting of NSC, Thursday 30 July 1953. Whitman File, NSC Series, box 20 (DDE Library).

24 NSC 5422/2, 'Tentative Guidelines Under NSC 162/2 for FY 1956', 14 June 1954. OSANSA, NSC Series, Policy Papers Subseries, box 11, NSC 5422/2 (DDE Library).

25 NSC 5422.

26 Memorandum for NSC, Project Solarium, 22 July 1953. OSANSA, Records, 1952–61, NSC Series, Subject Subseries, box 10, Project Solarium, 1953 (2) (DDE Library).

27 Discussion at 229th Meeting of NSC, 21 December 1954.

28 *Ibid.*

29 The South East Asian Treaty Organization (SEATO) was established at Manila in late 1954. It included Australia, France, Great Britain, New Zealand, Pakistan, the Philippines, Thailand and the USA. The 'Associated States' of Indochina were excluded in accordance with the 1954 Geneva 'Final Declaration', while Indonesia excluded itself from military alignment with the West.

30 Memorandum of Discussion at 229th Meeting of NSC, 21 December 1954.

31 *Ibid.*
32 *Ibid.*
33 *Ibid.* Upon referral to the Operations Coordinating Board (OCB), this project was designated OCB 014.12, and was redesignated the OISP in 1957.
34 Report of NSC 1290-d Working Group, 16 February 1955, p. 1. White House Office, OCB Central File, box 16, OCB 014.12 (1), (2).
35 'Organization Arrangements for Internal Security', NSC 5425/1, 10 September 1954. OSANSA File, NSC Series, Policy Papers Subseries, box 11, NSC 5425/1 (Internal Security) (DDE Library).
36 Working Group, 16 February 1955, p. 2. Also see NSC 5425.
37 Working Group, 16 February 1955, p. 4.
38 *Ibid.*, p. 1.
39 *Ibid.*, p. 4.
40 *Ibid.*
41 The original 1290-d target countries were Afghanistan, Bolivia, Brazil, Burma, Cambodia, Chile, 'Free Vietnam', Greece, Guatemala, Indonesia, Iran, Iraq, Korea, Laos, Pakistan, the Philippines, Syria and Thailand. Their number would roughly double before Eisenhower left office.
42 Working group, 16 February 1955, p. 7. Also, State Department Circular Telegram no. 559. White House Office, NSC Staff Papers, 1948–61, OCB Central File Series, box 16 (DDE Library).
43 OCB, 'Report to the NSC Pursuant to NSC Action 1290-d', 23 November 1955, p. 3. White House Office, NSC Staff Papers, 1948–61, OCB Central File Series, box 17, OCB 014.12, file no. 2 (5) (DDE Library).
44 *Ibid.*
45 *Ibid.*, p. 4.
46 *Ibid.*, p. 18.
47 *Ibid.*, pp. 28, 29, 34.
48 1290-d absorbed the diverse programmes previously undertaken to strengthen internal security forces in threatened countries, most of which had been developed from policies outlined in NSC 5501 (which had been approved in early January 1955). The 5501 programmes, like earlier efforts in Greece and Indochina, tended to be piecemeal efforts to 'put out fires', to address situations that had already become critical. In contrast, argued the OCB, 'the NSC 1290-d project [wa]s an effort to provide a coordinated approach to this problem. It envisage[d] "fire prevention".' OCB, 23 November 1955, p. 7.
49 OCB, 23 November 1955, p. 7.
50 Defense Telegram no. 997798, 24 February 1956. White House Office, NSC Staff Papers, 1948–61, OCB Central File Series, box 17, OCB 014.12 (3) [January–November 1956] (DDE Library).
51 OCB Report to the NSC Pursuant to NSC Action 1290-d, 23 November 1955. Working closely with recipient militaries and paramilitary police caused considerable dissent among USIA personnel.
52 Attachment to ICA Report on NSC Action 1290-d, 22 June, 1956, p. 3. White House Office, NSC Staff Papers 1948–61, box 17, file OCB 014.12 (3) (DDE Library).
53 Attachment to ICA report on 1290-d, 22 June 1956.
54 Supplemental Progress Report on Actions Taken Pursuant to NSC Action 1290-d, 6 September 1956, p. 8.

55 Attachment to ICA Report, 22 June 1956, p. 22.

56 CIA, Working Draft Paper on the OISP, attached to CIA memorandum to Joseph Jacyno, OCB, 13 January 1959. NSC, OCB, box 1, OCB 014.12 (1). National Archives. In most of the 1290-d documents obtained in researching this project, CIA responsibilities are contained in separate annexes that have, for the most part, been exempted from this author's Mandatory Review requests. Attempts to have these materials declassified will continue. In the meantime, there is adequate declassified material available to support the description of CIA activities contained herein.

57 NSC Directive on Covert Operations, NSC 5412, 15 March 1954. White House Office, OSANSA, NSC, Policy Papers, box 10, file: NSC 5412 (covert operations) (DDE Library). This emphasis on perceived need for aggressive countersubversion measures within the CIA had built steadily through the first part of the Eisenhower presidency. See John Prados, 'The Central Intelligence Agency and the Face of Decolonization under the Eisenhower Administration', in Kathryn C. Statler and Andrew L. Johns (eds), *The Eisenhower Administration, The Third World and the Globalization of the Cold War* (Lanham, MD: Rowan and Littlefield, 2006).

58 NSC 5412.

59 OCB Report to NSC, 23 November 1955, p. 7.

60 'The OISP Program', Memorandum, ICA Director J. H. Smith, Jr, to CIA Director Allen Dulles, 28 November 1958. NSC, OCB, box 1, file: OCB 014.12 (1), p. 1 (DDE Library).

61 Discussion at 269th Meeting of NSC, *FRUS*, 1955–57, vol. 10, p. 51.

62 *Ibid.*, p. 54.

63 *Ibid.*, p. 56. An excellent analysis of the origins of US military assistance, including its psychological role, is contained in Pach, *Arming the Free World*.

64 OCB, 15 January 1957, p. 1.

65 OCB, 'Supplemental Progress Report on Actions Taken Pursuant to NSC Action 1290-d, 6 September 1956, p. 3.

66 OCB, 6 September 1956, p. 9. Also OCB Status Report, 27 December 1956, p. 2.

67 NSC Directive on Covert Operations, NSC 5412 (emphasis added).

68 John Prados, *Presidents' Secret Wars* (New York: William Morrow, 1986), ch. 8.

69 NSC 5412, 15 March 1954.

70 Discussion at 269th Meeting of NSC, 8 December 1955. *FRUS*, 1955–57, vol. 10, p. 44.

71 NSC Action 1486-c, 8 December 1955.

72 Circular Telegram, State Department to all Chiefs of Mission, 24 July 1956. *FRUS*, 1955–57, vol. 10, pp. 83–84.

73 Action taken by OCB, 19 September 1956, revised and approved by the Board 26 September 1956. White House Office, NSC Staff, OCB Central Files, box 17, OCB 014.12 (3) [January–November 1956] (DDE Library).

74 Eisenhower to Dulles, 6 December 1955. Whitman File, Dulles-Herter Series, box 6 (DDE Library).

75 'Status of Mutual Security Program, as of June 30, 1955' (NSC 5525), pt 2, p. 25. White House Office, OSANSA Records 1952–61, box 6, file NSC 5525 (4) (DDE Library).

76 Discussion at 269th Meeting of NSC, 8 December 1955. *FRUS, 1955–57*, vol. 10, pp. 46–49. Ohly identified six, 'high-cost' country programmes, which together totalled roughly 50 per cent of the entire US foreign aid budget. These six were Iran, Korea, Pakistan, Taiwan, Turkey and Vietnam.

77 'Status of Mutual Security Program, as of June 30, 1955' (NSC 5525), pt 2, pp. ICA-35–37. White House Office, OSANSA Records 1952–61, box 6, file NSC 5525 (4) (DDE Library).

78 See, for example, 'Department of Defense report to the NSC on Status of Military Assistance Programs as of 30 June 1955, section 1: Area and Country Report', 1 October 1955, pp. 27–28. White House Office, OSANSA, records 1952–61, box 6, file NSC 5525 (2) (DDE Library).

79 See Kaufman, *Trade and Aid,* chs 7 and 8.

80 Eisenhower letter to Dulles, quoted in W. W. Rostow, *Eisenhower, Kennedy and Foreign Aid* (Austin, TX: University of Texas Press, 1985), p. 112.

4

The aid war and reassessment

Throughout the course of 1955, while the OCB were formulating the 1290-d̲ measures to attack the 'communist apparatus' in developing areas and thereby address the threat of political subversion, Eisenhower and his advisers grew increasingly concerned with a recent and pronounced shift in Moscow's foreign economic policy. In a marked departure from the policies of the Stalin era, the USSR had opened trade and aid relationships with the nations of the developing world. By the end of that year, Washington had declared these new Soviet economic initiatives to be an 'economic offensive', another tactical shift in the bloc's expansionist drive. Even as Washington formulated and implemented the countersubversive measures described in the previous chapter, US security planners moved to assess and respond to this new Soviet economic challenge in the developing world. What amounted to an aid war was soon underway.

Washington's perceptions of and response to these Soviet economic initiatives are highly significant because they focused US attention on economic development assistance as a *security* measure; such aid gained salience as a Cold War weapon. In response to the Soviet initiatives the Eisenhower administration launched the first significant programme of public-sector economic aid to the developing countries, the Development Loan Fund or DLF. The aid war also triggered a sweeping reassessment of the appropriate balance between military and non-military aid instruments in Washington's security assistance policy, and it redirected the course of US aid policy for the next decade.

Returning to the prescriptions of NSC 68, the 'military shield' was intended to protect the processes by which recipient societies would be strengthened to the point where they could resist the threat of communist subversion. However, outside of Europe and Japan, US aid efforts had emphasized the shield aspect over – and often at the expense of – efforts to build up the political and economic strength of free world countries. While Washington strove to protect developing countries from communist aggression, either overt or subversive, far less effort and far fewer resources had gone into developing the 'moral and material strength' of these countries needed to 'frustrate the Kremlin design' of world domination.[1]

Through the early years of the Eisenhower presidency, development efforts *per se* focused on continuing programmes of technical assistance that the Truman administration had initiated, as well as on increasing levels of private sector investment in, and trade with, developing countries. Eisenhower's 'trade, not aid' approach had resembled Truman era policies in two important respects: first, in that development was simply a matter of promoting economic growth; and second, that such development would depend primarily upon local efforts – it was up to the people of new states to make the most of development opportunities that came their way. Technical assistance would help provide recipients with the scientific know-how to develop the basic infrastructure needed to attract foreign commerce; the rest was up to the dynamics of the market. The NSC summarized the situation in 1954 as follows:

> In the economic field, there are two basic problems: (a) the industrialized areas seek expanding markets and (b) the underdeveloped areas seek to develop and modernize their economies. It should be within the capacity of the free world, with US initiative and leadership, to turn these two problems into mutually supporting assets for the promotion of appropriate economic strength and growth.[2]

At best, the 'trade, not aid' approach amounted to a slow and indirect route to development for the countries of these underdeveloped areas, and, by the mid-1950s, they had made little headway. Private corporations remained hesitant to invest in less developed areas. These companies expressed concern over the possible loss of their overseas investments through expropriation by the local government, and continually pressed for US guarantees of their foreign investments. Additionally, Congress had proven generally unwilling to lower tariff barriers and, thus, give products manufactured in these areas access to the lucrative US market. Without such market access, Eisenhower's 'trade, not aid' approach could make little progress.

This conservative approach was rudely shaken by the new threat of Soviet policy initiated by Khrushchev in 1955. The Soviets' launching of their own trade and aid initiatives in the developing world in the mid-1950s thoroughly undermined the administration's conviction that private capital would be adequate to bring about real economic development. Private commerce alone could not keep radicalism in check, as it could not develop in these regions the economic strength necessary to keep up with rising popular expectations.

The Soviet initiatives lent urgency to the cause of development in these areas; US programmes that promised slow and indirect routes to economic progress were outshone by the promises of rapid industrialization and economic progress offered and exemplified by the USSR. Increased prestige for the Soviet development model also translated into increased prestige for leftist factions in developing countries, thereby undermining US nation-building efforts. Local communist parties and leftist movements, previously shunned by Moscow, could now look to the USSR for support. These groups could also point to the USSR (and, increasingly, the PRC) as shining examples of what the communist development model could produce in a relatively short time. Towards the end of 1955, Washington observed that the communist example, rather than that of the free world, was proving the most compelling among the peoples of the underdeveloped areas, especially in Asia. Bolstered by their increased prestige, leftist factions actively promoted themselves as credible alternatives to incumbent regimes.

This trend toward intensifying factional competition and rising expectations among the peoples of new states compelled American policy-makers to search for ways of strengthening moderate, non-communist regimes and of bolstering their credibility and prestige as a means of securing for them the allegiance of their populations. In the context of the new Soviet foreign economic policy, Eisenhower and many of his advisers recognized that such credibility did not stem primarily from military deterrent capabilities; it was instead a matter of offering these populations some hope of economic progress. In their efforts to meet the Soviet economic challenge, US policy-makers were forced to reassess their security assistance programmes to determine whether the existing balance between military and economic elements was appropriate in light of that challenge. This reassessment marked a turning point in the development of US Mutual Security Assistance policy.

US perceptions of global communist threat

Our analysis of the impact of the Soviet economic initiatives on Washington's security assistance policies must begin with an overview of those initiatives themselves and of Washington's perceptions thereof, particularly Washington's perceptions of the threat these initiatives posed in the developing world.

Soviet initiatives

The Soviets had been developing the necessary capabilities for trade with the developing world since 1952. As the massive task of postwar reconstruction neared completion, Soviet economists anticipated an exportable surplus of machines and other capital goods, and sought avenues for marketing these in exchange for raw materials. Towards this end, the Soviet government established in the spring of 1952 an organization known as *Mashinoexport* to coordinate the export of machinery to less developed countries.[3] Soviet economists recognized that such trade arrangements, essentially of a barter nature, would appeal to developing countries. Raw materials producers could trade with the USSR without the risks inherent in the international capitalist market, with its price fluctuations, tariffs and exchange barriers.

In the years following the death of Stalin, the Soviet leadership also began to offer aid and technical assistance to new states emerging from the decolonization process. Moscow observed Washington's project to encircle the USSR with Mutual Security organizations, such as SEATO and the Baghdad Pact, and employed aid initiatives to establish amicable relations with emerging new states, thus undermining US efforts to shepherd them into anti-communist coalitions. Additionally, Moscow sought to guide new states onto the Marxist–Leninist path to development. The Soviet leadership, like its American counterpart, observed that the erosion and withdrawal of Western colonial authority from underdeveloped areas had left many newly decolonised states in political disarray. However, while Washington viewed such situations as fraught with dangers, the Soviets saw in them opportunities to engage emerging political elites and channel the blossoming social forces of these new states toward development along socialist lines compatible with the USSR. In the re-examination of Soviet international relations theory that followed Stalin's passing, Soviet social scientists embraced the idea that while the social class structures of developing countries posed a challenge to classical Marxist analysis, it was nonetheless possible that these countries could progress toward socialism within a Marxist–Leninist framework.[4]

The Soviet aid initiatives were tailored to the economic aspirations of many new states. In addition to forming trade links on a barter or otherwise concessional basis, Moscow launched extensive technical assistance programmes in developing countries. Like the Americans, the Soviets provided assistance in developing and extending basic infrastructure in recipient states and provided technical advice for improving production methods in extractive industries. Convinced of the centrality of heavy industrialization to any successful development programme, Moscow also helped build industrial plants such as the Bhilai steel mill in India.[5]

Moscow supplemented such tangible and highly visible aid with a concerted propaganda drive. The USSR promoted itself as the natural ally of the newly independent states, and as a concrete example of how, through communism, a country could achieve the rapid industrial and technological development that so many of the newly decolonised states aspired to. Rather like the Americans, who presumed that new states shared their goal of containing communism, Khrushchev repeatedly maintained that there existed a fundamental commonality of interest between these states and the USSR in advancing communism.[6]

In many newly independent countries, the often radical political tempers of emerging elites made them understandably receptive to the alternatives Moscow offered to anything that smacked of continued domination by the West. While both the USA and the USSR were trying to manage and direct the changes taking place in the developing world, the USA was, in essence, attempting to retard change and dampen the political upheaval produced by decolonisation.[7] Thus, Moscow could easily put political pressure on Washington to demonstrate its commitment to development in the former colonial areas. For example, as they toured South and Southeast Asia in

1956, Khrushchev and Bulganin actively encouraged the new states of these areas to use offers of Soviet assistance as bargaining levers to pressure the West, especially the US, for additional aid. In this manner Moscow could, and did, claim that increased aid these countries received from the West was in fact 'indirect assistance' from the USSR.[8]

Moscow pointed out that its aid came free of military obligations, in stark contrast with Washington's efforts to use aid in cementing military alliances. The post-Stalin leadership of the USSR was more tolerant of neutrals than either their predecessor had been or the Americans were. American observers in Moscow noted that the Soviets had replaced the zero-sum 'two camps thesis' of the Stalin years with a somewhat different view of international relations that recognized three camps: 'communist, enemy and neutral'.[9] This 'third zone of peace, neither socialist nor capitalist', which could draw upon the achievements of the communist world and receive aid 'free of any political or military obligations' was described by Khrushchev at the Twentieth Party Congress of the Communist Party of the Soviet Union (CPSU) in 1956.[10]

Moscow's aid initiatives were hardly free of political considerations, however. As Valkenier points out, the Soviets generally did not offer aid to moderate, pro-Western governments; instead, the USSR routinely used aid to encourage or reward anti-Western activities or orientation. Although the Soviet initiatives had originally been based on sound economic objectives, the control of these trade and aid programmes had been taken from Soviet economists and transferred to the political leadership, in whose hands it became part of 'an all-out political offensive aimed at encouraging the developing countries to nibble away at the territorial, strategic, and political domain of the West'.[11] The American mission in Moscow reported that a 1955 programme for increasing the production of consumer goods for domestic use in the USSR had been reversed in order to ensure an exportable surplus of industrial equipment and machinery for the developing world.[12] As Khrushchev declared in 1955: 'We value trade least for economic reasons and most for political purposes.'[13]

The American perception

Khrushchev's words resonated throughout the Eisenhower White House, confirming American suspicions that Moscow's new economic initiatives ultimately had political objectives. Washington interpreted these changes in Soviet foreign economic policy as a new 'economic offensive' in the Cold War. As one State Department analysis described the situation, the Soviet initiatives were aimed at 'economic penetration' of new areas, the long-term goals of which were to undermine and eventually replace the capitalist world market. According to this analysis, the USSR was positioning itself to:

> disrupt trade relations between the underdeveloped countries and the indus-
> trialized capitalist states, including the United Kingdom, West Germany
> and Japan. By encroaching on the traditional foreign trade markets of the

capitalist trading countries, it may be possible to simultaneously increase capitalist competition for remaining markets and to gain Bloc control of raw material supplies, such as Middle East petroleum, upon which the Western countries are dependent. It has for some time been a Soviet aim to create a 'democratic' world market which would rival and ultimately supersede the capitalist world market.[14]

Aware of how attractive Soviet offers of barter deals would appear to developing countries, US analysts worried that the USSR could eventually acquire the capability to manipulate and 'disorganize' important commodities markets and strangle Western industries by interrupting the flow of raw materials from developing areas. Washington also feared that the Soviets could disrupt the West's industrial exports to developing countries by competing for sales on terms below Western, or even Soviet, cost.[15]

If the bloc could gain control of commodities flowing from the developing world, American analysts reasoned that Moscow could exercise great leverage over the economic policies of the industrial states of Europe. Such leverage posed potentially dire strategic consequences for the Western Alliance. The State Department believed that if, for example, the Soviets could limit West Germany's export markets, they might create enough leverage to force long-term capital exports from West Germany to China on the Soviets' terms, countering US efforts to maintain its existing boycott of China and restrict trade with the bloc as a whole. Similarly, American analysts argued that interference in Britain's foreign markets could result in serious internal political pressures for reductions in that country's defence spending and even for a 'neutral accommodation' in the Cold War.[16]

While the above could be dismissed as something of an extreme over-reaction, the Soviet initiatives did pose a real political threat to the underlying containment strategy. The new Soviet foreign economic policy's principal challenge to the free world was that it threatened free world cohesion by easing the fear of communism, and, from Washington's perspective, fear was the most effective glue for holding the network of Mutual Security alliances together. Eisenhower expressed this concern in a letter to Dulles in late 1955: 'So long as [the communists] relied on force and the threat of force, we had the world's natural reaction of fear to aid us in building consolidations of power and strength in order to resist Soviet advances.'[17] Presidential adviser C. D. Jackson put it another way: 'So long as the Soviets had a monopoly on covert subversion and the threat of military aggression, and we had a monopoly on Santa Claus, some kind of a see-saw game could be played.' However, with their new foreign aid initiatives, the Soviets were clearly 'muscling in on Santa Claus'.[18]

Foster Dulles summed up his own view of how the situation had changed:

> So long as the Soviets under Stalin continued to behave so badly in public, it was relatively easy for our side to maintain a certain social ostracism toward them – and I stress the word 'social'. The whole post-war relationship between ourselves and our allies and the Russians can be analyzed and

described with great accuracy in terms of how a society, a community, a family responds to the behavior of an obvious bad egg ... And behind that social ostracism, which everybody understood even so some did not necessarily applaud, it was possible fairly quickly and easily to reach mutual defense agreements in order to see that this socially impossible person was kept out – and if he did threaten to break down the door or set fire to the house, that there would be sufficient friends and neighbours around to make him think twice.

Now all of a sudden the outward Soviet appearance, mood and behavior has materially changed, and speaking in social terms, it is becoming extremely difficult to maintain the ostracism – and maybe we should not even want to maintain it. Frowns have given way to smiles. Guns have given way to offers of economic aid.

Now I don't know if they are sincere or not, if this is a trick or not – but I do know two things. The first is that this 'change' is not superficial, is not limited to a few speeches and *Pravda* editorials. It goes quite deep, and of course the deeper it goes the less chance the new collective leadership has to disregard it or reverse it ... The other thing I know is that with all of these outward improvements ... it is very difficult for the United States to say to its allies that all of this means nothing, that it is a trick, that the ostracism must be maintained.[19]

Washington had worked steadily to discourage other free world nations from trading with the communist bloc. Now, with the new Soviet 'charm offensive' and lucrative terms offered to countries willing to trade with the bloc, the Americans found it increasingly difficult to maintain cohesion among their industrialized allies, and to effect a common stand on trade restrictions. US analysts viewed any easing of these restrictions as a threat, because from Washington's point of view, trade with the bloc simply helped fuel the Soviet economic offensive.

The less developed areas were viewed as particularly vulnerable to the Soviet offensive, and Washington expected that Moscow's economic activities in the backward regions were bound to resonate through those areas still under European control. Joseph Dodge, head of Eisenhower's Council on Foreign Economic Policy, asserted that the European states should be reminded of the threat the Soviet initiatives posed to European economic interests in Africa, the Far East, and the Middle East, before entering into trade relationships with the bloc. 'The further the Soviets go in their economic and trade offensive, the greater the penalties should be on its [*sic*] domestic economy.' Dodge argued that relaxation of Coordinating Committee on Multilateral Export Controls or Co-Com controls on trade and an increase of imports from the West eased burdens on the Soviet economy and thereby contributed to Moscow's aid offensive in developing areas.[20] From Washington's point of view, any allies advocating relaxation of Co-Com ultimately acted against their own interests. However, in the context of the new Soviet economic initiatives, the bloc was showing a far more amiable countenance to the world, undermining Washington's efforts to isolate it.

The US found ostracism of the bloc particularly difficult to maintain among the newly independent governments of the developing world. In the event that developing nations began to rely on trade with the bloc, American efforts to organize regional trade associations, largely modeled on the European Payments Union and other economic arrangements developed within the ERP, would never come to fruition. Fostering such regional trading arrangements had been a cornerstone of US development policy since the late 1940s, and if developing countries junked such arrangements in favour of increased trade with the bloc the resulting economic dependency would, from Washington's viewpoint, give Moscow considerable leverage in the economic decision-making of developing countries.[21]

The Soviets were well positioned to encourage increased trade with the developing world because of the complementary relationship between the economies of many new states and that of the USSR. Not only did the bloc have the sorts of capital goods that so many of these countries desired, they also had tremendous capacity to absorb the exportable surpluses characteristic of many developing economies. Moscow's decades of emphasis on heavy industrialization had left agriculture lagging, so the Soviets could readily absorb many surplus agricultural commodities for which the developing countries had been trying to find markets. In contrast the USA was more often a competing producer than a potential market for such products.[22]

American analysts estimated that, if the trade and aid 'offensive' continued, it would translate into substantial economic growth for the USSR. As it was becoming ever more costly to increase the output of the agricultural and extractive sectors of the Soviet economy, exchanging capital goods for surplus commodities supplemented net bloc resources considerably. Moscow could effectively employ such resources in expanding the industrial capacity of the bloc, with growth in production estimated as high as ten per cent per year. This would result in an increased capacity to export manufactured goods as well as a steady increase in the demand for raw materials, which could in turn result in steady expansion of the Soviets' economic drive in the developing world.[23]

The political threat in the developing world

Washington viewed the Soviet economic offensive in the developing world as a serious political challenge at two levels: in its effect on the foreign policy orientation of new states; and in its contribution to the power of communists and leftists in the factional struggles that characterized the internal politics of developing countries.

As it coincided with a rising tide of nationalist assertiveness in the decolonising areas, the Soviet economic offensive reinforced a growing tendency among new states to seek a neutral path with respect to the Cold War. Washington had been carefully trying to coax such neutralist nations as Burma and Indonesia into the pro-Western fold, but with the new Soviet economic initiatives the objective was shifting towards keeping new states from going over to the communists. Burma had unilaterally suspended its aid relationship with the US and asked Washington to withdraw its mission there.[24] Cambodia's government continued to accept aid from the USA and from France while opening new economic relationships with China and the USSR. From the US perspective, neutralism suddenly seemed more acceptable in the face of a worsening political environment.

Washington worried that newly independent states, while professing a neutral course in their affairs, were in fact drifting into the arms of the communist bloc. The Americans, along with some of their European allies, found the April 1955 Bandung Conference of Afro-Asian nations particularly unsettling. The strident anti-Western tone of the conference, as well as the highly visible and active participation of communist China in the proceedings, struck an unnerving chord in Washington. One after another, delegates to the conference declared that the threat to their new nations was not communism but Western colonialism.[25]

To Eisenhower, it seemed that these developing countries were being duped into an accommodation with communism that would ultimately prove their undoing. The President told Congress that, if he could believe that the Soviets had abandoned their 'sinister objectives', he would welcome their new economic initiatives. In fact, he saw these initiatives as merely communist expansionism in a different guise; the Soviets' fundamental objective was still 'to disrupt and in the end dominate free nations'.[26] Still the questioned remained; how to reverse the political gains scored by the communists in their economic offensive in the developing world?

Response: reassessment and a move toward redirection of effort

Washington urgently needed a means of combating the communist *idea*, along with the increasingly popular view that communism was the 'wave of the future' in Asia. Communism was riding a rising tide of popular expectations in the developing world. The new political elites of these regions, emerging from long periods of colonial domination, demanded rapid economic progress and development. The communist model appeared to offer a more rapid means of attaining such goals than did the path proffered by the West.[27]

Washington also needed a way to erode the prestige and enhanced credibility that had accrued to local communist parties and other leftist movements as a result of the Soviet economic offensive. The USIA information programmes launched under the 1290-d programme, as described in Chapter 3, and similar efforts to decry the 'false promise' of communism, rang hollow in the context of Moscow's new trade and aid policies.

The US attempted to address the political threat embodied in the Soviet economic offensive, at both the levels of external orientation and internal politics, through efforts to build confidence in non-communist paths to development. If US efforts could help bolster a citizenry's confidence in its government's ability to bring about some semblance of economic progress or even prosperity, such confidence could help that government resist challenges from local communists or other extremists. Similarly, if Washington's efforts helped recipient countries achieve significant economic success, then that country's success could become a showpiece of what could be achieved without adopting the communist development model, a showpiece that could outshine the apparent success being made by communist China.[28]

Thus, the Soviet trade and aid initiatives pushed Washington to institute its first substantial programme of direct economic assistance to the developing world, the Development Loan Fund (DLF). More importantly, the Soviet 'economic offensive' had precipitated a far-reaching reassessment of Washington's entire Mutual Security approach, a reassessment that questioned not only the effectiveness of the various aid instruments used but also the philosophy and objectives of US foreign aid programmes as a whole. Towards the end of 1955 the Eisenhower administration began work on a series of such assessments.

Early assessments: a question of balance

It seemed obvious to security planners in Washington that the Cold War was expanding along two dimensions: first, the communist threat had broadened from one based on military force and intimidation into the areas of political subversion and now economic competition with the West; and second, this Cold War competition had spread into new areas of the globe as new states emerged from the decolonization process. Additionally, Western Europe's 'retraction' from former colonial areas demanded that the USA provide support to maintain the independence of these areas.[29] The State Department also observed that Moscow's aid offensive scored great political successes against the USA, even though the Soviets spent far less on their aid programmes.[30] As any substantial expansion of the US foreign aid budget was unlikely to gain Congressional approval, the Eisenhower administration turned to assessing existing Mutual Security programmes to ascertain ways in which the current aid policies could be made more effective in achieving their goals.[31]

In the context of the new Soviet 'offensive', one area of particular concern to all involved was the lack of progress less developed recipients were making toward economic self-sufficiency. By this time, no further economic aid was flowing to European recipients, but the biggest developing-world recipients demanded more rather than less aid every year. To investigate the nature of this drain on Mutual Security resources, an interdepartmental committee was formed of representatives from the Defense and Treasury Departments and the ICA, and chaired by the Deputy Under Secretary of State for Economic Affairs, Herbert V. Prochnow.[32]

Prochnow's committee was charged with examining the impact and effectiveness of security assistance on the economic development and military

capabilities of the programme's largest recipients, the majority of which
were located in Southeast Asia and virtually all of which were developing
countries.[33] In particular, the committee would look for situations wherein
US-supported military programmes might be causing an undue burden on
the recipient's economy.

Prochnow delivered his report on behalf of his committee the following
summer. Prochnow's study found that most US assistance went to support the
budgets and balance of payments of recipient countries. Little or no money
went to promoting development or economic self-sufficiency; instead, the
military establishments of recipient countries continued to swell, demanding
ever more support from Washington. Their conclusions suggested that US
security assistance policy was seriously out of balance:

> It appears, generally speaking, that the US may have participated in the
> expansion of military plant in these countries beyond a point justified
> in terms of economic and security considerations. The further we go in
> this direction the greater are our contingent responsibilities. In this situ-
> ation, unless more real economic development assistance is forthcoming
> from somewhere, these economies may experience little or no increase in
> strength.[34]

Furthermore, since most aid went towards budget support, the US had
little control over how it was used, and thus had little hope of shifting aid
to an emphasis on economic development. The committee speculated that
such shifts, or any cutbacks in aid, 'would be politically very difficult' and
would grow more difficult as time went on, since recipients tended to build
security assistance into their budgets 'as anticipated income'. To make a
start in addressing this problem, Prochnow's committee recommended a
re-examination of recipient force goals and then 'reassessing the proportion
of our aid for military as compared to economic expenditures' in light of the
Soviet economic offensive, and that 'the US should look toward a negotiated
adjustment downward in military aid. It appears further desirable to
accompany this course with greater emphasis on economic development
projects'.[35]

As Prochnow's committee was beginning its work, a second assessment of
US foreign aid policies was launched by the administration, in this case by an
independent group, the International Development Advisory Board (IDAB).
Eisenhower expressed a personal interest in the study, which he thought
would be worthwhile in light of the new Soviet tactics.[36] Although the NSC
as a whole passed on the idea, the study went ahead with the understanding
that its findings would be reported in a personal communication to the
President.[37] In January of 1956, ICA Director Hollister sent a letter to
IDAB Chairman Eric Johnston, recommending that the Board study such
questions as: should mutual security programmes be adapted to the bloc's
economic offensive; and should aid programmes be shifted to a long-term

planning basis in accordance with the position that the Cold War would be a long-term effort?[38]

The IDAB presented its findings and recommendations in early 1957, and rather than being a private report to the President, the report was published. The Board called for an increased emphasis on development assistance, and recommended creation of a new 'International Development Fund' (IDF), quite similar to what would soon take shape as the DLF (see below). Johnston's group further recommended that those elements of Defense Support that served development objectives should be taken out of military assistance and placed under the proposed development fund. IDAB also recommended that Congress should fund the IDF on a three-year authorization basis.[39]

Yet, even before the IDAB submitted its recommendations, a third assessment of Mutual Security policy had been launched. This effort, formally dubbed the President's Citizen Advisers on the Mutual Security programme, also known as the Fairless Committee, had two special purposes. One was to serve as a 'well-publicized counterweight' to a Senate special committee to 'investigate' the foreign aid programme.[40] The other was to gain corporate America's support for foreign aid. The Eisenhower administration, in accordance with its 'trade, not aid' approach to development, had relied on private investment for the capital needed to promote economic growth in less developed areas. In the face of the bloc's mounting economic offensive, Eisenhower attempted to encourage greater enthusiasm for foreign aid and development among the business community by gaining the corporate world's seal of approval. Toward this end, the administration made sure that the Fairless Committee was dominated by leaders of American industry, including Bank of America board chairman Jesse W. Tapp, Procter & Gamble board chairman Richard R. Deupress, and retired United States Steel president Benjamin F. Fairless, the chairman of the committee.[41]

To some extent, the Fairless ploy backfired: the committee put itself in the government's shoes and evaluated aid programmes from the standpoint of sound business principles. The administration had been formulating a new programme of development assistance, much like that recommended by the IDAB, that featured concessional loans to developing countries. Of course, to the Fairless Committee, such soft loans were not good business practice, and the committee's report accordingly contradicted the IDAB's recommendations and argued against soft lending. The committee also maintained that loans should be denied to recipients who might prove unable to pay, and that grant aid should be made only in exceptional cases. Additionally, Fairless and his colleagues recommended that grants for development purposes should be severely limited, and would be appropriate in only the most unusual cases.[42]

Despite its criticism of what it viewed as unsound business practices, the Fairless Committee did endorse increased US financing of overseas development, albeit through less concessional measures than those advocated by the IDAB. All three of these assessments, Prochnow, IDAB and Fairless, recognized that the existing balance between military and economic components of American foreign aid seemed inappropriate to the current threat, and that substantial public funding would be required to promote economic growth and strengthening of recipient societies. However, any efforts undertaken to correct that imbalance by increasing development assistance faced entrenched opposition.

Resistance to development assistance

Eisenhower himself was, for the most part, quite receptive to the arguments for greater development assistance contained in the IDAB and Prochnow findings. In late 1956 he told his NSC that he had 'felt for a long time' that the administration had been going about containment the wrong way and that the US had 'not chosen the best path'.[43] The President had expressed his sentiments on the urgent need for development efforts in his 1957 inaugural speech, declaring 'wherever in the world a people knows a desperate want, there must appear at least a spark of hope, the hope of progress – or there will surely rise at last the flames of conflict'.[44] Although the President and some of his close advisers may have seen the time had come for a greater emphasis on development in security assistance policy, they faced substantial resistance to such a shift in emphasis. Such resistance came from powerful individuals in Eisenhower's own administration and in the Congress.

Within the Eisenhower administrations, the debate over foreign aid tended to polarize between two factions. On one side were the 'young turks', including Harold Stassen, C. D. Jackson, Nelson Rockefeller, and Vice-President Nixon, who believed that overseas economic development was central to US security interests and thus warranted the application of public capital. Opposing the young turks were the '4-H club', so named because of the initials of their last names; ICA director John Hollister, Budget director Rowland Hughes, Undersecretary of State Herbert Hoover, and perhaps the most conservative of all, Treasury Secretary George Humphrey. This group opposed foreign aid for any purpose other than short-term military security.[45] Fiscal conservatives all, the 4-H club's members evinced an opposition which stemmed from concerns that foreign aid represented a veritable haemorrhaging of the Treasury that would pose grave balance of payments problems and, if unchecked, would cripple the economy. To these individuals foreign aid represented only needless 'give-aways'.

Although the 4-H club represented a more powerful group than the young turks, the balance of power in the administration began to swing toward the pro-development side in the late 1950s. One reason for this shift was the President's own deepening conviction that the bloc offensive called for increased economic assistance, but the main tilt in the balance came from changes in personnel in the first year of Eisenhower's second term, making 1957 something of a watershed year in US foreign aid policy.

In February, Christian Herter, a true advocate of development aid, replaced Hoover as Under Secretary of State. In July, Treasury Secretary Humphrey was replaced by the more flexible Robert Anderson, and John Hollister resigned his position as director of ICA. In addition, the balance was tipped further toward the pro-development aid side by the return of C. Douglas Dillon from his ambassadorial post in Paris to take the position as Deputy Under Secretary of State for Economic Affairs.[46]

Congress represented a serious obstacle to development aid as well. While Congress had traditionally been sceptical of foreign aid programmes, legislators tended to be more receptive to aid programmes that the administration could clearly justify in terms of their benefits to US security. However, while Eisenhower and many in his administration had come to recognize the importance of development assistance as a security matter, this connection seemed a bit too oblique to most legislators. As Republican Senator William Jenner saw it, attempts to apply a security rationale to development aid reflected a 'will o' the wisp nonsense that ... American spending in poor areas of the world will keep the communists from getting in. This idea is so completely fallacious that it has been used again and again by the communists to help us spend our way into bankruptcy'.[47]

Modest moves in the direction of development aid

Despite such resistance the Eisenhower administration did attempt to adjust the imbalance between military and development aid in security assistance policy by augmenting the development-oriented, economic component of US foreign aid to developing areas. One such increase came in the form of the Development Loan Fund, or DLF, which was the first significant programme of direct, public-sector economic development assistance for less developed areas that was to be approved and funded by Congress. However, even while the administration was battling to get the DLF through the appropriations process, Eisenhower began providing development aid, in amounts much larger than those provided by the DLF, under the rubric of Defense Support within the military assistance programme. Both of these efforts will be described below.

The DLF is rightly viewed by many as a milestone in US foreign aid policy, or, as Rostow put it, a break in a 'log-jam' of resistance to development aid.[48] Established by the Mutual Security Act of 1957 and administered as a government corporation, the DLF was a programme of 'soft' loans to developing countries.[49] The DLF went some way in placating those in Congress, such as Congressman John M. Vorys, who had long demanded that a greater portion of US foreign aid be made up of loans rather than grants, although the DLF's provision for accepting payment in local currency made the programme far from popular with many on Capitol Hill.

Soft loans to aid recipients had been authorized by the Mutual Security Act of 1954, but the total amount of such loans declined steadily over the years 1954–57. As often as not, such loans were supposed to be made in foreign currencies that had been derived from the sale of US agricultural surpluses, as authorized under the Mutual Security Act of 1951 and later by Public Law (PL) 480 in 1954. Recipient countries were often unenthused at the prospect of receiving concessional terms on agricultural commodities in lieu of aid dollars, and as a result the proceeds of such local currency commodity sales did not keep up the fund intended for use in making local currency loans. The amount available for such soft loans fell from $350 million in 1954 to $175 million in 1957.[50]

In contrast, Congress authorized $300 million of the administration's requested $500 million for 1957, and had more than doubled this amount by 1959, funding $625 million of the administration's $750 million request. Each year the struggle for the DLF represented a stiff fight for the Eisenhower White House, yet the amounts appropriated by Congress were nonetheless significant, considering the concessional terms under which DLF loans were made: the loan of dollars for repayment in inconvertible currencies.

In an effort to get around this problem, Eisenhower turned to the Military Assistance Program. Increased development funding was provided under the category of Defense Support, as authorized by the Mutual Security Act of 1951. Defense Support legislation had provided two subcategories: direct and indirect support. Direct support was to help recipient countries meet the direct burdens of maintaining military forces, and this was directed to such items as budget support for armed forces, and infrastructure development programmes with direct military relevance such as defence highways and the building and maintenance of ports, airfields and other military facilities. Indirect support had originally been focused on military-relevant infrastructures that could provide significant 'spin-off' benefits for the recipient economy, such as road building and large-scale electrification projects, the type of improvements that could help attract private sector investment.

However, as Washington's concern over the Soviet economic challenge grew, and its faith in the ability of the private sector to provide development capital waned, the Eisenhower administration became convinced of the need to shift more resources into development aid, a need highlighted by Prochnow's committee report. As described in Chapter 3, the USA faced serious political resistance from recipients if existing security assistance should be redirected away from the military establishment and toward development. At the same time, the Eisenhower administration's potential for gaining more development aid from Congress was limited, as evidenced by Congressional opposition to the amounts the administration requested for the DLF.

In 1957 the Defense Support eventually authorized by Congress, including road and railway building programmes, electrification projects, irrigation and agriculture improvement programmes, and food aid in the form of agricultural surpluses, totalled over $1.6 billion. This is an impressive figure compared with the DLF's $300 million or even the $587 million that Congress authorized as *total* US 'economic aid' for 1957.[51] The period 1957–58 marked a significant turning point in US foreign aid policy, wherein for the first time since the outbreak of the Korean war the administration had asked for less aid in the form of military hardware than for various economic aid programmes, including those falling within the Defense Support category.[52]

The Draper reassessment

Despite this shift in the aid balance, and despite the resistance of fiscal conservatives in Congress, many in Washington argued that the reassessment of security assistance priorities had not gone far enough. By 1958 these individuals were in a position to push for the most sweeping reassessment of military assistance that had been undertaken.

The Democrats' mid-term election victory in 1954 represented a setback for fiscal conservatives on the right wing of the Republican Party, who had been the principal obstacles to many of Eisenhower's aid programmes, and significant gains for the 'internationalist' group of mostly Democratic legislators. This group, including J. William Fulbright, the new chairman of the Senate Foreign Relations Committee, Walter F. George, Hubert Humphrey and John F. Kennedy had helped save many of Eisenhower's aid proposals from defeat in the past.[53] The internationalists were strongly in favour of increased development aid, but differed sharply with the President over the 'military orientation' of existing foreign aid programmes. Seeking to *reverse* the existing balance between military and economic elements of US foreign aid, the internationalists began to pressure the administration to justify the military components of its mutual security requests. In letters to the President in August and September of 1958, Fulbright and another internationalist senator, Theodore Green, called upon the administration to justify its military assistance programme in a 'forthright and explainable' manner, or else face increasing pressures for 'indiscriminate cuts' in military aid in the interest of devoting the resulting savings to economic development programmes.[54]

Eisenhower and Dulles responded with another assessment of Mutual Security Assistance policy, this time focusing on military assistance. This examination was to serve the dual purposes of providing the justification the Congressional internationalists demanded on the one hand, while on the other reassessing the military aid force goals that the Prochnow committee had called into question.[55] To carry out this examination, Eisenhower appointed a distinguished committee chaired by retired Lieutenant General William H. Draper.

Draper took his appointment quite seriously, and as a result the Draper committee proceedings represent the most thorough examination of security assistance undertaken in this period. Along with its final public report, the committee was to produce a separate, classified annex dealing with the implications of its findings for future security assistance policy.[56] With this in mind, the administration ensured that the Draper committee had broad access to classified material. Draper also consulted academic sources, including Robert Bowie and Lincoln Gordon at the Harvard Center for International Affairs, Max Millikan at the Massachusetts Institute of Technology's Center for International Studies, and the Institute for Defense Analysis at the University of Pennsylvania's Foreign Policy Research Institute. Draper consulted representatives from all relevant agencies at virtually all levels, from cabinet officers to unified military commanders to field operatives, and sought from these individuals not only general comments and observations but also answers to a fairly standard set of questions on military aid.

In the course of the Draper proceedings there emerged three distinct positions on security assistance: namely, those of the Pentagon and the Joint Chiefs, the academic research institutes consulted by Draper, and the State Department. These three factions were not so much at odds with each other as they represented three perspectives on how to meet the communist threat in the developing world. As each of these viewpoints influenced the development of subsequent security assistance policy, they will be discussed in turn.

The essential position of the Joint Chiefs was that communism's military threat had not in any way abated and was in fact greater than ever. While acknowledging that the bloc had shifted tactics in its expansionist drive, the Pentagon pointed out that, according to intelligence sources, the communists had not shifted their resources from military forces, and in fact the bloc's political and economic offensives were in *addition* to their unwavering military posture.[57] Therefore, it would surely prove unwise to cut back on military assistance to US allies, as such a move would send a nebulous message about American resolve to these allies as well as to Moscow.

In the face of criticisms from State and ICA about the 'unrealistic' or 'subjective' force goals used in determining levels of military aid allocated to a given country, the Joint Chiefs responded that such force goals were derived from requirements set down by the NSC, not the Pentagon.[58] From the military's perspective, the real problem in allocations of military aid was not existing force goals, but an increasing tendency on the part of the State Department to allocate already scarce military aid resources for political purposes. The Pentagon taxonomy of military aid programmes exhibited three classifications: *military*, or aid to recipients that could contribute significant military capabilities to a collective effort in a general war; quid pro quo, or, in effect, the payment for such 'services rendered' as basing or transit rights; and *political*, i.e., bribes to influence some non-military aspect of a recipient state's behaviour.[59] The JCS cited military aid for Ethiopia, Jordan, Lebanon, Tunisia, Burma and Indonesia as being, in their view, examples of 'purely political' programmes, and complained of a disturbing trend wherein State devoted an increasing portion of available military aid for political purposes to counter Soviet aid promises.[60]

Academics consulted by the Draper committee tended to question the very notion that military aid and development aid were separate and distinct, arguing that military assistance programmes were a driving force behind the political and economic development of new states.[61] One such argument held that, in developing countries, military service amounted to something of a national technical school. Military personnel received training in a variety of technical skills, ranging from engineering to basic medicine, by US advisers or even at US training facilities. Such individuals would take these skills back into the civilian sector at the end of their military service. These studies went on to note that in some countries such military programmes represented the only technical training available.[62]

The academic analysts pointed to the military's civic action role as a powerful force for political as well as economic development. Civic action duties, such as work on civil engineering projects, not only built up badly needed infrastructure in recipient countries, but built a positive image of and support for the local government as well. Military service also served a socializing function by binding diverse populations together within a single institution.[63]

Additionally, the increasingly influential 'modernization' theorists had great faith in the local military's effectiveness as a 'modernizing elite' in the political development of new states. Often Western-educated, the officer corps of these recipient militaries seemed the logical source for the managers needed to set their young countries on the path to development. To enhance their abilities in this role, the USA had attempted to indoctrinate subtly local military officers in such skills as proper civilian–military relations through IMET, the international military education and training component of US military assistance. From the point of view of the academic analysts contributing to the Draper proceedings, military aid had tremendous potential to advance the cause of development, and as such should be viewed not just as a military programme but also as a 'broadly gauged sociological and organizational undertaking'.[64]

A contrasting view came from within the State Department. This faction, including Under Secretary of State for Economic Affairs C. Douglas Dillon and members of the PPS, did not directly take issues with the above perspectives so much as they argued that long-term development processes could be thwarted in the near term by the current Soviet economic offensive unless Washington took immediate action to offset that offensive. The immediate threat was not military but political, and it stemmed not from the agency of outside agitators but from the internal political upheaval that characterized many of these new states.

From Dillon's point of view, military assistance to developing countries proved least effective when allocated to the role of deterrence.[65] Therefore, aid resources devoted to maintaining local forces as a deterrent to external military aggression should be shifted to direct economic assistance. In the face of the bloc economic offensive the US would have to invest in strengthening the economic, and thereby the political viability of many of these new states. Rather than taking the widely held view that economic growth would naturally promote development and political stability, Dillon argued that without some tangible evidence or even a hope of economic improvement the governments of these new states would soon be lost to the more extreme political factions vying for power.

Dillon identified what he called 'politically relevant' sectors of developing societies as the linchpin of political stability. These were the 'politically literate' or 'urban middle groups' in a society, and in Dillon's view, recipient governments had to secure the allegiance of these groups above all others to survive. According to Dillon's observations, the problem in many of the states emerging from colonial empires was one of rising aspirations and expectations, and expectations ran highest with these politically relevant groups. If local leaders could make no headway in delivering economic progress and prosperity for their societies, if they could not even begin to keep up with the tide of rising expectations, these politically relevant groups would, in their frustration, turn to extremists who promised rapid economic advancement. Dillon did not presume these 'extremists' to be communists; rather than simply mistaking extremists of any shade for communists, he believed that extremists' close association with communists in many developing countries would lead to their co-optation and eventual domination by the communists.[66]

With the bloc economic offensive, and the resulting accrual of prestige to communists and the communist development model, there had come an increased tendency towards political polarization among these politically relevant groups. Leftist and more radical political factions could now point to communist development as a viable alternative to the practices of the incumbent leadership, and as a result, these incumbents found themselves under increasing domestic pressure to produce tangible results:

> Here is an area of great danger. The practically total mobilization of Communist China for economic production is a serious threat of major proportions. Should China succeed in achieving rapid development by totalitarian methods while the rest of Asia stagnates or grows only at a slow pace, we are in for serious trouble. The failure to develop, even without the comparison with China, would in itself likely lead to internal tensions with the danger of the people discarding moderate leadership and adopting totalitarian methods.[67]

In this situation Dillon saw a recipe for increasing instability:

> In India, for example, prolonged economic stagnation will be taken as evidence that the Congress Party leadership has failed, and polarization of political sentiment will be accelerated. In some countries, governments may try to avert such political deterioration by raising external claims (e.g., West Irian[68]) which temporarily distract attention from domestic problems, but which may over the long run increase the risk of foreign conflicts and worsen the prospects for domestic progress.[69]

Dillon argued that an urgent need existed for substantial economic aid to non-communist governments in these new states; in effect, the USA should directly invest in the success of these governments' economic programmes. Doing so would

> assure the receiving government that [their domestic economic develop-ment] policies, if adopted, need not fail for lack of capital. Many gov-ernments will hesitate to assume the political costs of rigorous domestic measures unless they feel that resources will be available to exploit the opportunities which these policies create.[70]

In a contrasting position to Dillon's focus on the 'urban middle groups', James Smith, of the PPS, recommended that aid should be concentrated on what he called 'community development' projects, designed to bring about 'changes in the outlook and the habits' of the recipient country's population. These projects, such as rural production investment schemes or infrastructure-building efforts in remote areas, were intended to give the people 'a sense of involvement in the development process' as well as tangible evidence of the local government's success. Aid was crucial in promoting these types of projects; although efforts of this kind were fundamental in promoting investment and overall development, they were generally not considered 'sufficiently self-liquidating' to merit funding through hard loans or private investment.[71]

The goal of all of these approaches, Dillon asserted, was to help bind important segments of the population to their government by helping that government keep up with rising popular expectations. The USA could not and should not attempt to prevent revolution and instability in developing areas, as the political processes underway there could not be stopped. However, it should be the goal of the USA to '*moderate* such instability'. 'A *major* expansion of aid' was hardly a sufficient condition to keep non-communists in power; however, in the context of the bloc economic offensive and the political changes underway in Asia and Africa, such an expansion of aid 'is almost certainly a *necessary* condition'.[72]

The Draper conclusions in the context of Eisenhower's own reassessment

In their report to the President, the Draper committee gave a qualified endorsement to the idea of increased economic aid for development. The Committee recommended that funding for economic development loans such as the DLF be raised to one billion dollars, as compared with the 550 million dollars that Congress had appropriated for the fiscal year 1959. However, Draper argued *against* increasing development funding if it would mean corresponding offset reductions in military aid programmes; economic aid should be increased only as part of an overall increase in aid funding.[73] Draper's committee concurred with the Joint Chiefs that the military threat was greater than ever:

> We must not forget that despite their shifting tactics the communists have continued to build up their military might and thus we need to continue to improve free world forces. *Therefore, the Committee believes that a substantial reduction in military assistance would involve an unacceptable security risk.*[74]

In various ways, the Draper recommendation represented a return to a pre-1954 approach to Mutual Security policy. Unlike the State Department and many in the Eisenhower administration, Draper and his committee believed that the main battlefield of the Cold War had not shifted to the developing world but remained in Europe. The committee emphasized the threat of communist military attack in Europe and went so far as to recommend a 400 million dollar increase in military aid to NATO countries, an increase that was to be paid for by making cuts in security assistance to areas other than NATO.[75] With respect to promoting development in the underdeveloped areas, the Draper recommendations echoed the rhetoric of the Truman years, stressing the importance of technical assistance and relying on 'local efforts' in promoting economic progress.[76]

In the end, Eisenhower could agree with only a handful of the Draper recommendations, these falling mostly in the areas of the administration and coordination of aid programmes. The President concurred in the committee's argument that more Mutual Security planning responsibilities should be decentralized and delegated to the field, and that a Mutual Security Operations Plan (MSOP) should be formulated for each recipient country.[77] Like the earlier reassessments of security assistance described above, Draper pointed to the need for long-term, multi-year authorizations for aid. Eisenhower's administration had been fighting to wrest such authorizations from Congress for several years and was involved in such a fight, in this case over the DLF, as the Draper Committee delivered its report.[78]

Like the preceding reassessments of aid policy, the Draper committee recommended the separation of development aid from military aid in the authorizations and appropriations processes. On this point, Eisenhower still demurred, acting from an enduring conviction that such separation would make development aid an easy target for Congressional budget-cutting. At one point the President had advised members of the NSC that in presenting aid programmes to Congress they would be well advised to call these programmes 'national security assistance', whether the programmes were military or not. The Vice-President concurred, noting that Congress was 'as generous in providing funds for military assistance as it was niggardly in providing funds for assistance for political purposes'.[79] Eisenhower personally believed that the USA 'could sustain peace more effectively by economic aid expenditures than by the provision of military equipment to other nations, even though military assistance may be more popular in Congress and perhaps among the people'.[80] Although Fulbright and the internationalists were increasingly assertive in pushing for greater emphasis on development assistance, they faced the same obstacles as Eisenhower faced in a handful of powerful, fiscally conservative legislators.[81] For its own part, Congress concluded in early 1960 that America's guiding foreign aid legislation needed an overhaul, and pledged to undertake a complete revision of the Mutual Security Act in the next session (after the election of 1960).[82]

Effectiveness

In the context of the ERP, the concept of the 'military shield' had worked well, from Washington's perspective, in 'protecting' the rebuilding of what had been thriving industrial economies. Security assistance provided under the MDAA of 1949 reassured Western European governments worried about the possibility of attack by the Red Army or the potential threat of a resurgent Germany, and proved effective in controlling domestic radical-leftist political parties, especially in France and Italy. Underneath this 'shield' the USA had injected billions of dollars in Marshall Plan aid to provide the material resources with which Europe could rebuild, and begin to integrate its economies.

In contrast, in developing areas, while Washington was quick to extend its security assistance 'shield' over new states, American assistance provided to spur economic prosperity often amounted to 'technical assistance' and little more. The provision of such assistance was rather like a rich patron offering to build one's family a house and then providing a carpenter but no materials. From Washington's point of view, the material and labour for development in these 'peripheral areas' should come from 'local efforts'. The recipients themselves, with the help of technical experts and advisers, would provide the necessary level of infrastructure development to attract private industry and investment. Private capital would be the life blood of development in these areas; no massive infusions on the order of Marshall Plan aid would be forthcoming.

However, Washington did not take the measures needed to encourage such private investment. Eisenhower proved no more effective than his predecessor in providing the concessions and investment guarantees that would encourage corporations to take a chance on investing in the less developed areas. To the end of his presidency, Eisenhower fought to persuade Congress to lower trade barriers and thereby give products manufactured in these areas better access to the US market, and provide tax breaks for income earned in the less developed countries.[83]

When the USSR launched its economic programme of trade and aid in developing areas, the Eisenhower administration was forced to junk the already failing 'trade, not aid' approach. Even with the administration's new appreciation of the urgent need for development assistance in new states, Washington's ability to institute effective programmes to promote economic and political development was compromised by several chronic problems.

Problems with interagency coordination

In the course of the Draper proceedings, John O. Bell, now the State Department's Special Assistant for Mutual Security Coordination, in a forthright criticism declared that after ten years of security assistance, the guiding principles of Mutual Security were still those spelled out in the Mutual Defense Assistance Act of 1949 (see Chapter 2). However, while billions of dollars had gone to military aid in those years, a coherent mutual security policy had yet to take shape:

> The translation of these principles into effective procedures to govern the development of the military and economic segments of the Program is perhaps our most troublesome problem. This is particularly true at the present time in the case of the military assistance Program, where the effectiveness of Program coordination has been impaired by our continued inability to identify adequately and understand clearly the bases on which Programs are now developed and presented for review.[84]

Mutual Security Assistance, like all US foreign aid, was ultimately under the control of the Secretary of State, and coordinated by his special assistant, in this case, Bell. However, interagency coordination in the area of foreign aid left much to be desired, especially when it came to sharing information. Information was highly compartmentalized, making the coordinator's job virtually impossible. As Bell put it:

> the Coordinator must be in a position to understand reasons underlying recommended force levels, and in particular to evaluate any political or economic judgments which may have entered into their formulation and identify the political and economic implications of maintaining such forces. He must be able to control the issuance of guidance relating to the economic capabilities or political orientation of individual countries insofar as they form the basis for the generation or elimination of military requirements. And he must receive sufficient information and justification for Programs presented to be able to form a judgment as whether fulfillment of the requirements presented would in fact further US foreign policy objectives.[85]

In effect, then, a situation existed wherein the NSC approved a basic policy objective and the individual agencies involved in foreign aid operations then developed policies in accordance with their own agency viewpoint of US interests. Each participating agency developed its own policy guidance regarding US objectives in the area of foreign aid, with no coordinating supervision.

The Draper committee, using its fairly standard set of questions to solicit views from participating agencies, revealed this policy disarray. As shown above, the State and Defense Departments held *very* different views of the nature of the threat to US interests in the developing world, and of the appropriate policy response to promote US interests in the face of that threat. In the absence of any overall mutual security concept to guide foreign-aid policy-making, interagency coordination proved an unattainable goal.

Problems coordinating multilateral aid efforts

Effective coordination of US aid with the aid efforts of allies and international organizations proved unattainable as well, although for different reasons. American policy regarding multilateral aid efforts reflected a tension between the desire, on one hand, for burden sharing in aid to the developing world in the face of the bloc economic offensive, and, on the other, a desire to retain control over how aid funds were spent. Similarly, the USA remained cautious when it came to contributing to the aid programmes of international organizations. For example, when in 1957 the IDAB recommended that its proposed fund be allowed to contribute to multilateral development organizations, the State Department attacked this proposal, arguing that such contributions to such organizations should be carefully considered by Congress and reviewed on a year by year basis.[86] US contributions to multilateral aid organizations remained a very small part of the overall US aid effort.[87]

Simply put, Washington did not like disbursing aid through organizations to which the Soviets belonged.[88] To the growing group of newly independent UN member states, who did not share Washington's presumptions regarding the nature of Soviet foreign policy, such American reluctance to fund international development programmes lent credence to the communists' anti-American and anti-Western rhetoric. For this reason the Eisenhower administration's reluctance to support the establishment of the Special United Nations Fund for Economic Development (SUNFED) cost the US considerable prestige among the states of the developing world.[89]

Ideological distortions and problems of general assumptions/doctrine

The process of formulating US aid policy toward the developing world in this period was hampered by the simplistic assumptions upon which such policies were based. Specifically, the Eisenhower administration's efforts to find a workable doctrine for prosecuting the Cold War in the developing world were impeded by its flawed assumptions regarding the nature of development processes and of neutrality.

At the beginning of the Eisenhower presidency, US foreign aid policy remained uninformed by any theories of development *per se*. As a result, decision-makers formed policies based on the simplistic assumption that development was simply a matter of economic growth. Walt W. Rostow and Max Millikan, development economists at Massachusetts Institute of Technology, had presented their report to the administration in 1954 along with a range of policy recommendations, and these were well received by some of Eisenhower's advisers. However, this 'modernization theory' approach would not begin to have any noticeable policy impact until late 1950s, and even then such impact was dampened and diffused by Congressional resistance and the interstices of the appropriations process. Throughout much of the Eisenhower presidency, analysis of trends and events in the developing regions tended to be rather superficial.

American policy-makers had been quick to point out that the development challenges in these 'backward areas' were fundamentally different from the challenge of rebuilding Europe. However, Washington's economic policies toward developing areas suggest that these policy-makers devoted little thought to just how these challenges differed from those of the developed world. Adequate investment capital in the hands of an industrious population would promote growth and thereby development, and such investment capital would naturally come from the private sector.

Douglas Dillon's arguments were innovative in that they represented a positive step in the administration's understanding of how politics and economics interacted in new states. Dillon recognized that rising expectations among the peoples of newly independent states created considerable pressure for political change and economic improvement. Dillon's argument resembled what T. R. Gurr would later articulate as 'relative deprivation theory'.[90] While many in Washington envisioned developing societies advancing steadily toward self-sustaining economic growth, Dillon offered a scenario in which the trend might go in the other direction; popular frustration over slow rates of economic progress could lead to instability that would not only discourage further foreign investment but also cause existing investors to flee. These events would in turn lead to even poorer economic performance, resulting in heightened frustrations and instability and a populace that might well turn to local Communists for solutions.

By 1958, Dillon, along with others in the Eisenhower administration, recognized that aspirations were indeed running high in states in the transition from colonial rule to independence, or as Eisenhower himself put it, making reference to the time of America's own independence, 'the spirit of '76 is running wild' in many colonial and former colonial areas.[91] The administration's appraisal of this situation is significant as it marks a departure from the previous assumption that such political pressures were whipped up by external, communist agitators. Here was a threat that was *internal* in origin yet no less dangerous from Washington's perspective; the resultant upheaval and rebellion could be exploited by communists or other extremists, and, as a result, the country would ultimately be 'lost' to communism. Washington could no longer simply focus on protecting recipient countries from infiltration by communist subversives, or on suppressing the activities of 'fellow travellers', through such measures as those contained in the 1290-d programme. US aid would now need to be targeted at relieving the political pressures within these societies by helping recipient regimes keep up with the rising expectations of their populations; this was Dillon's approach to 'moderating revolutions' in these new states. To promote the security of these new countries, US aid would now have to promote their development. This goal required Washington to rethink its simplistic assumptions about the nature of development and begin bolstering endangered, non-communist regimes with public-sector development aid.

During the Eisenhower presidency the USA was also forced to modify its conception of neutrality; Washington had to reconsider its assumption that neutrality was simply not a viable position in the Cold War. The Bandung Conference in 1955 had been an opportunity for many new states to declare their intention of remaining neutral and non-aligned. Washington had observed that the Geneva Agreement of 1954 and the subsequent partition of Vietnam contributed to regional tendencies toward neutralism that had long been exhibited by Indonesia and Burma. Now, under Sihanouk's influence, for example, Cambodia had been 'drifting toward neutralism'. Washington had for several years been observing trends toward neutralism in the Far East in the form of assertions of independence in action, and espousal of 'a sense of cultural affinity with other Asian neutrals, despite awareness that their security remain[ed] dependent upon benevolent exercise of Western power'.[92]

After observing the successes scored by the Soviets in these countries through Moscow's trade and aid initiatives, the USA could hardly maintain its previous 'if you're not with us you're against us' stance. The Eisenhower administration remained uneasy about new states adopting a neutralist course, as Eisenhower and his advisers believed the Soviets laboured incessantly 'to turn allies into neutrals and neutrals into communists'.[93] However, as more and more emerging new states established economic relations with the bloc, Washington was forced to revise its position on neutrality. Genuine non-alignment in the foreign policies of new states was preferable to seeing the Soviet economic offensive draw them closer to the bloc.[94] The President himself was forced to keep faith that the fervent nationalism of these new states would keep them truly non-aligned, believing as he did that nationalism had become a stronger force than communism in the developing world.[95]

In the case of the Soviet economic offensive, the ideological lens through which Washington viewed Soviet actions yielded a distortion that in turn may have produced a positive outcome with respect to the developing world. Although the Soviet trade and aid initiatives of the mid-1950s may have eroded many nations' fear and 'ostracism' of the bloc, Eisenhower's own assessments of Soviet actions reflected an enduring belief that communism was acting in pursuit of 'sinister objectives'.[96] Eisenhower continued to interpret all Soviet actions in light of the presumed communist objective of world domination, and rejected suggestions from advisers that the Soviet economic initiatives could actually promote economic development and stability in developing areas and thereby ultimately serve US interests and save US aid dollars.[97] In retrospect, several of Eisenhower's close advisers agreed that the President was oversold on the Soviet economic threat in the developing world.[98] Nevertheless, Eisenhower's perceptions of the dangers embodied in that economic offensive led to a massive reassessment of US aid policies, and the President's conversion to the cause of development aid in the late 1950s helped bring about the first substantial programme of public-sector economic assistance to developing countries. While the DLF may seem rather modest in retrospect, it was a hard-won first step, and had the President and his key advisers not perceived such dangers in the new Soviet foreign economic policies, Washington might have ignored the economic plight of developing areas for years to come. On the other hand, Washington's perception of Moscow's success in its 'charm offensive' led to the implementation of urgent, often heavy-handed security measures in Southeast Asia and elsewhere in the developing world (as will be discussed in Chapter 5).

Side-effects

Perhaps the most serious economic side-effect stemming from Washington's security assistance policy was the creation of bloated military establishments through Defense Support funding, as identified by Prochnow's committee (and described in Chapter 3). A no less significant side-effect, stemming from the Soviet economic initiatives and Washington's perceptions of the threats embodied therein, was the increased political leverage recipients derived from the aid war.

Providing aid to neutral countries proved a thorny proposition as it could bring the administration into conflict with the 'Battle Act', or Mutual Defense Assistance Control Act of 1951. This legislation stipulated that US aid be denied to any country exporting any sort of strategic materials to the bloc or otherwise not 'effectively cooperating' with East–West trade controls. Thus, through adjusting the definition of 'strategic materials', Congress could interdict Eisenhower's efforts to offer aid to developing nations that pursued a neutral course and opened trade relations with a communist state.

In the context of the Soviet economic offensive, such Congressional resistance to aiding neutrals put the administration in a bind. Using aid for political leverage is, in essence, exploiting a dependency on the part of the recipient.[99] However, in the presence of a competing donor, the leverage is easily reversed; if the recipient perceives that the donor has a strategic interest in the aid relationship, the recipient will remain confident that the donor will not shut off the flow of aid. Stanton Burnett refers to this scenario as the 'frozen spigot'.[100] If the recipient can play one donor off against the other, as Khrushchev advised developing world recipients to do in their dealings with the US, the recipient can apply increased leverage against the donor and thereby extract additional aid and trade concessions.

When the USSR became a competing donor in the mid-1950s, and in the context of the Eisenhower administration's perception that the Soviets were 'making every effort to turn US allies into neutrals and neutrals into communists', recipients began to exert leverage on Washington to extract increased aid.[101] Despite Congressional reluctance to aid neutrals, Washington made increased use of aid simply to bribe recipients into forgoing aid from the bloc.[102] The State Department policy attacked by the JCS in the Draper proceedings, that of using security assistance resources to counter promises of aid from the bloc, became an ever more prominent feature of US foreign aid policy as recipients learned to exert leverage against Washington by raising the possibility of a relationship with the USSR. Some aid recipients in the developing world would become quite adept at manipulating this lever against Washington by the end of the 1960s.

Closing the Eisenhower chapters

As the Eisenhower presidency progressed, Mutual Security programmes in the developing world underwent a shift in emphasis; while at the time of Eisenhower's first inauguration in 1953 such programmes were largely military in nature, by the end of Eisenhower's presidency the majority of Mutual Security funds requested from Congress were for economic rather than military programmes. However, in formulating responses to perceived tactical shifts in the communists' strategy, Eisenhower and his NSC were never able to strike a balance between providing the 'shield' component of security assistance policy and promoting the development that was to take place beneath that shield.

The Eisenhower presidency represented a period of considerable reassessment of the communist threat and subsequent modification of the measures designed and implemented to meet that threat, to 'seize the initiative'. The language of NSC 68 and other Truman-era statements of basic US national security policy had reflected a subtle presumption that the bloc could be immobilized through adequate military deterrence and isolated economically and politically while the processes required to strengthen the free world were underway. As Eisenhower and his advisers discovered shortly after taking office, this static conception of containment was being undermined by two processes. The first challenge to such a static concept of containment was the progress the Soviets were making in their own nuclear weapons programme. A more fundamental challenge to containment was embodied in the process of decolonization underway in the developing world.

Both of these processes put time pressures on Washington's containment policies. As Washington lost its monopoly in nuclear weapons and its immunity from Soviet nuclear attack, US decision-makers fully expected the bloc to grow bolder in pursuing its presumed expansionist aims. At the same time, the emergence of new states from what had been the West's colonial possessions, and the often turbulent character of their internal politics, presented the bloc with new opportunities to expand its influence through political or 'subversive' means. As the developing areas increased in importance as Cold War battlefields, the USA was forced to introduce such measures as the 1290-d programme to counter the bloc's subversive threat. When the Soviets began expanding their influence through their 'economic offensive' in the mid-1950s, the US was compelled to respond with economic instruments as well, including public-sector development aid.

Throughout this period security planners in Washington perceived an increasingly urgent need to secure some semblance of order and stability in recipient societies, to encourage outside investment and to permit the development of functioning internal institutions. While the 1290-d programme was supposed to provide such order and help protect development processes in recipient states, Washington understood that the internal strengthening of the type called for in NSC 68 would require more than just the 'shield'. The financial resources needed to fuel such development were expected to come from private investment; the US Treasury could hardly bear the burden of a Marshall Plan for Southeast Asia, much less all of the developing world. To provide such funds, NSC 149 had recommended that the USA should 'increase emphasis on lowering trade barriers and encouragement of reciprocal trade', encouraging the 'increased use of private capital' along with 'expanded trade and offshore procurement' as means of promoting regional economic cooperation and growth that would eventually remove the need for American security assistance in developing areas.[103] However, Congress's stubbornly protectionist agenda and continued refusal to lower America's trade barriers undermined these aspects of Eisenhower's policy towards the developing world. Even if developing countries' political environments could be adequately stabilized to provide a secure investment environment, corporations were unlikely to help develop the economic capacity of these countries if their goods could not be sold in the USA. Without such market access, the 'trade, not aid' approach became a travesty, and the need for the USA to resort to public-sector development aid grew ever more severe.

By the end of his time in office, Eisenhower had moved a long way from the 'trade, not aid' philosophy. His shift in attitude and more favourable stance on development aid was driven not only by the Soviet economic offensive but also by the world political climate that made that offensive seem so dangerous. By the end of the 1950s Eisenhower and his NSC clearly recognized that the Soviets were only exploiting opportunities as these were presented to them, throwing fuel onto an already smouldering fire of social unrest that was sweeping through the developing world and breaking out in a 'rash of revolutions'.[104] Eisenhower's awareness of this unrest and its dangers, alluded to in his 1957 inaugural address and in his classified discussions from late 1954 onwards, was reinforced by tours he made through less developed areas in 1959 and 1960. The President seemed deeply impressed by the stormy climate of 'Castroism' and anti-Americanism he encountered in Latin America and the upheaval he encountered throughout his travels.[105] The political upheaval of the decolonization process – what Eisenhower referred to as the 'spirit of 76' sweeping through the less developed regions – generated and was characterized by a rising tide of popular expectations. Eisenhower and his closet advisers understood that, should these popular expectations go entirely unfulfilled, popular frustrations would intensify, and that the upheaval generated thereby was far more likely to benefit the bloc than the West.[106] The most effective means of deflating and defeating the communist idea would be through economic assistance, either to moderate radicalism born of frustrated aspirations within societies, or by contributing to showpieces of non-communist development. Accordingly, by the late 1950s the USA was forced to implement a programme of direct economic aid to selected, non-communist regimes in new states in an effort to keep these regimes from being crushed and swept away by that rising tide of popular expectations, and in the hope that their eventual success might keep other new states from adopting a pro-communist orientation.

While Eisenhower's own views of the importance of development aid to US security clearly changed during this time, one significant question remains: in light of Washington's reassessment of its security assistance approach, why was no bold, new aid programme forthcoming? The DLF was a significant first step, but why did the Eisenhower administration not shift foreign aid to a greater emphasis on economic assistance?

Part of the answer rests with Congress. Eisenhower repeatedly complained that the constitutional restraints on his freedom to make policy handicapped him in responding to the Soviet initiatives, that his administration was forced to submit changes in policy to Congress for authorization and funding, and the protracted and open debate that process entailed. In contrast, the President observed, his communist counterpart was subject to no such restraints, and could shift resources quickly and decisively.[107] Additionally, Eisenhower was repeatedly frustrated by his inability to convince Congress of the value of foreign aid to US security. Toward the end of his presidency he stressed to Congress that, if it came to such a choice, he would rather see the defence budget cut than Mutual Security programmes.[108]

Another factor hindering the development of a bold, new approach was the accelerating pace of political change in the developing areas as decolonization accelerated. By the end of the Eisenhower presidency the USA was assembling its Mutual Security programmes under the dual pressures of the 'economic offensive' and the decolonization process itself, which was producing a stream of new and often unstable states. 'The old order is gone,' observed a State Department report, 'but the new order has yet to be achieved'. The situation in the developing world was changing so fast that US agencies were increasingly resorting to developing short-term programme concepts on an *ad hoc* basis. A 1960 Mutual Security Program status report argued that the US 'must view aid as a political investment' in newly independent countries. 'Survey teams are trying as rapidly as possible to evolve Programs in these new nations which make sense in terms of our objectives and interests'.[109] The decolonization process was simply outpacing the development of Mutual Security doctrine. 'We must never confess', the President had told his Secretary of State, 'that we have gotten to the bottom of the barrel in searching for ideas to stem and turn the tide of Soviet propaganda success'.[110] Like his predecessor, Eisenhower was leaving office in a time of crisis in the developing world. Into this context of increasing upheaval a new team of policy-makers was bringing to Washington a new way of looking at Cold War challenges in the developing world.

Notes

1   NSC 68, *FRUS, 1950*, vol. 1, p. 291.
2   Statement of Basic National Security Policy, NSC 5440, 13 December 1954. *FRUS, 1952–54*, vol. 2, pt 1, p. 817.
3   Elizabeth K. Valkenier, *The Soviet Union and the Third World: An Economic Bind* (New York: Praeger, 1983), pp. 2–7.
4   Margot Light, *The Soviet Theory of International Relations* (Brighton: Wheatsheaf, 1988), pp. 112–134.
5   'The Nature and Problems of Soviet Economic Penetration in Underdeveloped Areas', 29 February 1956, p. 3. Whitman File, Dulles-Herter series, box 6 (DDE Library). Also, Economic Intelligence Committee, 'Sino-Soviet Bloc Economic Activities in Underdeveloped Areas 1 January – 30 June 1959', 28 August 1959. White House Office File, OSANSA, NSC Series, Briefing Notes Subseries, box 5, p. 3 (DDE Library).
6   Robbin F. Laird, 'Soviet Arms Trade with the Non-communist Third World', in Robbin F. Hoffman and Erik P. Laird (eds), *Soviet Foreign Policy in a Changing World* (New York: Aldine, 1986), p. 718.
7   S. Neil MacFarlane, *Superpower Rivalry and 3rd World Radicalism: The Idea of National Liberation* (Baltimore, MD: The Johns Hopkins University Press, 1985).
8   'Nature and Problems', p. 2.
9   Moscow Embassy Telegram no. 1652, Bohlen to Secretary of State, 27 January 1956. Whitman File, Dulles-Herter Series, box 6 (DDE Library).
10 Report of the Central Committee of the CPSU, quoted in Light, *The Soviet Theory of International Relations*, p. 112.
11 Valkenier, *The Soviet Union and the Third World*, pp. 3–7.
12 Moscow Embassy Telegram no. 1652, Bohlen to Secretary of State, 27 January, 1956, p. 2.
13 Baldwin, *Economic Development*, p. 174.
14 'Nature and Problems'.
15 Memorandum attached to letters sent by John Foster Dulles to Business Advisory Council's ad hoc committee to study Sino-Soviet activities in world economic relations, 22 April 1958. John Foster Dulles White House Memorandum Series, box 6 (DDE Library).
16 'Nature and Problems'. In fact, according to Council on Foreign Economic Policy head Joseph Dodge, the Soviets had been making continuous offers to West Germany giving them a 'virtual trade monopoly' in the industrialization of China. Memorandum, Dodge to Herbert Hoover, Jr., 13 January 1956. Whitman File, Dulles-Herter Series, box 6 (DDE Library).
17 Eisenhower to Dulles, 5 December 1955. Whitman File, Dulles-Herter Series, box 6 (DDE Library).
18 Letter from C. D. Jackson to Rockefeller, 10 November 1955. Quoted in Burton

I. Kaufman, *Trade and Aid: Eisenhower's Foreign Economic Policy 1953–1961* (Baltimore, MD, and London: Johns Hopkins University Press, 1982), p. 66.

19 Dulles in interview with C. D. Jackson, 16 April 1956, quoted in Rostow, *Eisenhower, Kennedy and Foreign Aid*, p. 258.

20 Memorandum, Dodge to Hoover, 13 January 1956.

21 CIA, 'Sino-Soviet Bloc Aid 'Program'', 25 October 1956, p. 1. 'President's Citizen Advisers on the Mutual Security Program', records, 1956–57, box 4, file: CIA (DDE Library).

22 'Nature and Problems'; also CIA, 'Sino-Soviet Bloc Aid Program', 25 October 1956, p. 1.

23 *Ibid.*

24 Kaufman, *Trade and Aid*, p. 65. Also, 'Neutralism in the Far East', NSC Staff Papers, box 2, file: 'Bandung'.

25 D. G. E. Hall, *A History of South-East Asia*, 4th edn (New York: St Martin's Press, 1981), p. 911.

26 Message to Congress regarding the Mutual Security Program, 19 March 1956. Quoted in Kaufman, *Trade and Aid*, p. 67.

27 Kaufman, *Trade and Aid*, pp. 64–65.

28 Dulles held the opinion that the USSR was providing economic support to China to bolster the latter's image as an economic success; the PRC was, in effect, 'communism's created 'showpiece'. Discussion at 235th Meeting of NSC, 4 February 1955. Also, a CIA briefing paper for the Fairless Committee, dated 25 October 1956, noted that the developing world was 'watching with 'interest' the relative growth rates of India and China.

29 Discussion at 314th Meeting of NSC, 1 March 1957.

30 Department of State, Draft Memorandum prepared for NSC, 'Review of the Military Assistance 'Program', 28 November 1955, *FRUS, 1955–57*, vol. 10, pp. 37–39.

31 Department of State, Memorandum from Director of Office of International Financial and Development Affairs (Corbett) to Deputy Under Secretary of State for Economic Affairs (Prochnow), 28 October 1955, *FRUS, 1955–57*, vol. 10, pp. 25–28. Also, Memorandum from Executive Secretary of NSC (Lay) to Members of Council, 29 November 1955, *FRUS, 1955–57*, vol. 10, pp. 41–43.

32 'Terms of Reference for the Interdepartmental Committee on Certain US Aid Programs, 2 December 1955. *FRUS, 1955–57*, vol. 10, pp. 43–44.

33 Those mentioned in the committee's 'terms of reference' were Cambodia, Formosa, Iran, Japan, Korea, Laos, Pakistan, the Philippines, Spain, Thailand, Turkey and Vietnam. 'Terms of Reference for the Interdepartmental Committee on Certain US Aid Programs', 2 December 1955. *FRUS, 1955–57*, vol. 10, pp. 43–44.

34 'Memorandum from Deputy Under Secretary of State for Economic Affairs (Prochnow) to Secretary of State, 27 July 1956. *FRUS, 1955–57*, vol. 10, pp. 85–87.

35 *Ibid.*

36 Discussion at 269th Meeting of NSC, 8 December 1955. *FRUS, 1955–57*, vol. 10, pp. 58–61.

37 Rostow, *Eisenhower, Kennedy and Foreign Aid*, p. 126.

38 Letter, Hollister to Johnston, 16 January 1956. JFD Papers, Subject Series, box 5, folder: Mutual Security Program, 1957 (DDE Library).

39 State Department Comments on IDAB Report, 16 March 1957. *FRUS, 1955–57*, vol. 10, pp. 171–173.
40 See Rostow, *Eisenhower, Kennedy and Foreign Aid,* pp. 126–127.
41 Kaufman, *Trade and Aid,* p. 72.
42 Memorandum from Chairman of Council on Foreign Economic Policy (Randall) to President's Assistant (Adams), 14 March 1957. *FRUS, 1955–57,* vol. 10, pp. 146–167.
43 Discussion at 301st Meeting of NSC, 26 October 1956. *FRUS, 1955–57,* vol. 10, p. 130.
44 Quoted in Rostow, *Eisenhower, Kennedy and Foreign Aid,* p. 121.
45 Baldwin, *Economic Development,* pp. 168–169.
46 Rostow, *Eisenhower, Kennedy and Foreign Aid,* pp. 122–125.
47 Quoted in Kaufman, *Trade and Aid,* p. 55.
48 Rostow, *Eisenhower, Kennedy and Foreign Aid,* p. 121.
49 David Baldwin defines a loan as being 'soft' if it is offered at less than commercial terms with respect to rate of interest, time of repayment, or convertibility of currency in which the loan is to be repaid. Any of these characteristics makes a loan 'soft'. Baldwin, *Economic Development,* pp. 3–7.
50 Baldwin, *Economic Development,* pp. 128–133. (Public Law 480, the Agricultural Trade Development Assistance Act of 1954, was renamed by Kennedy 'Food for Peace' in 1961.)
51 'How Much Trade – How Much Aid?', Foreign Policy Association, 1957. White House Office, OSANSA, NSC Series, Subject Subseries, box 6 (DDE Library). This figure included not only the DLF but 'Point 4' technical assistance and UN contributions as well.
52 See Rostow, *Eisenhower, Kennedy and Foreign Aid,* pp. 86–87; also, Kaufman, *Trade and Aid,* p. 135.
53 Kaufman, *Trade and Aid,* p. 54.
54 Memorandum, Dulles to President, 13 September 1958. White House office, Office of Staff Secretary (Goodpaster), Subject Series, Alphabetical Subseries, box 15 (DDE Library).
55 *Ibid.*
56 Memorandum, Dulles to President, 13 September 1958.
57 CIA, 'The Present and Prospective Sino-Soviet Bloc Threat Relevant to US Mutual Security Programs', January 14, 1959. Draper File, box 8, Letter to A. Dulles, 15 December 1958, reply of 14 January 1959 (DDE Library).
58 'Notes from Meeting with General Twining, 8 December 1958. Draper File, box 8, Misc. Memoranda for the Record (DDE Library).
59 Marx Leva notes on briefing by JCS, 15 December 1959. Draper File, box 8, Misc. Memoranda for the Record (DDE Library).
60 *Ibid.*
61 Institute for Defense Analysis, 'A Study of US Military Assistance Programs in the Underdeveloped Areas', 3 March 1959, pp. 3–4. Draper File, box 12 (DDE Library).
62 Harvard Center for International Affairs, 'General Framework for Analysis of Military Assistance', 6 January 1959. Draper File, box 4 (DDE Library).
63 *Ibid.,* p. 5.
64 Max Millikan's comments, drawn from 'Notes of dinner meeting, December 2, 1958', Draper File, box 6, Misc. Memoranda for the Record (DDE Library).

Also, 'A Study of Military Assistance in Underdeveloped Areas', p. 4.

65   Dillon, 24 January 1959 reply to Draper letter of 18 December 1958, pp. 1–3. Draper File, box 9, folder 10 (DDE Library).

66   *Ibid.*

67   'Economic Growth of the Free World', p. 3. Draper File, box 9, folder 28 (DDE Library).

68   Dillon refers to Indonesian President Sukarno's demands for Indonesian control over the Western, Dutch portion of the island of New Guinea, or Irian Jaya, now West Papua.

69   Dillon letter to Draper, file: Letter to C. Douglas Dillon and reply of 20 February 1959, p. 2. Draper File, box 9 (DDE Library).

70   *Ibid.* (Dillon, reply of 20 February 1959).

71   James Smith, 'Talking Paper', file: Letter to C. Douglas Dillon and reply of 20 February 1959, p. 2. Draper File, box 9 (DDE Library).

72   *Ibid.*, p. 22 (emphasis in original).

73   Draft of Final Report, section 5, pp. 18–19. Draper File, box 5 (DDE Library).

74   *Ibid.* (emphasis in original).

75   Draft of Final Report; also Kaufman, *Trade and Aid,* p. 172.

76   Draft of Final Report, section 5.

77   Discussion at 465th Meeting of NSC.

78   Kaufman, *Trade and Aid,* ch. 8.

79   Discussion at 388th Meeting of NSC, 3 December 1958, pp. 3–4.

80   Discussion at 427th Meeting of NSC, 3 December 1959.

81   In particular, Representative Otto Passman, Chairman of the House Appropriations Subcommittee. See Kaufman, *Trade and Aid,* pp. 202–203.

82   Department of State, Report on the Status of the Mutual Security Program as of 30 June 1960, p. 2.

83   Eisenhower resisted many such measures that would defer or limit taxes on *all* income earned overseas, in an effort to encourage investment in the less developed areas in particular. The overwhelming bulk of US private investment overseas at this time was in the industrialized countries of Europe. See Kaufman, *Trade and Aid,* pp. 156–159 and ch. 2.

84   Letter, Bell to Draper, 6 April 1959. Draper File, box 10, folder 42 (DDE Library).

85   *Ibid.*

86   State comments on IDAB; see note 39, pp. 173–174.

87   Draper final report.

88   Baldwin, *Economic Development,* p. 171.

89   Kaufman, *Trade and Aid,* p. 133.

90   Ted Robert Gurr, *Why Men Rebel* (Princeton, NJ: Princeton University Press, 1970). Simply stated, Gurr reasoned that a widening gap between a people's aspirations and their opportunities for meeting those aspirations led to popular frustration that could in turn lead to rebellion.

91   NSC discussion on 'Newly Independent Countries'. NSC Staff Papers File, DDE Library.

92   'Neutralism in the Far East', NSC Staff Papers, box 2, file: 'Bandung', p. 3.

93   Discussion at 465th Meeting of NSC, 2 November 1960.

94   The White House still faced an uphill climb in selling this modified view of neutralism to Congress. Dillon's approach to 'moderating revolutions' raised

questions regarding the wisdom of aiding 'neutrals' and the related 'issue of principle' that had generated Congressional debate over and resistance to the DLF; should US aid go to help develop non-allied or 'uncommitted' nations? See Rostow, *Eisenhower, Kennedy and Foreign Aid,* p. 126. In the course of the Draper study, analysts at Harvard University went so far as to recommended that the US should be prepared to agree to 'the neutralization of certain areas now receiving [US] military assistance'. See Harvard Center, 'General Framework', p. 4.

95 *FRUS,* 1955–57, vol. 10, p. 191.
96 Message to Congress regarding the Mutual Security Program, 19 March 1956. Quoted in Kaufman, *Trade and Aid,* p. 67.
97 Komer memorandum on 'Countering the Bloc Trade and Aid Campaign', 29 January 1959. Draper File, box 8 (DDE Library).
98 Author interviews with Herbert Brownell, C. Douglas Dillon and Andrew Goodpaster.
99 O. M. Smolansky and B. M. Smolansky. *The USSR and Iraq: The Soviet Quest for Influence* (Durham and London: Duke University Press, 1991), ch. 1.
100 Stanton H. Burnett, *Investing in Security: Economic Aid for Noneconomic Purposes* (Washington: Center for Strategic and International Studies (CSIS), 1992).
101 Discussion at 465th Meeting of NSC, 2 November 1960.
102 Harvard Center, 'General Framework', pp. 8–10.
103 NSC 149, *FRUS,* 1952–54, vol. 2, pt 1, p. 312.
104 Discussion at 449th Meeting of NSC, 30 June 1960, p. 9.
105 Kaufman. *Trade and Aid,* pp. 199–200.
106 Discussion at 449th Meeting of NSC. For a discussion of how developing world radicalism and the concept of national liberation had far more common ground with the Soviet concept of development than with that of the West, see MacFarlane, *Superpower Rivalry and 3rd World Radicalism,* p. 6.
107 See, for example, Eisenhower's letter to Dulles of 6 December 1955.
108 Kaufman, *Trade and Aid,* p. 137.
109 Report on the Status of the Mutual Security Program as of 30 June 1960, pp. 1–5.
110 Letter, Eisenhower to Dulles, 26 March 1958. White House Memoranda Series, box 6, JFD Papers (DDE Library).

5

Kennedy, Johnson and the USOIDP: theory and practice

As John Gaddis has observed, Presidents Kennedy and Johnson shared the same intellectual framework for viewing the world.[1] They also shared many of the same advisers and cabinet officers. After the assassination of Kennedy in November of 1963, and even after Johnson's re-election in 1964, many members of Kennedy's team remained at their White House and agency posts. In the foreign policy sphere, these individuals included Secretary of State Dean Rusk, Secretary of Defense Robert McNamara, and Special Assistant for National Security Affairs McGeorge Bundy. Additionally, influential advisers such as Maxwell Taylor and Walt Whitman Rostow filled a variety of important posts in these administrations, with Rostow going on to succeed Bundy as Johnson's Special Assistant for National Security Affairs in 1966. For these reasons, this study treats both administrations as one era of US Cold War policy, and the period from 1961 to 1968 is the focus of this chapter.

The Eisenhower presidency had ended with furious efforts to come to grips with the 'new order' brought on by the accelerating decolonization process, and a search for new programmes to keep US security assistance policy abreast of the changes taking place in the world. In contrast, the Kennedy team felt assured that they understood this new order in the developing world, and, armed with the increasingly influential body of modernization theory, they believed they understood the processes at work therein. Whereas Eisenhower left the White House believing that his administration had hit the 'bottom of the barrel' in terms of ideas, the Kennedy administration came into office equipped with what its members considered a radical, new approach to containment, and a determination to avoid what they perceived to be the mistakes of their predecessors.

Containment in the Kennedy and Johnson era represented a shift in focus to the grassroots level in developing countries. While the Eisenhower administration operated from a Marxist–Leninist conception of the communist threat in new states, focusing on Dillon's 'urban middle groups', the Kennedy team viewed the threat in Maoist terms. Additionally, in response to the Maoist blueprint for revolution and people's war, the Kennedy administration assembled its own blueprint for combatting Maoist insurgency by promoting internal security, national cohesion and development. This blueprint was the United States Overseas Internal Defense Policy, or USOIDP.

The test-bed for the USOIDP would be Southeast Asia. In implementing the measures prescribed in the USOIDP Washington found itself ever more deeply involved in the internal affairs of target states. As US political involvement deepened Washington discovered the limits of its own ability to wield influence in recipients' domestic affairs. As America's military involvement deepened, US policy-makers learned just how easily the 'shield' element of security assistance could become unbalanced, and how easily this imbalance could undermine and destroy the more development-oriented elements of containment.

US perceptions of global communist threat

As with previous presidents, the Kennedy team's overall perception was that the Cold War was going badly, and their accession to office offered America the opportunity to 'seize the initiative'. The USA needed a policy designed to 'break the long chain of Sino-Soviet successes' in the world.[2] As the new Secretary of State Dean Rusk argued, in Latin America, Africa and Asia US policy had 'reached a watershed, where the holding operations of the past [we]re clearly inadequate and where new initiative [*sic*] of a dramatic and positive kind [we]re essential'.[3]

The need for a new US approach to the Cold War was acknowledged by the Defense Department as well. The US Military Program of 1961 recommended that:

> the US should shift progressively from a policy of mere reaction to communist moves to a strategy of initiative designed to effect, as soon as feasible, a radical change in the existing international situation. With a vigorous change of pace made now, the Free World by mid-decade should be in a position actually to take advantage of opportunities for the initiative as they arise. By the end of the next 10–15 year period, the US and its allies could well be creating their own opportunities.[4]

The difference between the Eisenhower and Kennedy approaches to containment reflects differences between Leninist and Maoist concepts of revolution. The Kennedy administration ushered in a shift of focus in security assistance programmes toward measures aimed at internal defence at the grassroots level. The fundamental difference in the Kennedy administration's perception of the communist threat was its tendency to analyse communist strategy and tactics in terms of Maoist doctrine, in contrast to the Eisenhower administration's scrutiny of Marx, Lenin and Stalin for insights into communist behaviour. Whereas Eisenhower, Dulles and the NSC had formulated policy on a belief that communism sought to expand through means short of violence, Kennedy's team saw an enemy who believed in the inevitability of armed struggle.[5]

This Maoist framework of analysis, with its emphasis on the efficacy of 'people's war' led the Kennedy administration to focus on prosecuting the Cold War in rural settings. Kennedy's team concentrated on the villages throughout the underdeveloped areas, in sharp contrast to Dillon's focus on 'urban middle groups' as the critical target of the Cold War.[6] As doctrine formed around this Maoist analytical framework, the rural counter-insurgency concept became the blueprint for nation-building as well as broader security assistance efforts in Southeast Asia and elsewhere.

Perceptions: communist threat in developing world

The Kennedy team observed that the principal battlefield of the Cold War would be the area witnessing the greatest change: the decolonizing, underdeveloped regions of the world. In this area, Kennedy's group of mostly young leaders saw their time in office as one of 'revolutionary change' and assumed for themselves and their country a leading role in managing such change in a world of turmoil. The emergence of new states was indicative of a world 'reshaping itself in a way that [was] at least as significant as the breakdown of the Concert of Europe'.[7]

Even as they formulated policy approaches for intervening in this 'reshaping' process, the Kennedy team also expected the communists to make every effort to exploit the upheaval produced by such change. To the Kennedy administration, these emerging new states would be the venue for 'the contest between communism and the Free World for primary influence over the direction and outcome of the developmental process'.[8] American analysts had viewed with unease a joint manifesto issued by eighty-one communist parties at a Moscow conference in December of 1960, and interpreted these proceedings as concluding that 'the policy of "peaceful coexistence" merely provides "opportunities for the class struggle in capitalistic countries and for the national liberation movement in colonial and dependent countries"'.[9] This unease in Washington intensified when in 1961 Nikita S. Khrushchev made a speech pledging Moscow's support for such wars of national liberation. Kennedy himself interpreted Khrushchev's declaration as a new Soviet initiative to take over anti-colonial and other revolutionary movements in the developing world.[10] Additionally, the PRC was emerging as a greater threat in its own right, stepping up its own foreign aid and other diplomatic activities in the developing world and calling for the broadening and intensification of popular armed struggle.[11]

Washington still perceived a need to combat the communist threat at two discrete levels, as described in Chapter 4. At the internal level, US policy was to attack the communist idea and lessen its impact on the factional struggles that characterized the internal political situation in many new states. At the external level, Washington sought to secure a favourable (i.e., non-communist) foreign policy orientation among new states. Perhaps the most pressing item on Washington's agenda in the developing world was to attack the pervasive perception that communism was the 'wave of future' in Asia.[12] If this powerful idea could be discredited it would represent a significant easing of the overall communist threat at both the internal and external levels. And, if Washington had any hope of discrediting this idea, two crisis areas demanded immediate attention: Indonesia and Indochina.

Indonesia

A leading proponent of the view that communism represented the 'wave of the future' in Asia and elsewhere was Indonesian President Achmed Sukarno. Sukarno saw contemporary trends in international affairs as a world undergoing fundamental changes. Propounding what Washington described as his 'simplistic foreign cosmology', Sukarno described a world in which the 'NEFO' or new, emerging forces, including the socialist states, newly independent states and 'progressive forces' within capitalist societies, were pitted against the 'OLDFO', or old, established forces, such as the USA and the former imperial powers. In this struggle there would be no room for peaceful coexistence; the NEFOs would continue militant confrontation until American and West European influence was purged from developing areas and 'puppet organizations' such as the United Nations (UN) were done away with.[13] US analysts recognized that Sukarno himself was a nationalist rather than a communist, but remained concerned that his association with communists would offer the latter increasing influence over him and his government. Given Sukarno's strident pro-communist rhetoric and close association with the very large Indonesian Communist Party (PKI), the Indonesian situation was extremely worrisome to Washington.

Even more worrisome was Sukarno's belligerent activity against Indonesia's neighbours. As Kennedy took office, Sukarno was intensifying his campaign to gain control of the Western portion of the Island of New Guinea, or Irian Jaya, which Indonesia claimed shortly after gaining independence. The Indonesian military's involvement in insurgent activities against West Irian, intended to destabilize the Dutch position there, was deepening. Washington further anticipated that Indonesia would steadily intensify regular military activity against West Irian, including limited air and naval attacks, as new Soviet-supplied military equipment became operational.[14]

However, Washington was less concerned with the direct impact of Indonesia's foreign adventures than with their domestic impact on the stability of Indonesian society. Sukarno had moved his chief political rival, the military, out of Jakarta to diminish its immediate political influence. As the Army became increasingly bogged-down 1,500 miles away in the West Irian campaign, the PKI was consolidating its position in Jakarta, positioning itself to reap the political benefits of any failure by the Army in West Irian, or to step into power if the chronically ill Sukarno died or became incapacitated. Washington observed that Sukarno had long played the Army and PKI off against each other, and as the Army was the only force that could keep the PKI from dominating Sukarno and Indonesia, US analysts were concerned over growing PKI influence in Jakarta at a time when the Army was away.[15] The Kennedy administration determined that the best course of action was to defuse the situation by pushing for and facilitating a negotiated settlement of the West Irian issue, one which, in the end, favoured Sukarno's ambitions.[16]

Fearing that domestic economic instability only improved the PKI's position, the USA also moved to bolster Indonesia's economic situation through a stabilization programme. Deficit spending in support of the West Irian campaign had exacerbated Indonesia's already serious economic problems. Foreign reserves were extremely low, resulting in falling imports of needed raw materials and spare parts for industry.[17] US Intelligence analysts also anticipated that Indonesia would soon suffer serious shortages of foodstuffs and expressed concern that such shortages would lead to explosive levels of internal disorder.[18] As an emergency measure, the Kennedy administration rushed a 70 million dollar emergency aid package to Jakarta in late 1962, consisting mainly of food and fibres.[19]

Even as Washington dispatched this emergency aid the USA was formulating a longer-term programme for Indonesia's economic recovery. However, this long-term programme was to be conditional upon Jakarta's commitment to addressing its own economic problems. The overall policy goal from Washington's perspective was to turn Indonesia's attention 'away from militant nationalism and towards development'.[20] Toward this end the US contemplated offering a substantial 'carrot' to Jakarta, a package of aid consisting of development loans, grants and food aid totalling some 600 million dollars over three years.[21] However, this offer would be conditional upon Jakarta's willingness to commit itself to taking the domestic measures necessary to reform its economy. The first, critical step in this long-term approach was, from the American point of view, to 'push Indonesia into an IMF stabilization program'.[22]

The proffered 'carrot' failed to turn Sukarno's attentions towards domestic affairs. In January 1963, only months after the West Irian settlement, Sukarno launched his campaign of confrontation or *Konfrontasi* against newly independent Malaysia. The *Konfrontasi* consisted mainly of paramilitary commando attacks into Malaysia in hopes of destabilizing that new state, forcing the new Malaysian government of Tunku Abdul Rahman to open negotiations with Indonesia on the future of the territory involved (primarily in North Borneo) and gaining a settlement more favourable to Jakarta.[23] While Sukarno declared himself opposed to the independence of Malaysia on the grounds that the new arrangement represented persistence of the British imperialist presence in the region, US analysts estimated that he was angered primarily because he had expected to inherit control of northern Borneo with the end of British rule there. Additionally, Washington believed that Sukarno was also concerned that a successful Malaysia would prove an attractive example and thereby encourage separatism among the peoples living in parts of Indonesia adjacent thereto.[24] *Disintegrasi* or the political disintegration of Indonesia had always been a sensitive issue with Jakarta, and had been aggravated by the Eisenhower administration's half-baked initiative to aid separatist movements in the outer islands.[25]

Malaysia's Tunku, for his part, sought to hang on and resist the *Konfrontasi* until Indonesia's economy, and perhaps Sukarno himself, collapsed. This was not an unreasonable expectation, in light of Sukarno's poor health and the debilitated state of the economy in the wake of the West Irian campaign.[26] Initiation of the *Konfrontasi* put new strains on Indonesia's resources and effectively killed any serious discussion of an economic stabilization plan.

Washington perceived serious danger in either event, as the *Konfrontasi* could produce a win-win situation for the communists. Acknowledging the PKI as second only to the Army as a political force in Indonesia, US analysts worried that, with the armed forces spread out through remote areas of Indonesia and Malaysia, they would be poorly positioned to block any PKI bid for power in the event that Sukarno died or became too weak to hold on. Thus, any interim gains made by Sukarno in his *Konfrontasi* would ultimately be inherited by the PKI.[27] Similarly, if the Indonesian economy did collapse, the PKI would be the most likely beneficiaries from resulting political upheaval.[28]

While US analysts perceived Indonesia to be sliding toward communism, they also recognized that their ability to arrest this slide was dwindling rapidly. The substantial aid programmes from the USA and multilateral aid sources had been conditional on Jakarta's commitment to internal economic reform, and Jakarta had scoffed at such conditions. Kennedy, and later Johnson, determined that future programmes of new aid to Indonesia would remain on a wait-and-see basis, pending internal economic reform as well as a toning-down of belligerence against neighbouring countries. Additionally, US actions were further complicated by Sukarno's 'to hell with your aid' speech, delivered at an event at which the US Ambassador was present. This outburst provoked the US Congress to amend foreign assistance legislation, suspending further aid to Indonesia except when the President could clearly justify it in terms of national interest.[29] Any aid the US granted Indonesia would now be a high-profile decision, which, in the context of Sukarno's *Konfrontasi,* put the USA in an awkward position. Continued aid to Jakarta could be interpreted internationally as a vote of confidence for Sukarno, who would certainly represent it as such. At the same time, Washington felt it could not simply cut-off all aid, lest Sukarno confiscate the considerable US and other Western investments in the country.[30]

Additionally, any substantial cuts in existing aid could drive Indonesia further towards the Soviets and the communist Chinese, who already enjoyed steadily increasing influence in Jakarta. The PKI had long been moving closer to the PRC and were, in the estimation of American intelligence analysts, 'clearly committed to the Peiping side of the Sino-Soviet Split'.[31] The Soviets, for their part, had been steadily stepping-up aid to Indonesia, the largest recipient of Soviet aid outside the bloc. As Jakarta's debt to Moscow increased, Washington estimated that Indonesia's patterns of economic interaction would be reoriented toward the USSR.[32] Moscow was also enjoying increasing influence among the military through their own military assistance training programmes, which, Washington seems to have assumed, were similar in their political purpose to American training programmes.[33] Through these Soviet military aid efforts, Washington feared, the Indonesian Army would moderate, or even lose, its anti-communist stance.[34]

While the USA perceived the situation in the Malayan archipelago as dangerous, one in which according to Rusk, the stakes were higher than Vietnam,[35] Washington was constrained in its actions by a target regime that would not let it have its way in reshaping internal economic and political structures. In Indonesia under Sukarno, the USA simply did not have the sort of access to public policy that it required to institute its political and economic development programmes. However, Washington could neither withdraw support from the regime nor depose its popular, charismatic leader, as the communists would be the most likely beneficiaries of the instability that would follow such a move. As a result, Washington would maintain cautious efforts to influence Indonesia's domestic and foreign policies, as it focused its security assistance efforts elsewhere.

Indochina

As Kennedy took office, the most immediate danger was perceived in Indochina. In a National Intelligence Estimate produced in early 1961, the US intelligence community warned that the crisis in Laos was being viewed in Asia as a 'test of wills and intentions' between the communist and non-communist worlds, and that the future foreign policy orientations of the countries of the region hung in the balance.[36]

According to American intelligence analysts, the possible 'loss' or partition of Laos was to be dreaded more for its political impact on the region than for any immediate military or strategic consequences. While there was concern that such a loss would bring increased communist military power to bear on the 'crucial Saigon defense complex', Washington was far more concerned with the political and psychological effects events in Laos would have on other regimes in Southeast Asia:

> The close proximity of a communist state would make more difficult Western efforts to starch up local resistance...The future course of all of the countries of Southeast Asia would be strongly influenced by the actual circumstances in which the loss or division of Laos had occurred as well as the local appraisals of the attitude and reaction of the US in response to the situation. The extent to which these countries would go in resisting Bloc pressures or in withstanding local communist threats would depend in great degree on whether they still assessed that the US could stem further

communist expansion in the area. They would feel more keenly than before a strong temptation to take a neutral position between the two power blocs, even though they recognize that the US is the only country with sufficient power to oppose the Communist Bloc in the area.[37]

Thus, in Washington's rationale, the mechanism of the 'domino effect' was psychological. US security assistance programmes had, from the outset, contained prominent psychological elements, being designed to bolster recipients' will to resist communist intimidation. As Pach put it, 'their most important and immediate goals were raising foreign morale, solidifying the will to resist communist expansion, and demonstrating American resolve and reliability'.[38] However, according to US intelligence estimates, the situation developing in Indochina went beyond efforts to stiffen any presupposed resistance on the part of Southeast Asian states. This situation was very much a contest, one that would, in essence, determine the foreign policy orientation of an entire region, and perhaps beyond.

Washington estimated that the communists were far more deeply committed to their efforts in South Vietnam than those underway in Laos, and attached far more importance to their Vietnamese objectives. Similarly, 'US prestige and policy' were 'particularly deeply engaged' in South Vietnam. 'Diem's policy of close alignment with the US is on trial in the current crisis. All countries of the area would attach great importance to a failure of the South Vietnamese Government to cope successfully with the rising tempo of Communist subversion and armed insurrection.'[39]

Based on such intelligence, and its estimates of the high stakes involved, Kennedy determined that the place to stop the expansion of communism in the region was in Vietnam.[40]

Response: nation-building

To the Kennedy administration, a successful US 'stand' in Vietnam would represent significant progress in meeting the communist threat at both levels. Such a success in Vietnam would 'break the long chain of Sino-Soviet successes' as alluded to above[41] and thus cast doubts on the widely held perception that communism was the wave of the future in Asia and elsewhere in the developing world. With respect to external alignment, such a success would address many of the concerns expressed in NIE 50–61 regarding the political and psychological impacts of further communist gains in the region. Internally, failure of the communists in Vietnam would represent a considerable loss of face and prestige for communist movements in the region and elsewhere.

To the Kennedy administration, the key to breaking the chain of communist successes in the developing world was at the grassroots level, in the villages where the communists were operating most actively and scoring significant political successes. The Kennedy–Johnson internal defence effort depended not only on protecting the villages from communist insurgents but also on denying the communists the allegiance of those villages' inhabitants and binding that allegiance to the recipient government. The resulting effort was a complex mix of measures to combat insurgents, increase cohesion and 'political awareness' among the population through community development programmes, while at the same time trying to increase the effectiveness and legitimacy of recipient regimes.

USOIDP

The Kennedy administration's Maoist framework of analysis shifted Washington's security assistance focus to counterinsurgency in rural settings, and the counterinsurgency concept became the framework for nation-building as well as broader security efforts in Southeast Asia. The philosophy and objectives as well as the practical measures embodied in this approach were codified in the USOIDP.

The USOIDP contained many features of the 1290-d/OISP discussed in Chapter 3. Like its Eisenhower-era predecessor, the USOIDP prescribed the creation of capable internal security forces, the extension of the recipient regime's presence and authority to outlying areas, educating the recipient population and leaders as to the dangers of communism, and enhancing the legitimacy and popularity of the recipient government and its security forces.

The difference between the programmes lay in that USOIDP was put forth as a comprehensive framework around which to build policy. Members and staff of the Eisenhower NSC tried to assemble such a framework in the form of the 1290-d programme, but found themselves modifying the overall internal security approach in the process of implementing its prescribed measures. The development of the 1290-d programme reflected feedback that steered policy. In contrast, the USOIDP, once it had presidential support, became the accepted doctrine; it was viewed as a broadly applicable plan for developing and executing a wide range of security assistance measures in developing countries. Additionally, Kennedy put even more support behind USOIDP than had Eisenhower behind 1290-d. To Kennedy, the USOIDP was much more central to US Cold War strategy. In August 1962 Kennedy approved the USOIDP as blueprint for *all* agencies' internal defence and counterinsurgency efforts.[42] The USOIDP became the basic framework for all US efforts to secure countries of the developing world from communism, whether these countries were pro-Western or 'basically neutral'.[43]

The President's approval of the USOIDP marked the beginning of what Blaufarb has dubbed 'the counterinsurgency era' in US security policy.[44] More importantly for the purpose of this study, Kennedy's acceptance of the USOIDP marks the beginning of a period in which modernization theory shaped almost every aspect of US security assistance policy in developing areas. The most direct conduit for modernization theory's influence was Walt Rostow, who, as Chairman of the State Department's Policy Planning Staff (PPS), had a central role in drafting the USOIDP.

While the military and paramilitary aspects of counterinsurgency doctrine have received significant criticism since the Vietnam war, the political development objectives embodied in the USOIDP have remained largely unexamined until recently.[45] For that reason it is worthwhile exploring USOIDP's perspective on the nature of the relationship between development and security.

According to the USOIDP, the communist threat in developing regions derived its urgency from the environment of upheaval and instability characterizing states in transition from traditional to modern societies, and from the potential for communist exploitation of that upheaval. It was summed up as follows:

> The principal forces at work throughout the underdeveloped world are: 1) the stresses and strains of the developmental process brought about by the revolutionary break with the traditional past and uneven progress toward new and more modern forms of political, social and economic organization; and 2) the contest between communism and the Free World for primary influence over the direction and outcome of the development process.[46]

Writing at a time when the pace of the decolonization process was still accelerating, Rostow and the PPS saw in this 'contest' opportunities for the USA and the West to shape that portion of the world currently emerging from collapsing empires. 'Social patterns and institutions in most underdeveloped areas are extremely malleable', wrote PPS. 'They are often a legacy of shapeless, frequently illogical political units which are derived, in part, from a colonial past.'[47]

Thus, 'traditional' society had already been disrupted by colonization, and it was the task of the West to help form the tattered remnants of this society, as well as the remaining vestiges of the colonial state, into a new, 'modern' society (as defined by modernization theorists like Rostow), ready to assume a place in the free world. What lent urgency to this process was, as the USOIDP implied, that the communists saw similar opportunities to shape from these same remnants new societies in accordance with their own social scientific perspective. The communists, from their own point of view, were simply helping along the processes of history.

From Washington's perspective, the very processes of political development and institutional formation increased the vulnerability of these new states to disruption and subversion by communism. As PPS noted, 'It is during the interim, between the shattering of the old state and its consolidation into a viable modern state of popularly accepted and supported institutional strength, that a modernizing state is vulnerable to subversion and insurgency', for 'the revolution of modernization can disturb, uproot and daze a traditional society. While the institutions required for modernization are in the process of being created, this revolution contributes to arousing pressures, anxieties, and hopes which seem to justify violent action.'[48]

According to USOIDP, this heightened susceptibility of transitional societies to subversion required the development of adequate indigenous internal security capabilities to assure the stability necessary for healthy economic and political development processes to take place. However, Rostow and PPS saw the enforcement of political stability as only one part of the answer, as:

> sheer repression of political unrest seldom does more than buy time. Unless used to political advantage, this time may favor the subversives or their communist mentors. Rebels of today may be the governments of tomorrow unless their grievances where legitimate are addressed by needed reforms.[49]

Thus, American help in providing an internal security 'shield' to ensure stability would have to buy time for the strengthening of the recipient society through reform of existing social, political and economic institutions and the development of modern ones to take their places. However, these new institutions should not simply be grafted on or installed by the USA. PPS stressed that efforts to ameliorate social unrest must be efforts of the local government, as insurgency was a 'uniquely local problem involving the aspirations and allegiance of local people. Only the local government can remove [insurgency's] causes, win back the support of the insurgents, and strengthen the society's cohesiveness.'[50] Washington understood that powerful nationalist passions were at work in many newly decolonized states, and sought to harness such forces for the benefit of recipient governments, without inflaming anti-Western sentiment. Therefore, participating US agencies would need to keep a low profile in their nation-building programmes so that 'any credit for success should accrue in the fullest possible manner to the local government'.[51] Expressing the sentiment that was the essence of what would become known as the 'win hearts and minds' approach, the USOIDP asserted: 'the US must always keep in mind that the *ultimate and decisive target is the people.* Society is itself at war and the resources, motives and targets of the struggle are found almost wholly within the local population.'[52]

Even though the USOIDP also assumed for the USA the ambitious task of managing these modernization processes, Washington's role would focus on supporting local efforts aimed at societal reform and political development. The USOIDP concentrated US support in several areas of political development.

'Community development' concept

Community development emphasized fostering a sense of participation among the population of a target country, including the development of a sense of community between outlying regions and their government.[53] The most prominent feature of such community development efforts was the extension of infrastructure to remote areas. Throughout much of Southeast Asia, US-funded road building and other infrastructure extension projects carried the government's presence to outlying areas.

Community development included efforts to enhance communications infrastructure and capabilities as well. For example, under programmes designed to 'increase national cohesion' in Thailand, hundreds of radio transceivers were supplied to villages along the Mekong to help link remote communities with regional or provincial centers.[54] In addition, the USIA, in collaboration with other US and local agencies, helped develop recipients' own mass-communication capabilities as well as producing information programmes to carry the government's voice to distant provinces, promote recipient governments' popularity, praise its security forces' counter-insurgency efforts, and the civic action accomplishments of the local military. One example was a 1,000 kw medium-wave transmitter installed in Bangkok for the *Voice Of America*, also justified as part of a programme to 'increase national cohesion'.[55] Similarly, a CIA-supported radio station transmitting to the Hmong areas of Laos broadcast under the name 'Union of the Lao Races' and carried programming intended to rally the tribal peoples towards the idea of a nationalist rather than an ethnic struggle.[56]

US programmes also contributed to recipient governments' physical presence in remote regions through the expansion of such initiatives as the 'strategic hamlet' programme in Vietnam and the introduction of similar 'agrimetros' in Thailand and elsewhere, the latter consisting of 'clusters of villages grouped around common security, health and other facilities'.[57] All such projects were designed to separate the insurgents from their support base, the rural population itself.

CIA participation in community development included the 'Citizens' Irregular Defense Group' (CIDG) concept, which armed civilians in villages and organized these into a militia with rather basic fighting capabilities. In the event of actual attack, these units could call for help from more combat-capable mobile response teams that were also formed from the local population. Like many US military aid efforts in the developing world, the CIDG programme was primarily psychological in its objectives rather than military. Participation in such units was intended to build a sense of common participatory defence among the villagers more than to develop effectiveness in actually killing the enemy.[58]

Leader groups

According to the USOIDP, 'leader groups' included local political leaders, foreign military (and other counterpart agency) officers, religious and educational leaders, the intelligentsia and 'the middle class generally'.[59] Actual leader group support programmes included 'political awareness' courses for local leaders, which featured material on the dangers of communism, methods of insurgent infiltration and 'information programmes' designed to enhance the image of the central government. Such courses were organized for leaders at various levels, from village headmen to provincial governors.[60]

Modernization theory's emphasis on the military as a 'modernizing elite' was reflected in USOIDP's 'leader group' support as well. Under USOIDP, the USA would seek to create in foreign officers:

> an awareness of the political process of nation-building, bearing in mind that national leadership often emerges from the military element of under-developed countries. It is US policy, when it is in the US interest, to make the local military and police advocates of democracy and agents for carrying forward the developmental process.[61]

Civic action

As defined by the USOIDP, 'civic action is the use of military forces on projects useful to the populace at all levels in such fields as training, public works, agriculture, transportation, communications, health, sanitation and others helpful to economic development'.[62] Kennedy-era policy built upon Eisenhower's Civic Action philosophy, and similarly advocated:

> encouragement and support of indigenous military forces in less developed nations to undertake constructive programs of economic, social and psychological activities as an added means of benefiting host countries generally and of creating for the populace a positive and friendly image of local military forces and of the United States.[63]

For, as one Army memorandum summed up the civic action concept, 'when the military and the people become close to each other there is no place for the enemy to hide'.[64]

Under the USOIDP, civic action projects undertaken by recipient military forces included the same sorts of activity that had been supported by the Eisenhower administration, such as the execution of sanitation and clean water projects by military engineering units, the extension of basic medical services and the provision of 'village kits' to Thai and Cambodian forces for civic action purposes.[65] As was the case under Eisenhower, such activities promoted a favourable image of the military, and thereby the local government, while contributing improvements to the country's basic infrastructure. However, the USOIDP envisioned an enhanced role for the military in the economic development of recipient states. Local military units would be expected to 'contribute substantially' to economic and social development, and such tasks would not be a sideline mainly for public relations purposes; they would become a 'major function of these forces'.[66]

Social projects

In accordance with the above civic action concept, the military would act as a primary vehicle for instituting social projects in recipient countries, projects 'designed to ameliorate discontent, i.e. low-cost housing, better sanitation, potable water, new schools and low-cost utilities'.[67] Examples included a project in Thailand to build one hundred schools in remote areas and provide these with water and sanitation facilities, to be undertaken by units of the Thai Border Police.[68] Another example was US support for the Thai Prime Minister's plan to assemble 'Mobile Development Units' within the Thai National Security Organization, comprised of technical experts in such fields as health and agriculture, to assist remote villages.[69]

Support for land reform

The USOIDP noted the 'primitive' and 'oppressive' forms of land tenancy characterizing much of underdeveloped world, and, recognizing the potential for unrest latent in these conditions, sought to promote and support 'sound land reform'.[70] Recognizing that none of the above efforts would bring internal stability unless they were undertaken in the context of necessary societal reforms, the Kennedy and Johnson teams proved far more willing to push recipients to institute these reforms than their predecessors had been.

In Latin America, Kennedy's Alliance for Progress had been designed to promote such reforms in land distribution and tenancy. As in other regions of the developing world, aid was often conditional upon recipients' demonstrated willingness to institute necessary social reforms. The Alliance went a step beyond conditionality by providing funding for such social change, including underwriting the logistical costs involved in such reforms and even providing compensation for land appropriated for redistribution.

However, Congress proved less prescient when it came to Southeast Asia, where similar, almost semi-feudal economic systems persisted. The Cuban revolution, and the appearance of a communist 'beach-head' in the Western hemisphere had lent a sense of urgency to the Alliance for Progress debate, and helped sway Congress to approve the 600 million dollars spent on the Alliance in its first year alone. Kennedy administration officials were not provided with similar 'carrots' for use in their efforts to secure social reforms in recipient countries elsewhere, and relied more heavily on diplomacy.

'Diplomatic' support

'Diplomatic support' described a role for US officials in persuading their counterparts among recipient leadership and the bureaucracy to accept the need to institute the local reforms necessary to defuse the threat of insurgency, and, once these counterpart officials were so persuaded, to help them actually institute these reforms.[71]

The USOIDP clearly asserted that US officials should push hard when necessary, and that they should be willing to use aid to achieve maximum leverage against recalcitrant counterpart leaders:

> In their desire to assure smooth short-run relations with traditional oli-
> garchies, US representatives often forget that in some cases local leaders
> may have no practical alternative to accepting the US recommendations,
> particularly if specific reforms become prerequisites to the continuance of
> US aid.[72]

Under the USOIDP, the US would readily marshal local opposition to bring pressure to bear on stubborn regimes:

> there are some cases where, despite the local suggestions for reform through normal U.S. diplomatic channels, the government and its leaders refuse to act. Experience has amply shown, in such cases, that through other means it is often possible with minimal risk to increase significantly the effectiveness of opposition leaders, political parties, institutional groups, and information media.[73]

Through such means the Kennedy administration anticipated that it could 'bring organized and broadly-based political pressures' to bear on reluctant local governments.[74]

Education, labour and youth

The USOIDP also called for supporting efforts to improve education in recipient states, and for extending education to a broader section of the population. The US role in such measures would include participating in the development of curricula as well as the development of teachers (see 'leader groups', above), and providing textbooks to 'prepare students for the modern democratic world'. PPS also directed that US resources be applied towards the 'development of healthy labor and youth organizations' in recipient countries.[75]

Nation-building within the broader Mutual Security approach

The Kennedy–Johnson period was one of continued and intensified efforts to reorient recipient military establishments away from external defence capabilities and toward an emphasis on meeting internal threats. Accordingly, the internal dimension of US military aid under Kennedy and Johnson emphasized the development of counterinsurgency capabilities in such forces.

The provision of adequate security assistance resources to recipient militaries still featured prominently in Washington's policies in developing areas. '[The] top priority objective of US policy in the underdeveloped countries [was] the achievement of a progressive internal environment secure from the ravages of communist guerrilla activity and the various other covert activities which characterize[d] the international Communist conspiracy.'[76] Securing that environment would certainly require indigenous internal security forces.

However, the Kennedy administration declared itself to be more committed to altering the prevailing balance between military and economic elements of security assistance. Kennedy impressed upon his cabinet his conviction that 'ultimate victory in the cold war [was] dependent on top priority being given to the achievement of self-sustaining growth by the underdeveloped countries'.[77] Less concerned with recipient reaction than Eisenhower, and in accordance with USOIDP's philosophy of putting pressure on recipients to institute necessary reform measures, the Kennedy and Johnson administrations sought to restructure and pare down recipient militaries and reorient these toward a primarily internal security mission.

In countries that had 'substantial fighting potential' (such as Greece, Korea, Taiwan and Turkey) the US attempted to reduce or 'compact' force structures to lessen the burden on the local economy in maintaining a military establishment. In countries judged to have less fighting potential, reductions would be even more severe. The security emphasis was to be on 'sub-limited', guerrilla warfare. In contrast, programmes providing 'prestige' military aid, such as heavy armoured units or high performance aircraft, would be curtailed. Such reductions were also planned for military aid programmes of a quid pro quo nature, as in countries where aid was essentially partial payment for base rights. According to the PPS, just because a country was an aid recipient for quid pro quo reasons, there was no reason why such aid should not serve 'other constructive purposes, such as nation-building, not just to tickle the vanity of recipients'.[78] By 1965, Johnson's Defense Department was advocating that provision of further aid should be made conditional upon recipients undertaking specific restructuring efforts.[79]

Effectiveness

Interagency coordination

Restructuring of US foreign aid organization under Kennedy had some immediate positive effects. One example was the transfer of authority for nominating countries as eligible P.L. 480 recipients to the President from the Department of Agriculture. Agriculture had closely guarded that authority for its utility in opening and developing new markets for US agricultural output.[80]

Other innovations met with resistance. The centerpiece of the Foreign Assistance Act of 1961, USAID, got off to a rocky start. Reorganizing all non-military aid under a new agency had been recommended by the Draper Committee, and early in his presidency Kennedy established USAID for this purpose. In October of 1961 Fowler Hamilton was sworn-in as director of the new agency.

At the same time, Kennedy's reorganization of executive decision-making structures and procedures, especially in realm of national security, impeded interagency cooperation and made USAID even more of a 'stepchild' than ICA had been. De-emphasis of the NSC as a decision-making forum and the subsequent delegation of specific areas of responsibility to powerful 'special groups' was troublesome, as these groups often overlapped and tended to seek regular presidential re-affirmations of their authority *vis à vis* other groups and agencies.

USAID provides a case in point. Early in its history, USAID launched a thorough review of the police programmes transferred to its control in accordance with the civil police responsibilities it inherited from its predecessor organization, the ICA.[81] Upon completion of this study, USAID began to reduce the scope of some police programmes while closing down others, intending to divert those resources to more conventionally development-oriented projects. In the Kennedy administration's reorientation towards a counterinsurgency emphasis, USAID's initiatives alarmed some of Kennedy's team, most notably Maxwell Taylor, McGeorge Bundy and Robert Komer. Taylor and Komer argued that, its own objectives aside, USAID should be intensifying its police efforts rather than de-emphasizing them, and took their concerns to Bundy. Together, these individuals and most of the 'Special Group-CI' (counterinsurgency) decided that a 'hortatory presidential prod towards USAID' was in order. With Bundy's concurrence, Komer drafted a letter for the President's signature, directing USAID's director Hamilton to either give greater emphasis to police programmes or give these programmes sufficient autonomy within the agency to operate without hindrance. In this way the Kennedy team's Special Group-CI re-oriented much of USAID's activity, over the head of its director.[82] Within a short time, USAID reported to the Special Group-CI that in Laos, Thailand and Vietnam, *all* programmes had been directed toward support of counterinsurgency efforts.[83]

The Kennedy team's reorganization of military aid proved troublesome as well. As one of the outspoken Senate 'internationalists' during the Eisenhower years,[84] Kennedy had long advocated a restructuring and reorientation of security assistance away from military measures and towards development aid. Early in his administration, the new President, in consultation with the Secretaries of State and Defense, directed Charles Burton Marshall to conduct a re-examination of the Military Assistance Program 'in light of the [current] environment of complex economic and political issues'.[85] This new environment notwithstanding, Marshall's recommendation proved quite conventional, emphasizing the importance of the undiminished Soviet military threat in the NATO area and recommending a substantial *increase* in military aid programmes for the fiscal year 1962.[86]

Within two months of receiving Burton Marshall's assessment the Kennedy administration launched yet another re-examination of military assistance – in this case, conducted by officials picked from the ranks of the State Department. This second study returned findings more in line with the administration's desire for a 'new look'. It concluded that, while 'sufficient military strength' was important to deter communist attack, the main thrust of US foreign aid efforts for the coming decade 'should be directed toward repelling the more likely Soviet threat of indirect aggression by furthering economic development and nation-building'. It also called for a gradual shift of resources from military assistance to economic aid programmes.[87]

Perhaps not surprisingly, the JCS were quick to express their reservations regarding Kennedy's efforts to restructure military assistance.[88] Similarly, senior US Army commanders resisted emphasis on political or 'unconventional' warfare, as represented by Kennedy's personal interest in increasing the strength and expanding the mission of the US Army's Special Forces or 'Green Beret' units.[89]

Neither did ambassadors take to Kennedy's 'new look' in foreign aid.[90] Not only had recipients grown comfortably accustomed to the prestige and material benefits derived from US military aid, but US ambassadors had also come to count on such aid as a useful lever or bribe in their dealings with host governments. Robert Komer, then a member of the NSC staff, described the ambassadors' resistance to what they saw as 'giving something up for nothing' as 'one of the most serious impediments to a rational "new look" at MAP':

> They argue that if they recommend a cut in MAP over the next five years they will simply be denying themselves at least one sort of country lever-age without any assurance whatsoever that this will be compensated for in other fields ... One ambassador said frankly 'If I play ball with you and tell you that I feel MAP ought to be cut because our chief problems here are internal and not external, but my colleagues in other countries don't play ball and continue making a big case for both economic and military aid, the result will be that my country takes a cut whereas they continue to get military *backsheesh*.'[91]

The Kennedy administration stressed the ambassador's role of coordinating the efforts of all participating agencies. Walt Rostow argued that this delegation of presidential authority to the ambassador was a remarkable, and successful, innovation of the Kennedy presidency.[92] However, such a position presumes that the ambassador, as the president's direct representative, was deeply committed to the president's conception of what the effort in the particular host country should be. An ambassador may not have a sense of agency mission or 'essence', to use Halperin's term,[93] especially if he or she is not a career diplomat. The ambassador may well come to identify with the host country, and strive to secure resources for it that might otherwise go elsewhere, as Komer pointed out.

Despite the use of USOIDP as blueprint for security assistance operations, turf battles continued to rage between the various executive departments and agencies. One example was the Defense Department's effort to wrest control of paramilitary operations from the CIA. In the wake of the Bay of Pigs debacle in 1961, a subsequent inquiry convened by the administration offered among its findings the suggestion that the CIA had neither the expertise nor the organization to establish or operate military or paramilitary forces. Accordingly, the administration moved to put all such CIA forces under the control of the Pentagon. This move took shape in 'Operation Switchback', in which control of such forces would 'switch back' to the military, even though they often had not been under military control in the first place.

This transfer of control completely defeated the paramilitary aspect of the community development concept, namely, the CIDG described above. Although Army Special Forces, working under CIA direction, had been implementing the CIDG programme as the political measure it ultimately was, once the Pentagon took control the Army command began using the CIDG as purely military units. The arms that had been given to the villagers were collected up and used to expand the CIDG's mobile response teams. These teams were in turn deployed to forward positions, far from their villages, for normal combat operations. Thus the political value of these forces was overlooked by the military and ultimately lost.[94]

In attempting to reorganize American security assistance policy the Kennedy administration, especially the President himself, saw a clear need to acquaint those participating in the internal defence effort with the many challenges particular to developing nations. However, in the end, even this effort was blunted by 'business as usual' rivalries among the various agencies. One of Kennedy's earliest actions in reorganizing the foreign aid effort was National Security Action Memorandum (NSAM) 131, which directed that personnel from all agencies involved with instituting US policy in developing areas receive extensive training and education in the situations and problems unique to these areas.

This training was to be provided to country team personnel in the Departments of Defense and State, USAID, USIA, CIA and other participating organizations. The President had assigned a high priority to this project, and it spawned a flurry of proposals for the establishment of an academic institution expressly for this purpose, variously referred to as the 'modernization institute' or the 'development institute' (also referred to in one White House memorandum as the 'Rostow Institute of Counter-Insurgency' and 'Taylor Tech').[95] The impact of the President's initiative became gradually diffused as virtually all of the participating agencies sent memoranda to the President stating: first, what a fine idea it was to establish such a school; second, they knew it was such a fine idea because their agency had established such a school years ago; and third, for that reason, their school should be the obvious choice for the training of personnel from all other agencies. In the end, the course was incorporated, in a less ambitious form than that originally envisioned, into the State Department's Foreign Service Academy.[96]

Coordination of recipients

Like previous US presidents of the Cold War era who envisioned the regionalization of Asian security, both Kennedy and Johnson strove to turn the anticommunist stand in Indochina into a regional effort. In doing so, they ran afoul of regional rivalries that long predated the Cold War. One example was Cambodia's continuing resistance to Washington's persistent efforts to persuade Phnom Penh to accept closer security ties and more security assistance, a reluctance based in part on Washington's close ties with two of Cambodia's traditional rivals, Vietnam and Thailand. Thailand, for its own part, remained perpetually uneasy over Washington's provision of aid to Cambodia. In 1962 Kennedy sent Maxwell Taylor to Bangkok to explain Washington's rationale in aiding the Sihanouk regime, but Taylor could not adequately reassure the Thai government. The State Department observed that, even after Taylor's mission, many high-ranking Thai officials remained uneasy, and were beginning to doubt the value of their alliance with the West as a result.[97]

Johnson intensified efforts to marshal Asia-wide support for the war in Vietnam, including the provision of funds to facilitate the participation of units from other Asian countries in the conflict. In some cases, such as the deployment of Korean combat units to Vietnam, such supplemental support was provided through normal military assistance programmes. In other cases, more surreptitious funding methods were employed. For example, in 1965 the Johnson administration made available roughly 4.5 million dollars to fund the deployment of an engineering battalion of the Philippine International Military Assistance Force (IMAF) to Vietnam. The project was funded covertly, using USAID funds, but this subterfuge was not for the benefit of the US Congress or electorate. Instead, both Johnson and USAID's David Bell sought to minimize the possibility that IMAF personnel might be labelled 'mercenaries' for the USA.[98]

Balancing the 'shield'

Washington's greatest overall problem in the region was coordinating the 'shield' elements of security assistance with the political and economic programmes spelled out in the USOIDP, especially as the conflict intensified in Vietnam. Of the several broad missions delegated to the military under Kennedy's overall military programme, two seemed in almost constant conflict. These were: to 'Preserve the integrity and enhance the effectiveness of US alliances by using military power as a protective shield and support for non-military programs designed to strengthen the free world' and to 'Deal swiftly and effectively with any local conflict situation in a manner best calculated to bring hostilities rapidly to a satisfactory conclusion and to prevent local war from broadening'.[99]

In part, this problem resulted from the administration's headlong rush towards its new counterinsurgency emphasis. The State Department had preferred the term 'internal defence' to 'counterinsurgency', and attempted to persuade the President that it should be used to include the entire counter-subversive effort, including but not limited to counter-guerrilla warfare. Nevertheless, the President declared a preference for the term counterinsurgency, and set the tone for subsequent efforts in Southeast Asia.[100] Kennedy's emphasis on counterinsurgency was conducted to the field by the agencies involved in the internal defence effort, including the military whose Kennedy-era mission was to 'revise' the communist doctrine regarding 'the exploitation of chronic civil war as a weapon of penetration and initial lodgement'.[101] The military side of counterinsurgency did not coordinate easily with other elements; it both dominated and obstructed the other components of the internal defence effort.

This problem was especially evident in Vietnam. Security assistance operations in Vietnam represented an extreme example of the inherent contradiction contained within America's Cold War nation-building approach: the security measures designed to protect development processes came to represent the greatest threat to those very processes. Incrementally increasing levels of force, ostensibly implemented with the objective of securing a stable environment for other aspects of the internal defence programme, ultimately undermined the broader, 'software' objectives of the programme. As William Colby later said of the Vietnam effort, the biggest problem with all the coordination efforts and directives emanating from both the ambassador and Washington was that they covered only civilian programmes and left the military 'independent to conduct the war on their own'.[102]

The Kennedy and Johnson years represent a period of almost constant escalation of military operations in Indochina. In effect, the introduction of US land-based air power at Bien Hoa in late 1964 marked the end of meaningful community development projects in much of rural South Vietnam. The subsequent introduction of regular US troops to protect US air facilities through 'sweep and search' tactics seriously disrupted the movement of aid and development officials and disrupted lines of communication between villages and local administrative and support centres.

Early in Johnson's presidency, the tempo of military operations rapidly increased in the face of a deteriorating military situation in the region. North Vietnam's introduction of regular troops into the South in 1964, along with Sukarno's intensification of the *Konfrontasi* and his bellicose references to a 'nutcracker' movement driving imperialism out of Asia, helped spur massive US intervention in the summer of 1965, as well as interventions by such allies as Australia and New Zealand. Sukarno's 'Nutcracker' suggested, to many in Washington, Wellington and Canberra, a coordination by the communists of events in the Malayan Archipelago and those in Indochina.[103]

At least in the American case, the objective of this massive escalation was largely to get North Vietnam to 'stop' intervening in the South by massively 'upping the ante', rather than to drive their forces out in any sort of decisive military victory. Shortly before the massive US escalation in the summer of 1965, Defense Secretary McNamara recommended a great expansion of military activity inside South Vietnam 'to prove to the VC [*Viet Cong*, or the National Liberation Front (NLF), the communist insurgency in South Vietnam] that they cannot win and thus to turn the tide of the war.' McNamara also estimated that North Vietnam and its communist allies would support the VC only so long as they perceived a possibility of early victory in South. Therefore, the immediate American objective was to remove any such anticipation of an early victory and to put military pressure on North Vietnam itself to make Hanoi change its strategy in the South.[104] Essentially, then, the *war* in Vietnam was the shield intended to protect economic and political development projects. However, the shield element became massively out of balance in Vietnam's case.

The resulting intensification of combat diverted available resources and completely disrupted political and economic development programmes while accomplishing little towards securing political development, as they stressed conventional operations at the expense of village-level response to the NLF's 'people's war'.[105] The conflict in Indochina was, in essence, a political contest with each side supported by military forces; but, from the middle of 1965, the US shifted its emphasis to the military side, to the 'shield', largely abandoning the political battlefield to the communists. Ironically, it was in the aftermath of the 1968 Tet offensive and the subsequent autumn communist offensive that the political and economic development programmes that Johnson called the 'other war' began to improve in South Vietnam.

In 1966, Johnson began an effort to wrest dominance of the Vietnam effort back from the military and rekindle political development efforts in the villages. He appointed Robert Komer from the NSC to the position of Special Assistant and dispatched him to Vietnam to take charge of coordinating all political development or 'pacification' efforts, both civilian and military.[106] Komer forged the civilian and military pacification efforts together; the 'Office of Civilian Operations' combined with the military's 'Revolutionary Development Support' programme to become the 'Civil Operations Revolutionary Development Support' or CORDS programme in 1967.[107] The activities of CORDS were very much in line with those support measures described in the USOIDP.

Initially, CORDS officers encountered the same problems operating in combat zones or NLF-dominated areas that had hampered nation-building efforts of the early 1960s. However, in the aftermath of the Tet offensive in early 1968, the CORDS programme began to make significant gains in the countryside. As the NLF reeled from its military defeat and the US reassessed its military commitment in the aftermath of its political defeat (even at that time Rusk referred to Tet victory for Saigon and allies as 'Pyrrhic'[108]), political and economic development advisers suddenly enjoyed greatly increased access to rural areas and freedom of movement in the countryside.[109] The tempo of insurgent activity and, consequently, of counter-guerrilla operations, subsided throughout much of the South. With the chances of being waylaid and ambushed by the now weakened NLF greatly reduced, the CORDS programme responded with expanded operations, deploying increasing numbers of US officials on field operations in the villages. According to one officer working for the CORDS programme, the conditions in the countryside began to resemble those of peacetime.[110] CORDS officers managed to make unprecedented progress in forging links between the local government centres and hitherto isolated villages until these operations were again swept aside by the North Vietnamese Easter Offensive of 1972.

General assumptions/doctrine and ideological distortions
The Kennedy era's more activist approach to political development as a security measure reflected a more crusade-like conception of America's role in the developing world than that held by the preceding administration. Just as Eisenhower had discerned only heinous motives in the Soviets' trade and aid overtures toward the developing world, so Kennedy perceived Khrushchev's pledge of Soviet support for peoples waging 'wars of national liberation' as simply another tactical shift in communism's expansionist drive. However, the new administration viewed this shift as particularly heinous in that the communists were evicting the USA from its 'rightful place' in the 'vanguard of [the] revolution of rising expectations'.[111] Kennedy and members of his team repeatedly expressed concern that the Eisenhower administration had allowed communism to 'distort the US position' on national liberation and was portraying the USA as 'defender of the status-quo' in the developing world. In contrast, the JCS suggested that many in the new administration might be more out of touch with the developing world than they realized, observing: 'the US, too, has a revolutionary heritage, but the nation has been rich a long time.'[112] In the end, while Washington's conception of its role in the developing world as one of a liberator continued to drive what would later be called the 'win hearts and minds' approach to internal defence, the actual policy approach devised and implemented by the Kennedy and Johnson administrations suffered from the flawed assumptions upon which it was predicated. These included assumptions regarding the external nature of the communist threat and an assumption that recipients shared American conceptions of good governance and bureaucratic ethos. However, most of the dangerously flawed assumptions that undermined Washington's internal defence effort during the Kennedy–Johnson era were those contained in the theoretical foundation of the USOIDP, 'modernization' theory itself.

Presumptions of modernization theory
Hubris shaded the administration's approach to internal defence, a hubris inspired by the modernization theorists' belief they had hit on a formula for developing societies. Like their communist counterparts, these theorists believed they had uncovered the scientific principles by which societies transitioned from 'traditional' to 'modern'. More importantly, from the standpoint of policy-making, they had hit on measures by which societies could make this transition, and these measures represented points where the USA could intervene in the modernization process.

The assumption that developing societies were so very malleable, as stated in the USOIDP, reflects the position of such theorists as Lucien Pye, who argued that, adrift in a state of transition, the peoples of Southeast Asia had no sense of their own history to anchor them.[113] Given this malleability, radical alterations of existing society seemed possible. Elements characterizing 'traditional' society had to go, as these obstructed modernization processes. To paraphrase Gabriel Almond, a 'modern' political system has no place for traditional elements, including, but not limited to religions, age-groups, and kinship and lineage groups.[114]

Among the most influential theorists of the time was political sociologist Karl Deutsch, whose social mobilization model, with its emphasis on communications infrastructure, stressed that, in effect, communication could overcome culture. In Deutsch's words, people are bound together by 'habits of, and facilities for, communication'.[115] Nationality, then, represented 'an alignment of large numbers of individuals from the middle and lower classes linked to regional centres and leading social groups by channels of social communication and economic intercourse, both directly from link to link and directly from the centre'.[116] Deutsch emphasized that *community*, established through a well-formed communications network, would ultimately determine the very nature of *culture*, by the nature of the information transmitted across that network. This view translated into American efforts to establish such a network of communications links in recipient countries throughout Southeast Asia and elsewhere, and, through these links, Washington's efforts to establish a national consciousness in each of these countries.[117]

Rather in the manner of Marx, Rostow himself maintained that societies would transition to modernization through a fixed progression of stages. In Rostow's conception of such development, the crucial transition point was that of 'take-off', at which a society's economy achieved self-sustaining growth.[118] As Rostow had written in *The Stages of Growth*, each of these stages could last many years; however, the Cold War lent urgency to this modernization process. The West simply could not wait and watch gradual transitions in developing countries with communist competitors on the scene, competitors with their own liberator's role conception and their own 'scientific' principles to apply to the development of these new states. Urgent measures were required, measures that would drive these 'malleable' societies toward take-off as soon as possible. This intervention would take place through the transfer of technical know-how to aid economic development and, to make these countries less vulnerable to insurgency, the rapid realization of basic societal reforms such as land reform.

One central challenge to the modernization theorists lay in the need to identify and strengthen a so-called 'modernizing elite', which would be relied upon to carry forth the process of modernization, instituting reforms, building democracy and necessary institutions. This approach was hardly new; as Tony Smith has pointed out, Americans had long shown a tendency to encourage reform by working with established power relationships in target countries, by co-opting existing elites.[119] However, in many if not most newly decolonized countries at this time, this elite was the military, which the USOIDP had nominated as 'agents for carrying forward the developmental process'.[120] Washington's focus on the military's suitability for such a role reflects an assumption that the recipient militaries, like the USA and other Western militaries, would be meritocratic in nature. However, in many recipient countries, militaries were products of, and reflections of, their countries' oligarchic elites. It was to these militaries that Washington entrusted the modernization process, overlooking the vested interest of incumbent elites in the status quo, and in resisting such reforms.[121] In the Vietnamese case, where American efforts were concentrated, there was no significant land reform programme undertaken until South Vietnamese President Thieu became convinced that a window of opportunity had appeared in the wake of the Tet Offensive. Going head-to-head against the traditional South Vietnamese elites, Thieu managed to institute the 'Land to the Tiller' programme only in 1970. While this reform came a bit late to adequately stabilize South Vietnamese society, it proved so popular among the peasantry that, upon taking over in 1975, the new communist government had to modify its own land policies to adjust to the positive popular view of land to the tiller policies in the countryside.[122]

Blinkered by modernization theory, US policy-makers tended to dismiss the importance of local cultures and social norms. For example, many American officials failed to recognize that the extension of infrastructure and central government authority to the villages would not be universally welcomed by the Southeast Asian peasantry, much less hailed as progress. In Indochina, villages had never experienced direct rule from the centre; the village was traditionally the place where 'the King's laws bow to village custom'.[123] Charles Maechling, one of the authors of the USOIDP observed in retrospect that it was a 'simplistic document' containing virtually no political guidance on which were the situations that called for its application.[124] Having reduced the variation between societies to the categories of traditional, transitional, and modern, modernization theory was presumed to be universally applicable throughout the developing world.

Another problem was that US officials tended to establish liaisons in recipient countries with counterparts drawn primarily from the Westernized urban elites. As the South Vietnamese coordinator of the Revolutionary Development Cadres, Tranh Ngoc Chau pointed out, not only did the USA not know the enemy they were facing in Indochina, they did not know the people they were trying to help. Western bureaucrats and high-level officials in Vietnam relied too heavily on their local counterparts for information and feedback on policy implementation.[125]

Rostow's predecessor at PPS, McGhee, had warned Secretary of State Rusk in 1961 that, while the new administration's emphasis on social and economic progress was laudable, the USA should avoid pursuing such goals through programmes that were inflexible and 'doctrinaire'. McGhee's PPS warned of the resistance the new aid approach might generate in many recipient countries as it would 'strike at the heart of entrenched interests' in these countries.[126] Rusk responded with a curt memorandum in which he declared that the USA should not assume the burden of 'persuading' recipients toward embracing the concept of self-help and accepting the need to institute domestic reforms; that burden should be on those countries seeking aid. Rusk also asserted that the USA would not compromise in the face of graft of corruption.[127]

Washington's problem with this attempt to maintain such a high moral position in foreign policy was the high stakes the USA perceived in its political competition with the communists in the developing world. In a memorandum to USAID director Hamilton, Chester Bowles suggested a set of standards that prospective recipients must meet in order to receive US assistance. However, he also allowed for a category of recipient countries that had made no effort to meet these standards, but had 'such over-riding military or political problems that we must give emergency aid without regard to standards'.[128] The USA simply could not write off stubbornly corrupt regimes if these were in geostrategically important locations, or if their ultimate 'loss' due to their unwillingness to reform contributed to the prestigious image of communism as the 'wave of the future' in the eyes of neighbouring states. Recipients understood Washington's position and exploited it in a manner described by Burnett's 'aid spigot' concept, as described in Chapter 4.[129]

Assumption of American-style 'bureaucratic ethos'

In American political culture, particularly the notion of bureaucratic ethos, popular legitimacy is directed toward the government office itself, not the individual holding it (i.e., the presidency, not any particular president). Steeped in that notion, the Kennedy administration saw no great danger in putting pressure on individual leaders whose unwillingness to move far and fast on modernizing reforms made them an obstacle to US objectives.

This approach had disastrous results in Vietnam, when the USA acceded to the removal of President Ngo Dinh Diem. For his many faults, Diem was the closest thing to an effective leader on the scene at the time. Bureaucratic confusion and a policy-making vacuum followed the coup in which Diem and his brother Nhu were killed, as well as subsequent coups in which South Vietnam's generals jockeyed for power. The resulting organizational disarray in the field stalled nation-building efforts in rural areas. The coup also emboldened the communists in the North as well as the South to step-up their own programmes in rural South Vietnam. These increased operations eventually triggered the increasing American military intervention that further undermined rural nation-building efforts. NLF leader Nguyen Huu Tho would later write that, from the communist perspective, the coup that toppled Diem was 'a gift from heaven'.[130]

Assumed external threat

Although recognizing the urgent need for internal reforms to defuse the insurgency threat, the Kennedy and Johnson administrations never wavered in their convictions that the communist threat was ultimately external. As a result, US policy continued to focus on the 'shield' aspect of security assistance, on protecting development processes from the agents of communist expansion. As Kahin and Lewis point out, Rusk's 'aggression from the North' theme ignored many complex causes of the insurgency.[131] However, Rusk's position should not be seen merely as a convenient device for calling the 17th Parallel a sovereign border and then justifying military responses to North Vietnamese activity in terms of 'external aggression'. Washington genuinely believed in the external nature of threat, in continuity with the Eisenhower administration's position. These administrations saw themselves regrouping behind the 17th Parallel in an effort to stop the communist advance in the region. From Washington's perspective, the initial 'loss' of North Vietnam in the first place was due to external communist subversion.

Johnson was even more convinced than his predecessor that communist activity in Indochina was part of a broader communist offensive in Asia, and even went so far as to talk of the conflict expanding to a 'second front' in Korea.[132] At the same time, Johnson recognized Ho Chi Minh's nationalist interests, and various US proposals for massive development projects in the Mekong region were attempts to decouple Ho from his communist allies and bring North Vietnam to the negotiating table.

In the case of Vietnam, the biggest flaw in American nation-building efforts was that, since the US presumed the threat to be primarily external, Washington failed to see that they were trying to build a national consciousness in competition with one that already existed. Washington therefore failed to grasp the power of this national idea that was promoted by North Vietnam[133] and centred on Ho and the Viet Minh. Ultimately, in Vietnam the US was engaged not so much in nation-building as in effecting a secession.[134]

Side-effects

The Kennedy team was far more willing to intervene in recipients' domestic politics than its predecessors had been, and it pressed more actively for domestic reforms. While Eisenhower's administration had approached the building of institutions in recipient societies with trepidation akin to that of a cautious bather approaching an icy pool, Kennedy's people ran to the edge and jumped in head-first. Armed with the USOIDP as a blueprint for policy, the Kennedy and Johnson administrations became more deeply involved in managing the processes of nation-building and institution formation in recipient societies than any previous presidents. However, these ambitious efforts produced significant and deleterious side-effects. Chief among these were the alienation of the rural areas from the recipient government as a result of the counterinsurgency approach, and the retardation of political development exacerbated by the USOIDP's emphasis on the military as a modernizing elite.

Alienation of the villages from the government
Eisenhower's emphasis on establishing civil police was replaced by Kennedy's earnest desire to build up local counterinsurgency forces. These were

paramilitary forces, armed and trained by the USA. Coupled with Kennedy's Maoist framework of analysis the shield was reoriented toward the rural sector. During the Kennedy era these new security forces were sent deep into remote areas of recipient countries, often to areas where previously there had been no government presence at all. Their presence in these areas often proved counterproductive. Characterized in most cases by poor pay, poor training and poor morale these largely conscript forces often resorted to 'foraging' (often of a brutal nature) for food and valuables among the rural population, presenting the worst possible image of the government. This problem was particularly acute in South Vietnam and Thailand and, later, in the Philippines.

Additionally, the counterinsurgency approach involved physically separating the insurgents from their support base, the rural population, while social and economic reforms were implemented. In various parts of Southeast Asia this effort took the form of 'Agrovilles', or 'Agrimetros', and in South Vietnam the 'Strategic Hamlet' programme, all of which were designed to keep the insurgents away from the peasantry by using village fortifications guarded by paramilitaries or by armed forces. However, the heavy-handed uprooting of existing villages and forced relocation required to institute these programmes, along with foraging and abusive treatment by local security forces, precluded the development of support among rural populations for their governments. Such measures lent credence to the insurgents' message and confounded nation-building efforts designed specifically to bond the population to their government.

Retarded political development

Like Eisenhower, Kennedy and Johnson relied upon the military and other security forces agents of development as well as a line of defence. In doing so, they retarded the development of other political and social institutions in recipient societies.

Modernization theorists put great stock in the impact of a Western education on reshaping the cosmologies of military officers from the underdeveloped regions, as well as their perception of their own role in society. As Edward Shils asserted at the time, those who had received such an education 'believe[d] in science; they believe[d] in the value of rational administration and written law and order' and that such elites would naturally 'aspire to modernity,' for themselves and for their societies.[135] However, given that the military leadership in these recipient countries was largely drawn from the dominant elites, the only sector of society that could afford to enjoy such Western training, their interests overlapped with those of Washington only so far as the need to implement anti-communist measures. The socializing power of military training and its way of life competed with the socializing power of immediate family, clan and class, and not always successfully. If anything, the officer corps' Western education served to accentuate these officers' perceptions that they held a uniquely enlightened perspective regarding what was best for their countries not only with respect to the population as a whole but also with respect to competing elite groups.

Like those of the Eisenhower years, the policies of the Kennedy and Johnson era acknowledged the importance of establishing 'healthy' social organizations among such groups as labour and youth while simultaneously relying on the military and other security forces to combat subversion. Like the Eisenhower administration, the Kennedy and Johnson administrations formulated their own efforts to identify and neutralize what Eisenhower had called the 'communist apparatus', or, in the language of the Kennedy and Johnson era, the communist 'infrastructure'. Both of these terms refer to the supposed agents of communist subversion, party cadres, the communist *agent provocateur* and the communist sympathizer or 'fellow traveller'. As was the case in the Eisenhower presidency, the military was trained in the acceptability of using extraordinary force and extra-judicial measures in its efforts to identify and neutralize 'subversives', and effectively set upon the other nascent institutions of the new state. Thus, while the USA counted on these other institutions, including 'opposition leaders, political parties, institutional groups, and information media' to pressure recipient regimes to institute the social and political reforms necessary for development, Washington was simultaneously arming and training the security forces to suppress the activities of these other sectors.[136]

While such contradictions characterized US security assistance programmes throughout Southeast Asia, in the Indochina conflict, Operation Phoenix stands as a well-known case in point. Phoenix was originally designed to identify and maintain a comprehensive database of communist counterpart operatives, the party cadres who were undermining the activities of CORDS operatives in the villages. Phoenix was a response to these cadres' success in targeting South Vietnamese aid workers, school teachers and other rural development cadres for assassination. However, even William Colby, who had nominal control of the programme, acknowledged the excesses of the South Vietnamese units who identified, apprehended and, far too often, executed elements of the communist 'infrastructure'. Phoenix's net was cast wide and many thousands of people having no involvement with the NLF were killed.[137] Colby later observed that Phoenix had become a 'campaign of reprisal' on the part of South Vietnam's military and para-military security forces.[138] Tens of thousands of individuals in South Vietnamese society, including many involved in teachers' and farmers' unions and other social organizations, were simply nominated as communists and eliminated. This suppression of social institutions and elimination of social and political activists crippled nascent institutions and could not help but deal a serious blow to political development in Vietnam and other recipient countries. Arguably, the hundreds of thousands of Indonesians purged in the bloodbath following the events of 30 September 1965, discussed below, would have had a similarly crippling impact on that country's development. Tragically, Washington's policy of encouraging local security forces to undertake such operations was one element of continuity in the USA's internal defence approach during the entire period of this study.

The Gestapu, or 30 September 1965

While Washington's massive efforts in Indochina failed to erode perceptions that communism represented the wave of the future in Asia, events in Indonesia in late 1965 and 1966 may have represented something of a turning point in this regard. At an NSC discussion in August 1966 Rusk observed that Indonesia's 'abrupt reversal of course', combined with Washington's determination to 'stand fast' in Vietnam, had produced a new sense of confidence among the states of the region.[139] Indonesia, among the largest and potentially the richest state in Southeast Asia, had been arrested in what the US State Department had called its 'slide toward communism', had turned away from its hitherto deepening relationship with the PRC and had officially ended its policy of *Konfrontasi* against its neighbours. The events of this period are indeed striking, but the question that remains is: did the US, through its security assistance programmes, play a role in shaping these events?

As was discussed earlier in this chapter, the USA had been observing trends in Indonesia with alarm for years. Washington had long observed that Sukarno had been playing off the Army and the PKI against each other, relying on the PKI to keep the Army in check while assuming that the Army would prevent an outright PKI takeover. However, as Sukarno's health deteriorated in 1965 he seemed to be losing any semblance of balance in this game.

D.N. Aidit, the leader of PKI, had been trying to neutralize and erode the power of the PKI's main rival, the Army, through its influence on the Sukarno regime. The PKI called for such measures as the appointment of political commissars in military units and the establishment of a 'people's militia' that would gradually supplant the Army.[140] Observing this trend, US intelligence analysts expected that the PKI would simply carry on quietly gathering influence and critical posts in government, making steady gains. Any shift in these tactics, they asserted, would probably be 'in response to provocation', such as an Army crackdown.[141]

In the end, the failing health of Sukarno precipitated the PKI's shift to more violent tactics. The communists, supposedly with Sukarno's blessing, had identified a group of key military leaders that they planned to remove and had set a date in 1966 for this *'putsch'*. However, a turn for the worse in Sukarno's illness forced their hand.[142] On 30 September 1965, the PKI, acting in conjunction with sympathetic elements of the military,[143] made their move. In this attempted coup, six of the targeted generals were assassinated, but the Army was alerted and mobilized against the PKI by a then relatively unknown General Suharto.

Over the next few months there ensued the destruction of the world's third largest communist party, in which Army units, Muslim groups and what the USA then identified as loose bands of disaffected youths set out on a 'systematic campaign of extermination' of PKI cadres, communist sympathizers and, in the process, many members of the country's Chinese minority. Contemporary US assessments placed the number of those killed in this initial period of blood-letting at over 300,000 while other estimates double that figure.[144] During this period a virtual second government was set up under Suharto, evolving into a triumvirate leadership that included Adam Malik, who served as Foreign Minister, and the Sultan of Jogjakarta, whose charismatic appeal helped secure the support of Muslim groups. The remnants of the Sukarno regime faded from power, and in March of 1966 Suharto forced the ailing Sukarno to cede power to the triumvirate leadership.

Indonesia's slide toward communism and toward Beijing had been stopped, but what role did the USA play? Declassified State Department and NSC documents from that time suggest that the USA had little direct input into the events of the counter-coup and subsequent purge.[145] William P. Bundy, then Assistant Secretary of State for Far Eastern Affairs, recalls NSC discussions at the time of these events at which President Johnson asked if anyone had assets on the scene in Indonesia that could provide an assessment of what was happening and what actions the USA might take under the circumstances. According to Bundy, no agency, including the CIA, could provide Johnson with such assets.[146] The relatively recent assertion that the US embassy in Jakarta provided the generals with lists of known communists and fellow-travellers would have been quite consistent with the Eisenhower-era OISP, discussed in Chapter 3.[147] One of the basic measures of the OISP was to compile such lists and provide these names to the host government so that the communists could be detained and 'judicial procedures' could be executed against them. The idea that the OISP contributed to the deaths of the estimated five thousand people on the alleged list is painful; that those people represented only about one per cent of the total number massacred is utterly horrifying.

Putting the Indonesian situation in the context of regional events, the State Department maintained that, while the upheaval was sparked by 'purely internal factors', and the ensuing 'decimation of the PKI was a direct response to the murder of the generals', the US presence in Southeast Asia was a decisive factor in the bloodletting. According to the State Department's Administrative History, the US military presence in the region

> enabled Indonesia's non-communists to attack the PKI without fear of intervention by Communist China. The fact that we stood in Viet-Nam between Indonesia and China gave Indonesia's new leadership greater flexibility in responding to the PKI bid for power.[148]

Despite Washington's vast expenditure of blood and treasure in Indochina, events in Indonesia did far more to combat the idea of communism as Asia's wave of the future. In retrospect, William Bundy observed that the spring of 1966, when Suharto's triumvirate consolidated control in Indonesia, represented a true turning point regarding the communist threat to Southeast Asia. According to Bundy, if there would have been an early de-escalation of US involvement in Indochina and in the region, it would have been at that time. However, like others within the Johnson administration, Bundy still believed that Beijing represented the principal threat in the region in 1966, and a growing one.[149] Rostow, who had succeeded McGeorge Bundy as Johnson's National Security Adviser by that time, maintained to the end that events in Indonesia and the destruction of the PKI contributed to Beijing's decision to embark on the 'Cultural Revolution' shortly thereafter.[150] If true, such a decision would have represented a victory as described in NSC 68; the bloc was forced to revise its conception of international relations and compelled to turn inward, toward reform of its own society.[151]

However, even if Rostow is correct, the question remains as to what role Washington's containment policies, particularly its security assistance policies, played in turning the perceived communist 'tide' in Southeast Asia. Contrasting Washington's efforts in Vietnam and Indonesia offers illuminating insights into this question.

The two cases differ sharply in the degree to which Washington's security assistance programmes penetrated government and society. In Indonesia, Washington enjoyed only limited access to government and bureaucratic processes. During the 1950s, most contact between US and Indonesian officials took place among military personnel. Other US government officials devoted much of their time to efforts intended to persuade their Indonesian counterparts to accept greater US involvement in internal security matters. US influence in Indonesia deteriorated rapidly after 1960, until, by the time of the 1965 attempted coup, American diplomats had evacuated their dependents and reduced staffing to minimum levels.

As for less direct US influence, the most likely place to find it is with the Indonesian military. Although Sukarno had limited US access for the purposes of implementing its internal defence policies, one channel through which the USA did exercise influence throughout the 1950s and early 1960s was the military education and training programme. In addition to training recipient military personnel in tactics and military science, these training programmes also sought to transfer elements of US political and military cultures. Indonesian military personnel were schooled in proper civil–military relations, the superiority of civilian rule and, of course, in accordance with Eisenhower's 1290-d objectives, an awareness of the dangers of communism and communist subversives.

The events following 1 October 1965 might tempt one to suggest that the lessons of such military training and the 1290-d programme were terrifyingly effective. However, nobody in the Johnson administration suggested this at the time. Instead, the intelligence community maintained that the Indonesian military was probably motivated less by ideological considerations than by the threat the PKI posed to their privileged position in society.[152] Additionally, one must remember that US policy-makers believed that the USSR had supplanted Washington's influence with the Indonesian military by 1965. And, after all, the Soviets would be at least as happy as Washington to see a pro-Chinese communist party removed as a contender for power in Indonesia.

The Johnson administration did not presume that the new Indonesian leadership would be an ally of the USA. The backlash to the PKI's coup attempt produced a regime that seemed more willing to focus on internal problems rather than on foreign adventures. The *Konfrontasi* was formally ended in August of 1966, and the new regime declared its intent to return to the UN, to reapply for membership in the International Monetary Fund (IMF) and the International Bank for Reconstruction and Development (IBRD, more commonly known as the World Bank), and to embrace a programme of domestic economic development. However, Washington observed that the best the US could hope for in Indonesia's foreign policy orientation was non-alignment, and noted that Indonesia would endeavour to maintain amicable ties with the USSR.[153] However, for the time being, the possibility of Indonesia becoming a communist state aligned with Beijing had, in Washington's view, gone from imminent to remote.

In contrast to the situation in Indonesia, US officials in Vietnam enjoyed access to their counterparts at every level of the Vietnamese government. Virtually every aspect of both the 1290-d and the USOIDP programmes were implemented in Vietnam during the 1950s and 1960s, under the close supervision of a steadily growing corps of US civilian and military advisers. Yet, in the end, Washington's security assistance measures failed in Vietnam and Washington's people were forced to withdraw under fire. Additionally, the failure of America's security assistance policies and programmes in Vietnam cast such a shadow over US foreign aid policy as to put the very future of aid as an element of US foreign policy in grave doubt.

In late March of 1968, Lyndon Johnson made the momentous decision to halt further military escalation of the conflict in Indochina. Although the recent Tet offensive in South Vietnam had resulted in a serious military defeat for communist forces there, it was already shaping up to be a crushing political defeat for Johnson and his Southeast Asia policy. The President's cabinet and staff had turned against the effort in Indochina. Johnson's new Secretary of Defense, Clark Clifford, worked steadily to disabuse the President of the long-cherished notion that military measures could dissuade the communists from prosecuting their objectives in South Vietnam. Even consultations with his informal gathering of senior advisers, collectively known as the Wise Men, indicated that there was in fact no light at the end of the tunnel in Southeast Asia. As one of the Wise Men, Dean Acheson told Johnson, 'We can no longer do the job we set out to do in the time we have left and we must begin to take steps to disengage'.[154] Johnson subsequently refused a standing request from his field commander in Vietnam, General

William Westmoreland, to send additional military units to Vietnam. Shouldering the responsibility for the failure of policy in Indochina, Johnson announced that he would neither seek nor accept nomination for another term as President.

While the situation in Indochina had been deteriorating, Johnson had also been facing growing activism and opposition from the US Congress as attempts were made to restrict the presidential ability to grant security assistance. Through measures such as the 1967 'Country X' legislation, Congress moved to exercise increasing oversight in presidential use of security assistance, lest the country be enmired in more Indochina-like conflicts.[155]

Military aid was not the only aspect of the foreign assistance programme that was under threat. A 1966 presidential study on the future of foreign aid, undertaken by a committee chaired by James Perkins, had found that foreign aid as an instrument of policy had been largely discredited by America's experience in Asia.[156] In considering the Perkins report, Johnson felt there was little hope for reviving flagging popular and Congressional support for US foreign aid programmes for the future. However, his successor would usher-in a very different, if less ambitious, approach to security assistance and foreign aid in developing areas.

Notes

1 Gaddis, *Strategies of Containment,* p. 201.
2 US Military Program for 1961, p. 3. NSF, Departments and Agencies (JFK Library).
3 Rusk, Memorandum to President, 10 March 1961. *FRUS,* 1961–63, vol. 9, p. 210.
4 US Military Program for 1961, p. 3.
5 See, for example, USOIDP, pp. 8–10. File: Re: NSAM 182, NSF, Meetings and Memoranda, box 338 (JFK Library).
6 See Chapter 4.
7 Rusk, quoted in Thomas J. Schoenbaum, *Waging Peace and War: Dean Rusk in the Truman, Kennedy and Johnson Years* (New York: Simon and Schuster, 1988), p. 264.
8 US Overseas Internal Defense Program.
9 US Military Program for 1961, pp. 2–3.
10 Carl M. Brasser, *Presidential Transitions: Eisenhower Through Reagan* (Oxford: Oxford University Press, 1986), pp. 117–119.
11 Memorandum to Secretary of State from Thomas Hughes, Bureau of Intelligence and Research (INR) reporting on the 'Tri-Continental Conference' in Havana, 1963 (Declassified Documents Retrieval System, accessed March 1991). Hughes reported on the proceedings of the conference (which included delegations from liberation movements in Africa, Asia and Latin America), at which China asserted its own role in promoting and aiding popular struggles in the developing world and lambasted the USSR for not putting enough pres-

sure on the Americans, thereby distracting US attentions away from the under-developed areas.

12 Rostow interview. Also see an earlier US assessment of this phenomenon in 23 November 1955 OCB Report to the NSC on the 1290-d programme, as described in Chapter 3.

13 Department of State, Administrative History, vol. 1, ch. 7, section L, 'Indonesia'. Administrative Histories, box 3, State (LBJ Library).

14 National Intelligence Estimate (NIE) 55-61, 7 March 1961, pp. 8–9. NSF, National Intelligence Estimates, box 6–7 (LBJ Library).

15 Rostow Interview, March 1993. Also see NIE 55-61, pp. 5–6.

16 For an excellent discussion of the US role in the West Irian/West New Guinea dispute, see Bradley R. Simpson, *Economists with Guns: Authoritarian Development and US-Indonesia Relations, 1960–1968* (Stanford, CA: Stanford University Press, 2008), ch. 3.

17 Memorandum attached to NSAM 195, 'Background Plan of Action for Indonesia', 2 October 1962, NSF, Meetings and Memoranda, box 339 (JFK Library).

18 NIE 55-64, p. 2.

19 The proposed aid package had originally included roughly 15 million dollars' worth of spare parts, which Kennedy deleted from the final package, out of concern that these would be diverted to the black market or otherwise 'sidetracked', probably by the Indonesian authorities themselves. National Security Action Memorandum (NSAM) 195, 22 October 1962. Also State Department Telegram no. 928, 5 November 1962. NSF, Meetings and Memoranda, box 339 (JFK Library).

20 Memorandum, 'Background Plan of Action for Indonesia'.

21 Joint Embassy/USAID Telegram no. 769, 12 October 1962. NSF, Meetings and Memoranda, box 339 (JFK Library).

22 *Ibid.* Also Forrestal, Memorandum to Kennedy, 11 October 1962. NSF, Meetings and Memoranda, box 339 (JFK Library).

23 NIE 54/55-63, 30 October 1963, pp. 4–5. NSF, National Intelligence Estimates, box 6–7 (LBJ Library).

24 *Ibid.*, p. 3.

25 For extensive explorations of these efforts, see Kenneth Conboy and James Morrison, *Feet to the Fire: CIA Covert Operations in Indonesia, 1957–1958* (Annapolis, MD: US Naval Institute Press, 1999), and Audrey Kahin and George McTurhan Kahin, *Subversion as Foreign Policy: The Secret Eisenhower and Dulles Debacle in Indonesia* (Seattle, WA: University of Washington Press, 1997).

26 NIE 54/55-63, pp. 2, 10–11.

27 NIE 55-64, pp. 6–7.

28 *Ibid.*

29 This amendment was signed into law with the Foreign Assistance Act of 1963 on 18 December 1963.

30 For a sample of such discussions, see Summary Record of NSC Meeting of 7 January 1964. NSF, NSC Meeting File, box 1 (LBJ Library).

31 NIE 55-64, p. 6.

32 Memorandum: Background of Plan of Action for Indonesia, 2 October 1962, pp. 3–4.

33 Special National Intelligence Estimate (SNIE) 55-61, March 1961. NSF,

National Intelligence Estimates, box 6–7 (LBJ Library).

34 *Ibid.*

35 For Rusk comments, see Summary Record of NSC Meeting of 7 January 1964. NSF, NSC Meeting File, box 1 (LBJ Library).

36 NIE 50-61, 28 March, 1961. NSF, National Intelligence Estimates, box 6–7 (LBJ Library).

37 *Ibid.*

38 Pach, *Arming the Free World*, p. 5.

39 NIE 50-61.

40 Timothy N. Castle, *At War in the Shadow of Vietnam: US Military Aid to the Royal Lao Government, 1955–1975* (New York: Columbia University Press, 1993), p. 41. Also see Stanley Karnow, *Vietnam: A History* (New York: Penguin, 1984), p. 248.

41 See note 2.

42 With NSAM 182, dated 24 August 1962, the President approved the USOIDP as 'a national counter-insurgency doctrine for the use of US departments and agencies concerned with the internal defence of overseas areas threatened by subversive insurgency' and 'directed its promulgation to serve as basic policy guidance' to all such departments and agencies at home and their missions abroad. File: Re: NSAM 182, NSF, Meetings and Memoranda, box 338 (JFK Library).

43 USOIDP, p. 1. File: Re: NSAM 182, NSF, Meetings and Memoranda, box 338 (JFK Library).

44 See Douglas Blaufarb, *The Counterinsurgency Era* (New York: Free Press, 1977).

45 Blaufarb, *The Counterinsurgency Era* and Shafer, *Deadly Paradigms*. For more recent explorations of the political development dimension, see Michael E. Latham, *Modernization as Ideology: American Social Science and 'Nation Building' in the Kennedy Era* (Chapel Hill, NC: University of North Carolina Press, 2000) and David Ekbladh, *The Great American Mission: Modernization and the Construction of an American World Order* (Princeton, NJ: Princeton University Press, 2010), especially ch. 6.

46 USOIDP, p. 5.

47 *Ibid.*, p. 3.

48 *Ibid.*, pp. 3–6.

49 *Ibid.*, p. 4.

50 *Ibid.*, pp. 13–14.

51 *Ibid.*

52 *Ibid.*, p. 8, emphasis in original.

53 *Ibid.*, p. 15.

54 Status Report on Southeast Asia, 8 August 1962, Department of State, Task Force on Southeast Asia. NSF, Regional Security, box 231, p. 7 (JFK Library).

55 Status Report on Southeast Asia, 19 September 1962, Department of State, Task Force on Southeast Asia NSF, Regional Security, box 231, p. 10 (JFK Library).

56 William E. Colby, *Lost Victory: A Firsthand Account of America's Sixteen-Year Involvement in Vietnam* (Chicago, IL: Contemporary Books, 1989), p. 197.

57 Status Report on Southeast Asia, 8 August 1962, Department of State, Task Force on Southeast Asia. NSF, Regional Security, box 231, p. 7 (JFK Library). For a critical account of the strategic hamlet concept, see Karnow, *Vietnam: a*

History, pp. 255–259.

58 Colby, *Lost Victory*, p. 165.

59 USOIDP, p. 16.

60 'Status Report of the Task Force on Southeast Asia, 21 August – 04 September 1962'. Department of State, Task Force on Southeast Asia NSF, Regional Security, box 231, p. 7 (JFK Library).

61 USOIDP, p. 16.

62 *Ibid.*, pp. 14–15.

63 Attachment to NSAM 118, p. 45, Re: NSAM 118, NSF, Meetings and Memoranda, box 333 (JFK Library).

64 *Ibid.*

65 Status Report on Southeast Asia, 22 August 1962, p. 12. NSF, Regional Security, box 231 (JFK Library).

66 USOIDP, p. 15.

67 *Ibid.*

68 Status Report on Southeast Asia, 22 August 1962, p. 8. Department of State, Task Force on Southeast Asia NSF, Regional Security, box 231 (JFK Library).

69 *Ibid.*

70 USOIDP, p. 14.

71 *Ibid.*, pp. 17–18.

72 *Ibid.*

73 *Ibid.*

74 *Ibid.*

75 *Ibid.*, pp. 15–16.

76 Memcon from meeting of Secretaries of State and Defense and the Director of the Budget, 25 February 1961. *FRUS*, 1961–63, vol. 9, p. 202.

77 *Ibid.*, p. 201.

78 PPS Memorandum, *FRUS*, 1961–63, vol. 9, pp. 189–190.

79 Department of Defense, International Security Affairs (Hoopes). Military Assistance Reappraisal, FY 67–71: vol. 1-A, June 1965. Box 20, NSF Agency File, Defense (LBJ Library).

80 Memorandum, ICA Director Laboussie to Kennedy. *FRUS*, 1961–63, vol. 9, p. 239.

81 The responsibilities of ICA's 'Civil Police Branch' were transferred to the new 'Office of Public Safety' within USAID.

82 Memorandum, Komer to Taylor, 19 February 1962; Komer, draft letter to Hamilton, 19 February 1962. NSF, Meetings and Memoranda, box 334, NSAM 114. Memorandum, Bundy to Taylor, 14 February 1962; Memorandum, Bundy to JFK, 19 February 1962, NSF, Meetings and Memoranda, box 332, NSAM 114 (JFK Library).

83 Memorandum from Frank Coffin to Chairman, Special Group (CI): 'AID Organization for Counter-Insurgency,' 18 July 1962, p. 4 (emphasis in original). NSF, Departments and Agencies, box 268 (JFK Library).

84 For a discussion of the 'internationalist' position, see Chapter 4.

85 Editorial note, *FRUS*, 1961–63, vol. 9, pp. 240–241.

86 'Military Assistance in the 1960s', 17 May 1961. *FRUS*, 1961–63, vol. 9, pp. 241–243.

87 Memorandum from Deputy Assistant Secretary of State for Politico-Military Affairs (Kitchen) to Secretary of State and Secretary of Defense, 12 December

1961. *FRUS*. 1961–63, vol. 9, pp. 280–281.

88 *Ibid.*

89 For an account of Army high-command resistance to the unconventional warfare mission, see Aaron Bank, *From OSS to Green Beret: The Birth of Special Forces* (New York: Presidio Press, 1986).

90 Kitchen, Memorandum, 12 December 1961.

91 Komer, Memorandum for the record, 23 October 1961. NSF, Departments and Agencies, USAID, 1/61 – 12/61, box 268 (JFK Library).

92 Telephone interview with Rostow, January 1994. For a description of Eisenhower's efforts to consolidate USOM agency coordination, see Chapter 3.

93 Morton H. Halperin, Priscilla Clapp and Arnold Kanter, *Bureaucratic Politics and Foreign Policy* (Washington, DC: Brookings Institution Press, 1974).

94 Colby, *Lost Victory*, pp. 163–167. Also, interview with Maj. Steven E. Courtney, US Special Operations Command (USSOCOM) Historian's Office, April 1996.

95 Belk, Memorandum, Re: NSAM 131. NSF, Meetings and Memoranda, box 334 (JFK Library).

96 Refer to the voluminous correspondence in the Re: NSAM 131 file.

97 State Department Status Report on Southeast Asia, 19 September 1962, p. 11.

98 Memorandum from A. E. Claxton, Bureau of the Budget, to Chester Cooper, NSC, dated 19 April 1965. See also memorandum to the President from David Bell, USAID, dated 20 February 1965. Both documents NSF, Country File, box 278, Philippines vol. 2 (LBJ Library).

99 US Military Program, vol. 1, p. 4.

100 'Report to the Special Group (CI) on Counter-Insurgency Training Objectives', 15 March 1962, p. 1. Also, Policy Planning Council (State) Memorandum, Henry Ramsay to Walt Rostow, 16 March 1962. Both in NSF, Meetings and Memoranda, box 334, NSAM 131, Training Objectives for Counter-Insurgency.

101 US Military Program, vol. 2, 'An Analysis of Requirements for US Military Power', p. 3.

102 Colby, *Lost Victory*, p. 192.

103 Peter Edwards, *Crises and Commitments* (Sydney: Allen and Unwin, 1992), chs 14 and 17. Also, Rostow interview, March 1993, and his paper, 'A Counter-Revisionist View', presented at the Vietnam Symposium at the LBJ Library, Austin, Texas, March 1991 (Photocopy), p. 2.

104 McNamara, Memorandum to President, 26 June 1965 (revised 1 July 1965). NSC Meeting File, box 1.

105 Colby, *Lost Victory*, p. 179.

106 According to Colby, the term 'pacification' was not coined by the Americans but was a leftover from the days of the French involvement in Vietnam. The term held no specific meaning, and became something of a catch-all expression for anything having to do with political development efforts in South Vietnam. Colby, *Lost Victory*, p. 214.

107 Shortly after the organization's launch, the 'Revolutionary' was changed to 'Rural'. Colby, *Lost Victory*, pp. 214–215.

108 Discussion at Meeting of 581st NSC, 7 February 1968. NSC Meeting File (LBJ Library).

109 Interviews with CORDS programme officer Michael Tolle and with Tran Ngoc Chau, Boulder, CO, 23 June 1996.

110 Interview with CORDS programme officer Michael Tolle, 23 June 1996.

111 Rusk, who also wanted to see the USA use its power to lead a 'revolution of economic and social progress' in the world, quoted in Schoenbaum, *Waging Peace and War,* pp. 264–265.

112 US Military Program, vol. 1, p. 1.

113 Lucien Pye, 'The Politics of Southeast Asia', in Almond and Coleman (eds), *The Politics of the Developing Areas* (Princeton, NJ: Princeton University Press, 1960).

114 Almond and Coleman, *The Politics of the Developing Areas,* ch. 1.

115 Tolle, 'In the Realm of Theory', p. 3.

116 Karl W. Deutsch, *Nationalism and Social Communication: An Inquiry into the Foundations of Nationalism* (Cambridge, MA: Technology Press, 1953) p. 75.

117 Tolle, 'In the Realm of Theory', pp. 3–4.

118 Rostow discusses this progression at length in W.W. Rostow, *The Stages of Economic Growth.*

119 Tony Smith, *America's Mission: The United States and the Worldwide Struggle for Democracy in the Twentieth Century* (Princeton, NJ: Princeton University Press, 1994), p. 180.

120 USOIDP, p. 16. For a thorough exploration of how this approach was implemented in Indonesia, see Bradley Simpson, *Economists with Guns: Authoritarian Development and US–Indonesia Relations, 1969–1968* (Stanford, CA: Stanford University Press, 2008).

121 For a more detailed discussion of the vested interests of elites in resisting reforms, see Shafer, *Deadly Paradigms.*

122 Tolle, 'In the Realm of Theory', p. 16.

123 *Ibid.,* p. 6.

124 Maechling, quoted in Shafer, *Deadly Paradigms,* p. 112.

125 Author's interview with Tran Ngoc Chau, at Boulder, CO, 23 June 1996.

126 McGhee, Memorandum to Rusk, attached to PPC 12-61, 26 October 1961. p. 272–274.

127 Rusk, Memorandum to McGhee, *FRUS, 1961–63,* vol. 9, p. 275. Roughly one month after this memorandum, McGhee was replaced by Rostow at PPC.

128 Bowles, Memorandum to Hamilton, 7 October 1961. *FRUS, 1961–63,* vol. 9, pp. 265–266.

129 Burnett, *Investing in Security.*

130 Quoted by Colby in *Lost Victory,* p. 158. Also author's telephone interview with Colby in November 1995 and interview with Tran Ngoc Chau, 23 June 1996. See also William Duiker, *US Containment Policy and the Conflict in Indochina* (Stanford, CA: Stanford University Press, 1994).

131 George McTurnan Kahin and John Wilson Lewis, *The United States in Vietnam* (New York: The Dial Press, 1967), p. 127.

132 By early 1968 Lyndon Johnson was talking of a 'second front' opening in the stand against communism in Asia, and he considered the Korean Peninsula the likely spot. In a meeting with key Congressional leaders in January 1968, Johnson noted the ten-fold increase in cross-demilitarized zone (DMZ) incidents initiated by the North between 1966 and 1967, and asserted: '[It is] very obvious that they want to put some pressure on us. We think try to [*sic*] divert us from Vietnam and try to divert the Koreans who now have two divisions there from sending another division which we hope to get from them.' Johnson also

opined that the communists were attempting to bring domestic political pressure to bear on the US Government: 'I think they expect that perhaps our people would rise up and say, "Here is a second war. We can't do that. Maybe we ought to come home." ... This all ties in, we think, to one large determined offensive of theirs that is calculated to try to put them back in the ballgame.' One week later, during a NSC discussion of measures being undertaken to contain the Tet offensive, Johnson asked, 'What about my second front in Korea?' The question seems to have drawn no response from other NSC members present. Summary Notes for the 581st NSC Meeting, 7 February 1968. NSC Meeting File. Also, meeting with Congressional leaders, 31 January 1968. NSF, Meeting Notes File, box 2 (both documents LBJ Library).

133 See Duiker, *US Containment Policy and the Conflict in Indochina*, pp. 265–267, for an account of Hanoi's debate over how to best structure and pitch their political appeals in the South.

134 Tolle, 'In the Realm of Theory', pp. 13–14.

135 Edward Shils, 'The Military in the Political Development of New States', in John J. Johnson (ed.), *The Role of the Military in Underdeveloped Countries* (Princeton, NJ: Princeton Univerity Press, 1962), pp. 13–19.

136 USOIDP, pp. 17–18.

137 Colby, *Lost Victory*, pp. 244–246.

138 Michael Maclear, *The Ten Thousand Day War, Vietnam: 1945–1975* (New York: Avon, 1981), p. 263.

139 Informal Notes of NSC Discussion of 4 August 1966. NSF, NSC Meeting File, box 2 (LBJ Library).

140 State Department, Administrative History, vol. 1, ch. 7, section L, Indonesia. Administrative Histories, box 3 (LBJ Library).

141 NIE 55-64, pp. 6–7.

142 State Department, Administrative History.

143 NSC Briefing Paper on US Policy Toward Indonesia, dated 2 August 1966, for NSC Meeting of 4 August, 1966. NSF, Confidential File, CO 110, box 9 (LBJ Library).

144 *Ibid.*

145 The author notes that, while none of the documents declassified for this study indicate such involvement by the USA, many pertinent documents remain classified. Some of the documents for which the author has requested review for declassification have been exempted from such declassification by the agency involved, usually the CIA. In short, numerous pieces of the puzzle are still unavailable.

146 Conversation with Bundy at Annapolis, MD, 21 June 1995.

147 Michael Wines, 'CIA Tie Asserted in Indonesia Purge', *New York Times,* 12 July 1990.

148 State Department, Administrative History.

149 Conversation with Bundy at annual meeting of the Society for Historians of American Foreign Relations, 21 June 1995, at Annapolis, Maryland.

150 Rostow interview, March 1993.

151 Of course, both of these observations rest on the assumption that China was embarked on an aggressive programme of fomenting violent revolutionary struggle in Southeast Asia. Such an assumption is supported by contemporary statements emanating from Beijing; however, a determination of Chinese objec-

tives in the region is beyond the scope of this study.

152 NIE 55-64, p. 4.
153 Informal Notes of NSC Discussion of 4 August 1966. NSF, NSC Meeting File, box 2 (LBJ Library).
154 Quoted in Richard Immerman, '"A Time in the Tide of Men's Affairs": Lyndon Johnson and Vietnam', in Warren I. Cohen and Nancy Bernkopf Tucker (eds), *Lyndon Johnson Confronts the World* (New York: Cambridge University Press, 1994), p. 78.
155 Chester Pach, 'Military Assistance and American Foreign Policy', in Michael A. Barnhart (ed.), *Congress and United States Foreign Policy: Controlling the Use of Force in the Nuclear Age* (Albany, NY: SUNY Press, 1987), pp. 144–145.
156 Letter from Perkins to Johnson. NSF, Subject Series, Foreign Aid, Perkins (LBJ Library).

6

Conclusion:
towards a 'tolerable state of order'?

In the summer of 1969 Johnson's successor, Richard M. Nixon, made his 'Guam Declaration', that the USA would henceforth provide recipients with military aid and honour security pacts, but would expect those recipients to look after their own internal security. En route to Asia in July of that year, the new president had diverted to the South Pacific to witness the return of the Apollo 11 astronauts from their successful moon landing. Later, in an officers' club at a US military base on the island of Guam, in the presence of the press, Nixon began to talk about the future direction of US security assistance policy in Asia. In response to a reporter's question, he was quoted as saying:

> I believe that the time has come when the US, in our relations with all of our Asian friends, should be quite emphatic on two points: one, that we will honor our treaty commitments … but, two, that as far as the problems of internal security are concerned, … the US is going to encourage and has a right to expect that this problem will be increasingly handled by, and the responsibility for it taken by, the Asian nations themselves.[1]

Nixon's comments were quickly dubbed the Guam declaration, and then the Guam doctrine, later changed by the press to the Nixon Doctrine.

The Nixon Doctrine reflected an approach to international security affairs that was not limited to Asia, one that involved transferring the responsibility and the necessary hardware for maintaining security to the local regime. As Kissinger pointed out in his memoirs, this statement simply reflected the conventional wisdom of the time.[2] However, it also reflected a position Nixon had maintained for many years, that the USA's role in shaping recipients' domestic politics should be minimized. Speaking at a meeting of Eisenhower's NSC in 1958, then Vice-President Nixon asked if US security assistance policy was in fact 'running against the tide of affairs in the world'. To Nixon, it seemed questionable 'whether or not the US could continue to try to promote democracy and free enterprise, in the forms we understand these systems, in the underdeveloped areas'. The Vice-President went on to state that the USA might have to learn to 'play ball' with political and economic institutions in the developing world even if they did not resemble those of the United States.[3] In essence, Nixon was so bold as to question the unquestionable, the fundamental assumption that Western-style political and economic institutions were broadly applicable and universally desirable. His enunciation of the Nixon Doctrine over a decade later suggests that the events of those ensuing years had done nothing to dissuade Nixon from this view, and his presidency began a phase in US security assistance policy best known for a perceived emphasis on 'bolstering dictators' with US foreign aid, especially military aid.

The CORDS programme, described in Chapter 5, continued apace in Vietnam as Nixon initiated gradual US troop reductions and attempted to 'Vietnamize' the conflict. Speeding-up political development programmes in Vietnam was one means by which the Nixon White House sought to extricate the USA from Indochina. However, there was no longer a broader, regional effort towards internal defence through political development efforts. The USA was stepping back from its broad nation-building project in the developing world. As mentioned in the introduction, US security assistance to developing countries had emphasized internal security at three levels: protecting the regime from overthrow, extending its authority throughout its territory, and promoting nation-building and government legitimacy. Nixon-era assistance represented a retreat to level two or, in many cases, level one, protecting recipient regimes from internal challenges.

Development-oriented aid programmes shifted away from their broad, nation-building approach toward what Washington intended to be a more 'basic human needs'-driven approach. With the Foreign Assistance Act of 1973, Congress expressed its will that US foreign aid be reoriented toward the 'poorest of the poor', and toward meeting basic human needs. This was reflected in USAID's 'New Directions' approach implemented from 1973, designed to concentrate on such basic needs. However, New Directions also relied on recipient governments to identify specific needs for development projects, and this proved to be a serious weakness in the approach.[4] Often, recipient regimes did not share USAID's commitment to meeting basic human needs and helping 'the poorest of the poor'. As a result, these aid funds often went to support grand, if inappropriate, capital-intensive development projects which provided numerous opportunities for local graft. Security Supporting Assistance, which had been known as Defense Support during the Eisenhower era, was renamed 'Economic Support Funds' or ESF in the 1978 legislation, and quickly became a 'carrot' designed primarily to elicit or reward specific actions on the part of 'politically important' recipients.[5]

In restructuring America's security assistance approach, Nixon did not step away from the 'world police' role the country had assumed for itself in the late 1940s. Neither did he reconsider the overall, American concept of security that viewed the entire world as its National Security Zone. He simply removed the USA from an active role in internal development and nation-building in less developed areas, using security assistance programmes to create and arm deputies in developing regions, his 'gendarmes', such as the Shah of Iran. Through this approach, he pursued his own version of the 'tolerable state of order' that was and is the overall goal of American foreign policy.

Overall, the Nixon presidency signalled a move away from an aid approach based on 'indirect' interest toward the more Realist 'direct' interest approach, a trend that continued with succeeding administrations. Washington's use of aid in developing countries was to be targeted less toward promoting internal stability through development and more toward quid pro quo, conditionality and bribes.

Rebuttals to presumption of Realist analysis

The post-1968 period in American security assistance policy was characterized by the very traits criticized by Krause, Ayoob, and other scholars cited in the introduction. Under Nixon and his successors US security assistance policies emphasized keeping recipient regimes in power with little regard for the internal political conditions of their states. However, as the preceding chapters have shown, these post-1968 policies stand in contrast to the containment policies of Nixon's predecessors. Lest recent events by their proximity obscure those more distant, we must review the ways in which these earlier policies differed from the dictats of Realism and flow beyond the bounds of Realist analysis.

Not power projection

Aside from maintaining basing rights, the security assistance policies of the Eisenhower–Kennedy–Johnson period demonstrate that security assistance policies in the Third World at this time were not about power projection or the maximization of power through proxy forces. Quite simply, Washington knew that these forces lacked the 'power' necessary for such a role.

A seemingly endless stream of reports from military assistance missions in the field, as well as reports by the Joint Chiefs to the NSC clearly indicated that security assistance was not succeeding in building effective military capabilities in most recipient countries. In fact, these military establishments were proving themselves to be 'money pits', black holes into which billions of dollars of US aid simply disappeared with little effect.

Defense Support, particularly 'direct support', had been formulated to address the 'substitutability' problem, to remove the need for recipients to divert resources from their fragile economies in order to support the military establishments and force goals Washington had recommended for them. However, in practice Washington's defence support simply allowed a continual swelling of recipient military establishments. Within these bloated establishments corruption was often rife, but actual military effectiveness was disappointing at best. A central objective of the 1290-d programme was to wean recipients off military aid by building separate internal security forces that might eventually replace and make redundant regular military forces that had been serving in internal security roles.

Similarly, the Mutual Security network did not constitute alliances in the traditional sense. Although the system of Mutual Security alliances expanded during this period, these 'alliances' were very one-sided, and often little more than instruments providing for US intervention in the event of conflict. Such pacts represented a formal extension of the US security umbrella to states around the periphery of the communist world. With the advent of Eisenhower's New Look defence philosophy these areas were ever more important in 'drawing the line' that the bloc could not cross without risking nuclear retaliation, as envisioned by the *Solarium* task groups. The objectives of alliances with less developed countries stressed the political message Washington would send to the bloc and the psychological impact that American security commitments would have on recipients' will to resist accommodating their communist neighbours or adopting a neutralist position. The military efficacy of recipient forces was generally negligible, and far less important. Third World 'allies' were able to contribute little in the way of military capabilities to US efforts. Johnson was particularly emphatic in pressing Asian members of SEATO and other Asian allies to make even token contributions of forces to the war in Vietnam, primarily to build the image of a united stand against communism in the region. In most cases, the combat effectiveness of such contributions was far less important than their political and psychological impact.

The Kennedy and Johnson era represented a massive swing toward counterinsurgency in military assistance. In the face of considerable recipient resistance, Kennedy's mutual security assistance programmes shifted resources away from prestige items for external defence (such as heavy armoured units and high-performance aircraft) and worked to reorganize recipient militaries for internal security missions. By the end of 1964 even the Department of Defense was firmly behind the idea of reorienting recipient militaries towards an internal defence role. A 1964 Department of Defense Military Assistance Reappraisal went so far as to recommend making future military aid deliveries conditional upon recipients' commitment to restructure their forces toward internal security and away from conventional combat units.[6]

Importance of internal politics

As described in the Chapter 1, the only value Morgenthau and other realist theorists saw in foreign aid was its promotion of *direct interest,* the quid pro quo approach that used aid as payment for services rendered, as in maintaining basing or transit rights. However, this direct interest approach was problematic in developing countries, as it presumed recipients to be unitary actors, or, at least, stable regimes. In the upheaval and economic strife that characterized decolonizing areas, policy-makers in Washington understood that they could make no such presumptions. Treaties and other agreements were ultimately unstable if forged with weak or otherwise unstable governments. By the mid 1950s, with the acceptance of the 1290-d survey and its findings, the NSC had become well aware of the need to promote recipient stability, not simply through repressive security measures but through efforts to promote internal cohesion and legitimacy. Central to this objective was the promotion of political and economic development.

True, economic development often was simply equated with economic growth. Development was in turn linked to Cold War security calculations via one of what Robert Packenham later referred to as 'poverty theses', popular arguments relating economic deprivation to political instability that, in turn, would be exploited by the communists.[7]

Packenham's critique of the poverty theses largely rests upon a perception of developing societies that seemed quite popular with many in Washington during the 1950s and even into the 1960s; while such societies were mired in hardship, they had always been so and were thus unlikely to expect better.[8] This was the view of Morgenthau and other contemporary Realist theorists as well.[9]

While Washington had indeed acknowledged the link between poverty and radicalism that communists could readily exploit, policy-makers from the Truman administration onwards recognized that the threat in the developing world stemmed from popular *aspirations*. The rising expectations and aspirations of peoples in developing areas were the main source of internal political pressures and of demands made on the governments of new states. If Washington could not help recipient regimes provide their populations with some hope of meeting these demands and expectations, they would face situations in which those populations would not only sweep away those regimes but, in the ensuing upheaval, would also abandon existing, non-communist systems of government in favour of the promise of communist alternatives. Accordingly, from the mid-1950s onward, America's security assistance policies were increasingly oriented toward internal security in a broad sense. This approach featured efforts to help recipients meet economic and political aspirations through economic development assistance and through attempts to foster the sound leadership practices and political institutions that would in turn promote popular legitimacy. During this period, US policy was intended to help favoured leaders or political factions win the internal political competition that characterized so many developing countries, not simply to suppress that competition.

Normative distortions rather than rational analyses

Finally, during this period, US policy toward the developing world deviated from realism in its irrationality. Washington simply could never acknowledge communism as a legitimate, political force and presumed communist activity in all cases to be heinous in motive, ultimately designed to promote the expansionist objectives of communism's power centre (originally Moscow; later, Moscow and Beijing). American analyses were distorted by a normative bias that kept policy-makers from seeing the genuine appeal the communist development model held for the peoples of many new states; Washington saw only 'false promises' designed to exploit popular discontent and co-opt local leaders. Similarly, their distorted view of communism kept American leaders from acknowledging local communist movements as indigenous, rather than as agents of the bloc.

Were they acting in a more Realist manner, American policy-makers would have had a less frantic perception of the 'communist threat' and its limitations. Washington would have acted from a clearer view of Moscow's limited ability to provide sustained high levels of economic assistance, much less its ability to orchestrate and manage a global 'communist conspiracy'. Instead, Washington's normative lens distorted the perception of threat in the developing world out of all proportion. This distorted perception of an immediate, ubiquitous and endlessly capable threat lent urgency to Washington's security assistance measures, and fostered an often shortsighted, heavy-handed approach to internal defence.

Effectiveness

If those who critique US foreign policy in the Third World on the basis of its simplistic Realist analysis are incorrect, than why was US policy during the Eisenhower, Kennedy and Johnson era so unsuccessful? If, as this study has demonstrated, 'software' considerations were very much a part of Washington's Cold War security effort in the developing world, then all the more interesting is the question of why and how these policies went so wrong. Through the preceding chapters, this study has tried to describe the formation of such Cold War policies, exploring the rationale behind them and offering critiques. This section offers overall critiques of chronic impediments to policy common to the entire period under study.

Problems of coordination

One chronic problem was that of interagency coordination, especially 'step-child' status suffered by successive aid-administrating agencies. The Economic Cooperation Administration, which successfully coordinated assistance under the ERP or 'Marshall Plan', differed from its successor agencies in that it was given a specified life-span at the time of its creation. The ECA was intended to complete its task and dissolve in 1952, and it did just that. In contrast, its successors were given vaguely defined missions in less-developed areas, and a very small fraction of the ECA's level of funding. The Mutual Security Agency (MSA), Foreign Operations Administration (FOA), International Cooperation Administration (ICA) and Agency for International Development (AID) were each formed with the intention that they would oversee ongoing efforts. Accordingly, they would have to jostle for position with the other executive agencies of the US government, cutting out a niche for themselves from what other agencies viewed as their policy 'turf'. In this environment they have suffered Congressional as well as Presidential whittling away of their statutory responsibilities (as in the case of the MSA), have atrophied from lack of direct responsibility and lack of cooperation from other relevant agencies (FOA), or ended up powerless due to other agencies' refusal to submit to their authority in coordinating security assistance efforts (ICA). USAID is still with us, but its own authority has been subject to frequent revision, and Congress regularly calls for its dissolution.

A more fundamental coordination problem stemmed from the close shepherding and compartmentalization of classified information. This problem was pointed out by agencies participating in the 1290-d effort,[10] and it intensified under Kennedy with the marginalization of the NSC as a forum for discussion of security policy and the subsequent rise of the highly compartmentalized 'Special Groups'. This close guarding of information, coupled with a Cold War tendency to classify virtually every piece of paper pertaining to security policy, seriously hampered and undermined cooperation in the multi-agency security assistance programmes described in this study, to the point where often one hand truly did not know what the other was doing. Ultimately, such compartmentalization impeded the dissemination of best practices and other lessons to be learned.

An even greater failure in coordination resulted from successive administrations' failure to share sufficient information with Congress, or the electorate, to secure their support for security assistance efforts in the developing world. These presidents hesitated to give Congress enough information to inform their debates and secure cooperation and funding for development efforts. When presenting foreign aid requests to Congress, Eisenhower refused to allow the economic elements of security assistance to be separated from the military elements, firmly believing that the Legislative branch would simply do away with the economic aid requests. During the Johnson presidency, contemporary foreign policy scholars remarked that the administration had appealed to the American people to close ranks behind its Indochina policy, and in doing so, '[the administration]would seem to bear a responsibility for providing the information necessary for [the people] to comprehend the situation that has actually developed in Vietnam. That has not been done.'[11] As a result, Congress remained an obstacle rather than an ally when it came to security assistance efforts in the developing world.

Securing such broad, popular support for security assistance was a cherished goal of Cold War presidents, from Truman onward. Truman himself had even approached film-maker Frank Capra, creator of the successful *Why We Fight* series of Second World War propaganda films, to create a series on *Why We Fight the Cold War*.[12] However, a comparison of NSC discussions with presidents' presentations to Congress and memoranda of conversations with Congressional leaders indicates that presidents rarely, if ever, shared with Congress the concerns that preoccupied them in their NSC deliberations. Such reticence may be attributable in part to these presidents' concern over the inevitable resistance born of traditional US isolationism. Another possibility is that presidents were unwilling to inform the Congress or the electorate of their beliefs that the USA was losing the Cold War. This realization was especially burdensome in Eisenhower's case.[13]

Another likely, if partial, explanation for these administrations' failure to coordinate Congressional support is the 'Madisonian labyrinth' that is the US government. The government is essentially designed to pit the executive and legislative branches against each other in the interest of keeping too much power from accruing with any one agency or branch. Accordingly, Congress is predisposed to critically scrutinize presidential policy initiatives. Eisenhower often bemoaned his having to suffer such scrutiny and debate of his policies while his counterpart in Moscow could act decisively, free of such restrictions. Kennedy managed to convince Congress – to some extent – that he represented a new approach to containment, a chance to seize the initiative from the communists. Kennedy succeeded in gaining increased Congressional support, for a time, for foreign aid as an instrument for promoting security interests. However, when his policy approaches, as implemented by his successor, failed to achieve positive results, there followed a Congressional backlash against such policies and against foreign aid in general. The Johnson White House even pondered the idea of 'quietly' establishing a political action organization to put pressure on Congress on behalf of foreign aid.[14]

In times of emergency, the President can ask Congress for measures that can straighten and simplify the 'labyrinth' and give the executive powers to act without Congressional restraint. The most straightforward such measure is to ask for a declaration of war, but this seemed inappropriate in a Cold War context. Johnson managed to gain some direct presidential powers to deploy US forces without Congressional approval through passage of the Gulf of Tonkin Resolution in 1964, but this hardly provided the broad powers that came with a declaration of war. Congressional approval was still required to fund security assistance measures, and successive administrations, upon sounding out key Congressional leaders, found a broad perception that aid to developing countries seemed too 'oblique' to US security interests to warrant broad Congressional and public support.[15] Since the Marshall Plan, no US president has successfully made a convincing case linking large-scale foreign development aid to US security interests.

As a result, US security assistance policy continues to embody an inherent paradox; in many US aid relationships, an emphasis on more immediate security concerns tends to undermine the other, longer-term objectives in the relationship. When the Executive, the Congress and the electorate perceive few if any urgent threats to US security, support for foreign aid languishes, and funding for long-term development and stability-building aid projects, which themselves might ultimately promote security, withers away. On the other hand, while perception of urgent threats may temporarily bolster support for foreign aid, the aid programmes formulated to meet those threats tend to be heavy-handed, short-term in nature, and prone to create the types of violent upheaval that undermines economic and political development projects, ultimately threatening recipient stability. In a sense, the situation is akin to a health-care system that provides critical care but no primary care or follow-up care.

Problems of basic assumptions and doctrine

Even if these presidents had achieved better coordination between participating agencies and gained the desired levels of funding from Congress, the assumptions upon which their security assistance approaches were founded remain questionable.

One of the revelations of Steven Hook's fine comparative analysis of foreign aid policy is the tendency of aid donors to strive to replicate their own systems, or what they imagine their own systems to be.[16] Nordic countries, traditionally the most generous on a *per capita* basis, targeted aid toward the development of thriving social democracies. The USSR at one time sought to identify promising 'Marxist–Leninist Vanguard Parties' as the focus of its own aid efforts. Therefore, it should not come as a surprise that the USA also viewed its own 'exceptional' system as a suitable blueprint for guiding and managing development processes across the world, and the model to which the developing world's leaders would naturally aspire. However, this assumption made it particularly difficult for Washington to balance the 'shield' element of these policies with other development measures. Arguably, this assumption leads to an emphasis on targeting the *obstructions* to such natural development. The resulting policies stress protection rather than cultivation, much like the gardener who neglects proper fertilizer in favour of herbicides and chopping away violently with the hoe.

Most questionable were American assumptions regarding development processes. The latter part of the 1950s represented a radical change in Washington's assessment of processes underway in the less developed areas, as the 'growth equals development' approach was replaced by the 'modernization' approach. By the end of 1955 the Eisenhower administration had begun to learn that the process of development in these areas involved a complex interaction of social, political and economic elements. However, Eisenhower's team did not claim to have a broad schematic by which they could analyse and intervene. Consequently, the Eisenhower administration focused the bulk of their efforts on keeping communism out of these development processes, while attempting to transfer US-style political institutions and provide the technical assistance that would promote private investment in these developing economies. Changes in the Eisenhower-era policies were shaped by feedback and reassessment, as well as by the shift in Soviet foreign economic policy that took place in the mid-1950s. By the end of his administration Eisenhower was admitting to himself, and to his Cabinet, that events in the developing world were overtaking the policies of his administration.

In contrast, the modernization theorists who so influenced the Kennedy and Johnson administrations assumed, like their Communist counterparts, that they understood these development processes. Security-assistance decision-making in the Kennedy–Johnson period involved relatively little feedback and reassessment. The Kennedy team stood firm in its conviction that the schematic it had for guiding development processes, as expressed in the USOIDP, was appropriate for Southeast Asia and the developing world as a whole. However, in order to shoe-horn the entire developing world into this framework, modernization theorists had to streamline or even eliminate the complexities of culture and other elements of identity from the equation, reducing states to the simplistic categories of traditional, transitional and modern.

Over time, Indochina became the main focus and the primary testbed for America's broad, nation-building approach to security assistance in the developing world, and the test was judged a failure. In the transition following the 1968 election, everyone, from the president to Congress, even USAID, made every effort to distance the USA from the aid and security assistance philosophy and approach of the pre-Nixon era.

Another dangerous assumption was that the communist threat was ultimately external. This assumption stemmed from Washington's normatively distorted view of the very nature of communism and had serious ramifications for US policy-making. Washington remained unable to see local communist parties and organizations as native to recipient societies. In retrospect, Washington's chronic problem in dealing with developing world radicalism was not so much a tendency to mistake nationalists for communists as a refusal to accept that communists could be nationalists. They were presumed to be agents of the bloc, solely concerned with bloc interests.

Assuming that local communists were not endogenous actors meant that the USA was loathe to accept their presence in recipient governments. The memory of the 1948 Czech coup continued to shape Washington's analysis of communist tactics throughout much of the period under study. Accordingly, many US policy-makers assumed that, once incorporated into the local government, the communists would work to undermine that government and deliver it into the bloc's control. US security assistance policies strove to make communist affiliation unacceptable in recipient societies, if not an imprisonable offence, thus eliminating a significant element from local political development processes. In such circumstances, communists and other leftists had little alternative to resorting to insurgency.

'Irrational' assumptions regarding the nature of communism
Finally, during this period, US policy toward the developing world deviated from the Realist conception of rationality; cold, carefully measured cost–benefit analysis.[17] In viewing the USSR and, later, the PRC not as competing powers but as fanatics, Washington deviated from the Realist rationality of great power politics and exhibited an unorthodoxy or even a fanaticism of its own.

The goal of political development was itself irrational in a Realist sense. The more Realist approach would simply have been to exert the sort of vice-like control over new states that Washington presumed communist governments exerted either directly or by proxy, or, at least, to behave more like a traditional imperial power.

Washington simply could never acknowledge communism as a legitimate, political force, and presumed communist activity in all cases to be heinous in motive, ultimately designed to promote the expansionist objectives of communism's power centres. In its struggles with the bloc, the USA did not exhibit a classic balance of power approach to international affairs; specifically, there was no concept of equilibrium. If communism was on the advance, there must be containment. If communism was halted in its advance, there must be 'roll-back' of communism's frontiers. Once entangled in a contest with its communist competitor, Washington was chronically unable to cut its losses and withdraw. Once embarked on a crusade, more than mere balance of power considerations were at stake. A normative, even dualistic, element coloured Washington's assessment of the ideational threat: if communism was indeed 'evil', then how could any 'balance' with evil be acceptable?

Similarly, just as they could never acknowledge locally grown communist movements, American policy-makers could never see the genuine appeal the communist development model held for the peoples of many new states. Washington saw only communism's 'false promises' designed to exploit popular discontent and co-opt local leaders.

The crusader-like zeal and evangelical rhetoric Washington exhibited in its efforts to meet the communist threat were not merely ploys to elicit domestic US support and mobilize resources. Instead, they were reflections of a deep and widely held perception of communism as an essentially evil force that threatened the wellbeing of all free (i.e., non-communist) peoples and, ultimately, humanity as a whole. As Anders Stephanson points out, the formulation of American views of communism was coloured by the recent struggle against the forces of fascism:

> The master signifier around which the [Cold War] struggle initially came to be articulated was World War II, or more precisely, what it had meant to negate fascism in World War II. No one could question that act in itself, it was a universal Right. But to claim the same role now and, obversely, to cast the former ally and present enemy in the role of fascism, was not mere repetition. It was a new constitution of the Other and a new affirmation of the Self as the negation of that which was thus being excluded.[18]

The USA had intended its Cold War policy in the developing world to be defined by far more than the 'negation of that which was being excluded'. The defining element was to be the spread of the fundamental elements of the American form of government and political culture to new states, a form of government that Washington presumed to be universally applicable and desirable. As indicated by the conclusions and recommendations of NSC 68, this fostering and strengthening of such free world institutions and their ultimate triumph by example represented the basic concept of Cold War victory over communism. However, such strengthening was conditional upon the ability of the USA and its allies to contain the spread of communist domination. As a result of Washington's irrational conception of the communist threat, the more 'positive' programme of transferring US-style institutions, ethos and governance was repeatedly overruled and set aside in favour of 'negative' measures, often based on force, to combat the communist idea and those who promoted it.

Side-effects

Bloated, entrenched military establishments

While critical security scholars rightly criticize Washington's building-up of military establishments in the developing world, they err in attributing this policy to a Realist emphasis on these states' external threats. Eisenhower, and to a far greater extent Kennedy and Johnson, tried to strengthen local militaries out of a conviction that they would serve as driving force in political development, as a modernizing elite similar to the 'young Turks' movement in Turkey.

David Shafer, among others, has observed that the Cold War saw both the USA and the USSR attempting to fill the role of 'managers of modernization' in the developing world.[19] In fact, both superpowers stifled the modernization process. Modernization efforts were not starting from traditional, premodern societies described by Rostow in *Stages of Growth* but, in most cases, with what Crawford Young referred to as a 'colonial state', an entity unlike either the metropolitan society or the traditional, precolonial society. Developing societies had their collision with modernity not as they gained independence in the 1940s, 50s and 60s, but much earlier with the onset of colonization. It was then that indigenous social structures, norms and cultural traditions were disrupted and destroyed, replaced with those impressed upon the society by the colonial power. The upheaval resulting from this disruption was held in check by colonial administrations, until the eventual removal of that authority led to a rising tide of social forces in these societies, effectively taking the proverbial lid off of the cauldron. In the resulting turbulence the social cleavages and factional tensions long suppressed by colonial administrations re-emerged while new, indigenous elites arose in competition to take the place of the colonials.

Into these turbulent situations stepped the modernization theorists. As Pye noted in the 1960s, contemporary nation-building efforts were yet a new phase in the disruption of traditional society. Modernizing elites (whether pro-Western or pro-communist) were attempting to impress 'modern' institutions onto transitional societies in the same way as had the colonial powers.[20] In these new states, the US sought to promote its version of the modernization process by entrusting it to the most prominent 'institution in being', the military.[21] This approach ultimately backfired in many cases. With US assistance, the military assumed such a powerful position in society that they effectively stifled political development.

Additionally, the economic costs of the military had a crippling effect on development processes, despite Washington's provision of Defense Support under Eisenhower and Security Supporting Assistance under Kennedy and Johnson. Although intended to cushion developing economies from the burden of supporting military establishments, these funds were often spent at the discretion of the recipient, usually as budgetary support. As shown in the preceding chapters, this assistance promoted an uncontrolled swelling of the recipient militaries, often at the expense of domestic economic priorities. For example, by 1966 the Indonesian military establishment was consuming at least 70 per cent of that country's national budget.[22] In other recipients such as Korea, Pakistan, Iran and Taiwan, the situation was similar.

In addition to promoting local military establishments, security assistance also shielded recipient regimes from having to make hard economic development decisions. By providing economic aid to bolster local support for regimes, often on an emergency basis, the USA undermined its own objectives of creating self-sustaining growth in recipient economies.

In crisis contexts, the USA often provided development aid as emergency measures to ease bouts of intense dissatisfaction with local regimes and thus promote short-term stability. For instance, the American military escalation in Vietnam in 1965 was coordinated with a large-scale programme for improving domestic rice and pig production intended to undermine popular support for the guerrillas and deny them their rural support bases.[23] Similarly, in Indonesia's case, even *after* the PKI threat had peaked and was receding, US policy-makers were troubled by the difficulty of balancing a clear need to provide aid to ease popular discontent and prevent resurgence of 'Sukarnoism' with the need to let the new regime make the hard economic choices necessary to put the economy on the path to stabilization.[24] Instead of strengthening local economies and promoting sound economic practices on the part of the local regime, such aid tended to breed dependency.

Crippling burdens of debt service

Despite Washington's efforts to expand 'soft' lending to developing countries, debt service had begun to cripple recipient economies by the mid-1960s. By 1965, total debt service payments by less developed recipients on public and private loans totalled some $4.25 billion dollars, roughly twice the 1960 figure. As a result, while total aid transfers looked substantial on paper, *net* aid transfers were dwindling rapidly. For example, as the result of debt service paid by Latin American countries, net aid transferred to Latin America had reached *zero* by 1965, despite the 'Alliance for Progress' programme.[25] These debt burdens rendered the *Alliance*, along with other development loan programmes, largely ineffective by the end of the Johnson presidency.

Increased recipient leverage

As Richard Emerson observed years ago, in aid relationships the potential to exert influence resides in the dependency of one actor upon another, the control by one actor over resources that the other actor desires.[26] While the donor derives leverage through aid, the recipient derives counter-leverage through exploiting the donor's own vulnerabilities. Stanton Burnett calls this the 'frozen spigot' phenomenon; if strategic or domestic political factors prevent donors from turning off the flow of aid, the spigot is effectively frozen open.[27]

As recipients of US security assistance recognized Washington's objectives and the importance of these objectives, threats to suspend aid lost much of their credibility. Washington lost leverage in these relationships even as recipients gained it. As Shafer observed, once developing-world recipients recognized the importance of their place in US Cold War objectives, it became increasingly difficult to prevail upon these regimes to mobilize their own resources for development. Instead, recipients exerted increasing leverage on the USA and, in many cases, managed to negotiate increasingly lucrative aid packages in return for continued cooperation on such issues as base or transit rights, or simply as an incentive not to enter into an aid relationship with the bloc.

Lessons

A central goal of the preceding study has been to offer lessons relevant to current and future US policy-making. These lessons are especially relevant now that political development objectives are once again in the forefront of US foreign policy toward developing areas and new states. Nation-building was rehabilitated on a limited basis as a security policy approach in Central America in the 1980s.[28] Political development, nation-building and democratization surged briefly in America's aid budget in the post-Cold War era, especially in policy towards new states emerging from the former Soviet Union as well as 'collapsed' states in other regions. In the aftermath of 11 September 2001, US policy confronted the limits of its early, mainly military approach in Afghanistan and Iraq and shifted to a somewhat more sophisticated approach, described by Condoleeza Rice as centred on 'defense, democracy and development'.[29] Secretary of Defense Robert Gates summed up the new insecurity environment as follows:

> The recent past vividly demonstrated the consequences of failing to address adequately the dangers posed by insurgencies and failed states. Terrorist networks can find sanctuary within the borders of a weak nation and strength within the chaos of social breakdown. A nuclear-armed state could collapse into chaos and criminality. The most likely catastrophic threats to

the U.S. homeland – for example, that of a U.S. city being poisoned or reduced to rubble from a terrorist attack – are more likely to emanate from failing states than from aggressor states.[30]

In the final years of the Bush presidency, the link between security and development abroad and security of the USA itself had been rediscovered and returned to the fore of US foreign policy. This shift included the adoption of the Provincial Reconstruction Team (PRT) concept in Afghanistan and Iraq, as well as broader efforts to more closely coordinate military, economic and political elements of nation-building. Now, as during the Cold War, policy seems driven by and formulated with an analytical framework other than Realism.[31]

In today's foreign policy environment, three lessons derived from Cold War policies remain particularly salient. These centre on challenges of interagency coordination, the challenge of balancing the 'shield' with development measures and the transferability of Western institutions.

Challenge of coordination

The complex constitution and structure of the US government tend to keep the executive and legislative branches at odds with each other and help to explain successive presidents' challenges in funding nation-building programmes. However, there is little in the 'Madisonian labyrinth' to explain competition between executive branch departments and bureaucracies. Now, as during the Cold War, coordination depends to a considerable degree on the management and leadership styles of the president and key officials, with the result that predictions are difficult to make beyond a given election cycle.

Coordination is bound to become more challenging. On one hand, the role in such operations for non-governmental organizations (NGOs) is bound to keep growing. Additionally, joint and multilateral operations are becoming the norm. The USA is working with NATO allies in Afghanistan now, and has cooperated with the European Union in crisis management and nation-building efforts in the Balkans and elsewhere. Recently, the USA has established AFRICOM, raising the possibility of increasing cooperation with the African Union as well as increased training and security sector reform missions with individual African states, missions remarkably similar in their goals to the 1290-d/OISP missions of the 1950s. The multilateral dimension seems certain to present new coordination challenges and to exacerbate those currently extant.[32]

Challenge of balancing the 'shield'

Today's nation-building efforts are still implemented in settings characterized by considerable political, social and economic upheaval, if not open conflict involving multiple factions. In these turbulent contexts, the questions confronting US policy-makers today are the same as they were in the 1950s and 1960s: how *much* order is a prerequisite for successful development, and what is the essence of the relationship between development, order and security?

There is always the danger that aid policy may again fall victim to the paradox described earlier, and that nation-building efforts will be undermined by the intensity and force-heavy nature of 'emergency' intervention. One area posing such a danger is intervention in ethno-nationalist or other factional conflicts within recipient societies. The constraints of the state system and corresponding international rules and norms such as the integrity and inviolability of borders, along with the inheritance of boundaries established in the days of empire, leave many states with the task of nation-building in multi-ethnic or multi-nation states. In such circumstances, an enigmatic relationship exists between nation-building and conflict; as nation-building efforts fashion a concept of citizenship separate from ethnic identities, increased participation among and interaction between ethnic groups can lead to frictions and even open conflict.[33] While the USA should hardly make a policy of standing-by and remaining aloof from such conflicts as they escalate into vast human tragedies, neither should US interventions go off on a 'hair trigger', attempting to stabilize the situation by shifting its aid emphasis to the state's security institutions. To do so would return US policy to the tendencies of the 1948–68 period, as a renewed emphasis on security measures would again undermine any progress made by more subtle institution-building projects.

Transferability of Western institutions

In efforts to promote Western-style notions of 'good governance', US security assistance went far beyond 'conditionality' in foreign aid. Instead, these policies featured efforts to shape the basic character of developing societies, to guide their political as well as their economic development. However, in formulating and implementing these policies, US policy-makers never really questioned whether Western institutions could be successfully transferred to any culture or society. A generation later, with reconstruction, development and nation-building at the forefront of security policy, the question of how universally applicable Western institutions really are still begs serious scrutiny before more blood and treasure are expended on ever more reconstruction and nation-building projects.

The applicability of the *ideas* underlying these institutions, such as democracy and respect for human and civil rights, is not in question. Rather, what is questionable is the notion that Western-style institutions can be taken off the shelf and plugged-in to recipient societies, impressed upon society from above. Political cultures are formed of ideas; but ideas, in turn, are shaped by experience.

During the Eisenhower administration, policy-makers assumed that Western, especially American, institutions and ways of governance were appropriate, and that these were aspired to by all leaders who would want the best for their constituent populations. While Eisenhower-era policies focused on security institutions, the USA presumed that these would be shaped and guided by the same sort of ethos as characterized Western institutions. In the Kennedy–Johnson era, the question of universal applicability was set aside by modernization theory's blockish categorization of all less developed countries into 'traditional, transitional and modern' societies. All such societies were presumed to be shapeless and 'malleable', and thus their institutions could be formed like clay. As events demonstrated, they were not, owing to their differing experiences and resultant political cultures.

More recently, top decision-makers in Washington sent waves of personnel, both military and civilian, into Afghanistan and Iraq with plans based on lessons derived from Western experience. In this case, the experience was the liberation and occupation of Europe in the mid-1940s. To an extent, referring to such historical experience served a simplifying, heuristic purpose by providing a broadly shared and accessible frame of reference.[34] However, upon closer scrutiny, it seemed that the lessons from America's experience in Europe were, at the highest levels of elite discourse, presumed to be appropriate bases for planning operations in Iraq.[35] While Defense Secretary Donald Rumsfeld made numerous references to Saddam representing another Hitler and the US invasion of Iraq as preventing another Munich, Assistant Secretary of Defense Paul Wolfowitz declared, 'If you're looking for a historical analogy, it's probably closer to post-liberation France [after World War II].'[36]

Faced with a very different reality on the ground, military commanders from theatre to company level sought lessons more relevant to the cultural as well as physical landscape in which they had to operate. Many turned to the works of a man placed in similar circumstances generations earlier, T. E. Lawrence, the British soldier-scholar who helped to organize and lead the Arab revolt against the Ottoman Empire in the First World War. His written works are packed with lessons and parables of working and fighting alongside people of a culture very different from his own. The works of 'Lawrence of Arabia', including his twenty-seven articles appearing in *The Arab Bulletin* in 1917 and his *The Seven Pillars of Wisdom: A Triumph*, have been cited repeatedly since 2001 in military training courses and manuals on counterinsurgency.[37]

In effect, those implementing policy had to relearn lessons that had been lost, valuable data, histories and doctrine from the nation-building projects explored in previous chapters. In the wake of America's bitter experience in Vietnam, these hard-won lessons were the proverbial baby thrown out with the bathwater as agencies, individuals and the nation as a whole attempted to distance themselves from that encounter. Officers who served in Iraq and Afghanistan have written books to preserve and disseminate their own lessons learned. These include David Kilcullen's *Accidental Guerilla* and John A. Nagl's *Learning to Eat Soup With a Knife*, both borrowing concepts (and the latter, his title) from Lawrence. Similar works have emerged from civilian operators involved in these reconstruction and nation-building projects in both governmental and non-governmental capacities. All of these should contribute to a substantial and ever-growing body of pertinent lessons for the future.

Ultimately, Nixon's approach to ensuring a 'tolerable state of order' was unsustainable. His emphasis on essentially stifling political development in recipient states amounted to clamping the lid on a boiling kettle; pressures would continue to build, and there was little in the Nixon-era policy to address that. Subsequent presidents, notably Jimmy Carter, attempted to modify this approach, manipulating aid flows to encourage internal reforms in recipient states, but he proved unable to effect significant changes in policy. Only the end of the Cold War and the evaporation of communism as an ideational threat allowed for significant change in policy. However, in accordance with the paradox mentioned above, when the threat abated, so did America's interest in promoting development and stability abroad. That changed after the events of 11 September 2001, and development abroad and security at home were again linked.

Ultimately, it has been America's own political culture, with its sense of exceptionalism and its late-1940s conception of its own role in the world, that has proven the most rigid and seemingly immutable of all. In the end, both the United States and the world are hostage to American political culture and the resulting paradox. Americans are impatient and action-oriented with a penchant for quick fixes. However, the lessons derived from the US experience in nation-building demonstrate that short-term incursions only serve to exacerbate long-term problems. The danger is that history might repeat itself: the US may become so disenchanted with its experiences in Afghanistan and Iraq that it will once again forget its lessons learned.

America and developed countries in general will have to prepare for the long haul.

Notes

1 Henry A. Kissinger, *White House Years* (Boston, MA: Little, Brown & Co., 1979), pp. 223–225.
2 Kissinger, *White House Years*, p. 225.
3 Discussion at 388th Meeting of NSC, 3 December 1958 (DDE Library).
4 E. R. Morss and V. A. Morss, *US Foreign Aid: An Assessment of New and Traditional Development Strategies* (Boulder, CO: Westview Press, 1982), pp. 25–30.
5 For an extensive critique of ESF programmes and policies, see Zimmerman, *Dollars, Diplomacy and Dependency: Dilemmas of US Economic Aid* (Boulder: Lynne Rienner Publishers, 1993).
6 Military Assistance Reappraisal, FY 67–71: vol. 1-A, June 1965. NSF, Agency File, Defense, box 20 (LBJ Library).
7 Robert A. Packenham, *Liberal America and the Third World* (Princeton, NJ: Princeton University Press, 1973), pp. 49–52.
8 *Ibid.*

9 See Morgenthau, 'Preface'. Morgenthau also maintained that these new states could only become a threat to US interests in the event that they *did* become developed.

10 As discussed in Chapter 3.

11 Kahin and Lewis, *The United States in Vietnam*, p. vii.

12 Declassified Documents Reference System. Also, Tricia Jenkins, *The CIA in Hollywood: How the Agency Shapes Film and Television* (Austin, TX: University of Texas Press, 2012), p. 8.

13 This was a regular topic in correspondence between Eisenhower and Dulles. For example, see letter, Eisenhower to Foster Dulles, 26 March 1958. White House Memoranda Series, box 6, JFD Papers (DDE Library).

14 Bator, Memorandum to President, 13 October 1966. NSF, Subject File, Foreign Assistance Programs, box 17 (LBJ Library).

15 For a discussion of public scrutiny of policy for clear security interests, see Stanley Hoffman, 'The Acceptability of Military Force', in *Force in Modern Societies,* Adelphi Paper no. 102 (London: International Institute of Strategic Studies, 1975).

16 Hook, *National Interest and Foreign Aid*. See especially ch. 7.

17 According to Morgenthau, for example, morality has no place in foreign policy-making. Rather, 'Realism considers prudence – the careful weighing of the consequences of political actions – to be the supreme virtue in politics'. Similarly, leaders 'think and act in terms of interest defined as power', and formulate and pursue policies that are calculated to improve the position of their individual country. See Morgenthau, *Politics Among Nations,* 5th edn (New York: Knopf, 1978), pp. 4–10.

18 Anders Stephanson, 'Fourteen Notes on the Very Concept of the Cold War', H-DIPLO, June 1996.

19 Shafer, *Deadly Paradigms*.

20 Pye, in Johnson, p. 73.

21 *Ibid.*

22 NSC Briefing Paper, 2 August 1966.

23 McNamara, Memorandum to President, 26 June 1965 (revised 1 July 1965). NSC Meeting File, box 1 (LBJ Library).

24 NSC Briefing Paper, 2 August 1966.

25 Rostow, Memorandum to President, 15 November 1966. NSF, Subject File, Foreign Assistance Programs (Perkins), box 17 (LBJ Library).

26 Richard Emerson, 'Power-Dependence Relations', in *American Sociological Review,* 27 (February 1962): 31–41, quoted in Smolansky and Smolansky, *The Soviet Quest for Influence,* pp. 2–4.

27 Burnett, *Investing in Security*, p. 5.

28 For an analysis of US political development approaches in El Salvador, see Benjamin C. Schwartz, *American Counterinsurgency Doctrine and El Salvador: The Frustrations of Reform and the Illusions of Nation Building* (Santa Monica, CA: RAND Corporation, 1991).

29 C. Rice, 'Welcome to my World, Barack', *New York Times Magazine,* 13 November 2008.

30 Robert M. Gates, 'A Balanced Strategy: Reprogramming the Pentagon for a New Age', *Foreign Affairs*, 88, 1 (Jan/Feb 2009): 28–40.

31 To make their position clear, leading Realist scholars including Robert Jervis,

John Mearsheimer, Kenneth Waltz and others took out a paid advertisement in the *New York Times* declaring that the US invasion of Iraq was *not* in American national interests. The advertisement appeared on 26 September 2002, roughly six months before the invasion.

32 Xymena Kurowska and Thomas Seitz, 'The EU's Role in International Crisis Management: Innovative Model or Emulated Script?', In Eva Gross and Ana Juncos (eds), *EU Conflict Prevention and Crisis Management: Institutions, Policies and Roles* (Abingdon, Oxon: Routledge/UACES, 2011).

33 For a discussion of this relationship, see Rebecca Kook, 'Towards the Rehabilitation of 'Nation-Building and the Reconstruction of Nations'. Paper presented at Annual Meeting of American Political Science Association, Chicago, IL, 31 August – 3 September 1995 (photocopy).

34 For an excellent exploration of this process, see Yuen Foong Kong, *Analogies at War: Korea, Munich, Dien Ben Phu and the Vietnam Decisions of 1965* (Princeton, NJ: Princeton University Press, 1992).

35 For evidence of this problem among the top civilian leadership of the Defense Department, see Thomas W. Maulucci, Jr., 'Comparing the American Occupations of Germany and Iraq', *Yale Journal of International Affairs* (Winter 2008): 120–130. Also, Jay Hallen, 'Can Baghdad Learn From Rome?' *National Review Online*, 16 May 2011. In contrast, the Army War College's Strategic Studies Institute drafted a far more nuanced and sophisticated overview of likely challenges to be faced in an occupation of Iraq. After noting the successes of the post-Second World War occupation of Germany, the authors declare, 'The world has changed a great deal since 1945, however'. In Conrad C. Crane and W. Andrew Terrill, *Reconstructing Iraq: Insights, Challenges and Missions for Military Forces in a Post-Conflict Scenario* (Carlisle, PA: USAWC Strategic Studies Institute, 2003).

36 Rumsfeld quoted in David Rennie, 'Attack Saddam now and let history judge, says Rumsfeld', *Daily Telegraph*, 21 August 2002. Wolfowitz quoted in Trudy Rubin, 'Paul Wolfowitz: not just any optimist', *Philadelphia Inquirer*, 17 November 2002.

37 See, for example, Alisdair Soussi, 'Lawrence of Arabia, Guiding U.S. Army in Iraq and Afghanistan', *Christian Science Monitor*, 19 June 2010. Lawrence's works are also quoted and cited in the most recent US Army and Marine Corps field manuals on counterinsurgency.

Bibliography

Acheson, Dean. *Present at the Creation: My Years at the State Department* (New York: Norton, 1969).

Adams, James. *Secret Armies* (New York: The Atlantic Monthly Press, 1987).

Ayoob, Mohammed. *The Third World Security Predicament* (Boulder, CO: Lynne Rienner Publishers, 1995).

Baldwin, David A. *Economic Development and American Foreign Policy, 1943–62* (Chicago, IL: The University of Chicago Press, 1966).

Banfield, Edward C. *American Foreign Aid Doctrines* (Washington, DC: American Enterprise Institute for Public Policy Research, 1963).

Bank, Aaron. *From OSS to Green Beret: The Birth of Special Forces* (New York: Presidio Press, 1986).

Bedeleux, Robert. *Communism and Development* (London: Methuen, 1987).

Bell, Wendell, and Walter E. Freeman. *Ethnicity and Nation-Building: Comparative, International, and Historical Perspectives* (Beverly Hills, CA: Sage Publications, 1974).

Berliner, J. S. *Soviet Economic Aid: The New Aid and Trade Policy in Underdeveloped Countries* (New York: Praeger, 1958).

Beschloss, Michael R. *The Crisis Years* (New York: Edward Burlingame Books, 1991).

Blaufarb, Douglas S. *The Counterinsurgency Era* (New York: Free Press, 1977).

Blum, R. M. *Drawing the Line: The Origin of the American Containment Policy in East Asia* (London: W.W. Norton & Company, 1982).

Brauer, Carl M. *Presidential Transitions: Eisenhower Through Reagan* (Oxford: Oxford University Press, 1986).

Brauer, Jurgen. 'Military Investments and Economic Growth in Developing Nations'. *Economic Development and Cultural Change*, 39, 4 (1991): 873–874.

Brazinsky, Gregg. *Nation Building in South Korea: Koreans, Americans and the Making of a Democracy* (Chapel Hill, NC: University of North Carolina Press, 2007).

Brown, Seyoum. *Faces of Power* (New York: Columbia University Press, 1968).

Browne, Stephen. *Foreign Aid in Practice* (New York: New York University Press, 1990).

Burnett, Stanton H. *Investing in Security Economic Aid for Noneconomic Purposes* (Washington, DC: Center for Strategic and International Studies (CSIS), 1992).

Buzan, Barry. *People, States and Fear: The National Security Problem in International Relations* (Brighton: Wheatsheaf, 1983).

Carleton, D., and M. Stohl. 'The Foreign Policy of Human Rights: Rhetoric and Reality from Jimmy Carter to Ronald Reagan'. *Human Rights Quarterly*, 7, 2 (1985): 205–229.

— 'The Role of Human Rights in U.S. Foreign Assistance Policy: A Critique and Reappraisal'. *American Journal of Political Science* 31 (1987): 1003–1018.

Castle, Timothy N. *At War in the Shadow of Vietnam: US Military Aid to the Royal Lao Government, 1955–1975* (New York: Columbia University Press, 1993).

Chandler, David. *Empire in Denial: The Politics of State Building* (London: Pluto Press, 2006).

— *International Statebuilding: The Rise of Post-Liberal Governance* (New York: Routledge, 2010).

Childress, Michael. *The Effectiveness of US Training Efforts in Internal Defense and Development* (Santa Monica, CA: RAND Corporation, 1995).

Colby, William E. *Lost Victory: A Firsthand Account of America's Sixteen-Year Involvement in Vietnam* (Chicago, IL: Contemporary Books, 1989).

Conboy, Kenneth, and James Morrison, *Feet to the Fire: CIA Covert Operations in Indonesia, 1957-1958.* (Annapolis, MD: U.S. Naval Institute Press, 1999).

Conteh-Morgan, Earl. *American Foreign Aid and Global Power Projection* (Aldershot: Dartmouth Press, 1990).

Cummings, Bruce. *Dominion from Sea to Sea: Pacific Ascendency and American Power* (New Haven, CT: Yale University Press, 2009).

Dacy, Douglas C. *Foreign Aid, War, and Economic Development: South Vietnam, 1955–1975* (Cambridge: Cambridge University Press, 1986).

Deibel, Terry L., and John Lewis Gaddis, eds. *Containing the Soviet Union: A Critique of US Policy* (Washington, DC: Pergamon-Brassey's, 1987).

Deutsch, Karl W. *Nationalism and Social Communication: An Inquiry into the Foundations of Nationalism* (Cambridge, MA: Technology Press, and New York: John Wiley & Sons, 1953).

Deutsch, Karl W., and William J. Foltz. *Nation-Building* (New York: Atherton Press, 1966).

Divine, R. A. *Eisenhower and the Cold War* (Oxford: Oxford University Press, 1981).

Duiker, William J. *US Containment Policy and the Conflict in Indochina* (Stanford, CA: Stanford University Press, 1994).

Eberstadt, Nick. *U.S. Foreign Aid Policy: A Critique* (New York: Foreign Policy Association, 1990).

Edwards, Peter. *Crises and Commitments* (Sydney: Allen and Unwin, 1992).

Ekbladh, David. *The Great American Mission: Modernization and the Construction of an American World Order* (Princeton, N.J.: Princeton University Press, 2009).

Etzold, Thomas H., and John Lewis Gaddis. eds. *Containment: Documents on American Policy and Strategy, 1945–1950* (New York: Columbia University Press, 1978).

Fukuyama, Francis. 'Soviet Strategy in the Third World'. In *The Soviet Union and the Third World: The Last Three Decades,* eds. A. Korbonski and F. Fukuyama (Ithaca: Cornell University Press, 1987), pp. 24–45.

Fulbright, J. William. *The Arrogance of Power* (New York: Random House, 1966).

Gaddis, John Lewis. *Strategies of Containment: A Critical Appraisal of American National Security Policy During the Cold War* (New York: Oxford University Press, 2005).

— *The United States and the End of the Cold War* (New York: Oxford University Press, 1992).

Garthoff, R. L. 'Assessing the Adversary: Estimates by the Eisenhower Administration of Soviet Intentions and Capability'. *Brookings Occasional Papers* (Washington: Brookings Institution, 1991).

George, A. L. *Presidential Decision Making and Foreign Policy: The Effective Use of Information and Advice* (Boulder, CO: Westview, 1980).

George, A. L., and G. A. Craig. *Force and Statecraft: Diplomatic Problems of Our Time* (New York: Oxford University Press, 1983).

George, A. L., et al. *The Limits of Coercive Diplomacy: Cuba, Laos, Vietnam* (Boston: Little, Brown & Co., 1971).

Graebner, N., ed. *The National Security: Its Theory and Practice 1945–1960* (Oxford: Oxford University Press, 1986).

Graves, Ernest, and Steven A. Hildreth, eds. *U.S. Security Assistance: The Political Process* (Lexington, MA: Lexington Books, 1985).

Grimmett, R. 'The Role of Security Assistance in Historical Perspective'. In *US Security Assistance: The Political Process*, ed. E. Graves and S. Hildreth (Lexington, MA: Lexington Books, 1985).

Guess, George M. *The Politics of United States Foreign Aid* (New York: St. Martin's Press, 1987).

Gurr, Ted Robert. *Why Men Rebel* (Princeton, NJ: Princeton University Press, 1970).

Halberstam, David. *The Best and the Brightest* (New York: Random House, 1972).

Hall, D. G. E. *A History of South-East Asia,* 4th edn (New York: St Martin's Press, 1981).

Halperin, Morton H., Priscilla Clapp and Arnold Kanter, *Bureaucratic Politics and Foreign Policy* (Washington, DC: Brookings Institution Press, 1974)

Heinrichs, Waldo. 'Lyndon B. Johnson: Change and Continuity'. In *Lyndon Johnson Confronts the World: American Foreign Policy 1963–1968*, ed. Warren I. Cohen and Nancy Bernkopf Tucker (Cambridge: Cambridge University Press, 1994), pp. 9–30.

Hilsman, Roger. *To Move a Nation: The Politics of Foreign Policy in the Administration of John F. Kennedy* (Garden City, NY: Doubleday, 1967).

Hoffman, Stanley. 'The Acceptability of Military Force', in *Force in Modern Societies*, Adelphi Paper no. 102 (London: International Institute of Strategic Studies, 1975).

Hook, Steven W. *National Interest and Foreign Aid* (Boulder, CO: Lynne Rienner, 1995).

Hoopes, Townsend. *The Limits of Intervention* (New York: W. W. Norton & Co., 1987).

— *The Devil and John Foster Dulles* (Boston, MA: Little, Brown and Company, 1973).

Hovey, H. A. *United States Military Assistance: A Study of Policies and Practices* (New York: Praeger, 1965).

Immerman, Richard H. '"A Time in the Tide of Men's Affairs": Lyndon Johnson and Vietnam'. In *Lyndon Johnson Confronts the World: American Foreign Policy 1963–1968*, ed. Warren I. Cohen and Nancy Bernkopf Tucker (Cambridge: Cambridge University Press, 1994), pp. 57–98.

— *The CIA in Guatemala: The Foreign Policy of Intervention* (Austin, TX: University of Texas Press, 1985).

Janowitz, Morris. *Military Institutions and Coercion in the Developing Nations* (Chicago, IL: University of Chicago Press, 1977).

Jenkins, Tricia. *The CIA in Hollywood: How the Agency Shapes Film and Television* (Austin, TX: University of Texas Press, 2012).

Jervis, Robert. 'Security Regimes'. *International Organization,* 36 (Spring 1982).

Johnson, John J., ed. *The Role of the Military in Underdeveloped Countries* (Princeton, NJ: Princeton University Press, 1962).

Jordan, Amos A., Jr, *Foreign Aid and the Defense of Southeast Asia* (New York: Praeger, Inc., 1962).

Kahin, Audrey and George McTurhan Kahin, *Subversion as Foreign Policy: The Secret Eisenhower and Dulles Debacle in Indonesia* (Seattle, WA: University of Washington Press, 1997).

Kahin, George McTurnan, and John Wilson Lewis. *The United States in Vietnam* (New York: The Dial Press, 1967).

Karnow, Stanley. *In Our Image* (New York: Random House, 1989).

— *Vietnam: A History* (New York: Penguin Books, 1984).

Katz, Mark N., ed. *The USSR and Marxist Revolutions in the Third World* (Cambridge: Cambridge University Press, 1990).

Kaufman, Burton I. *Trade and Aid: Eisenhower's Foreign Economic Policy 1953–1961* (Baltimore, MD: Johns Hopkins University Press, 1982).

Kerkvliet, Benedict J. *The Huk Rebellion: A Study of Peasant Revolt in the Philippines* (Berkeley, CA: University of California Press, 1977).

Kinnard, D. *President Eisenhower and Strategy Management: A Study in Defense Politics* (Lexington, KY: The University Press of Kentucky, 1977).

Kissinger, Henry A. *Years of Upheaval* (Boston, MA: Little, Brown & Co., 1982).

— *White House Years* (Boston, MA: Little, Brown & Co., 1979).

Klare, Michael T., and Peter Kornbluh, eds. *Low Intensity Warfare* (New York: Pantheon, 1988).

Klare, Michael T., ed. *Supplying Repression: U.S. Support for Authoritarian Regimes Abroad* (Washington, DC: Institute for Policy Studies, 1981).

Kolko, Gabriel, and Joyce Kolko. *The Limits of Power: The World and United States Foreign Policy, 1945–1954* (New York: Harper and Row, 1972).

— *Confronting the Third World: United States Foreign Policy 1945–1980* (New York: Pantheon Books, 1988).

Krause, Keith. 'Military Statecraft: Power and Influence in Soviet and American Arms Transfer Relationships' *International Studies Quarterly,* 35 (1991): 313–336.

— 'Insecurity and State Formation in the Global Military Order: The Middle Eastern Case'. Paper presented at annual meeting of the International Studies Association (ISA), Chicago, Illinois, February 1995. Photocopy.

Krause, K., and M. C. Williams. 'Broadening the Agenda of Security Studies: Politics and Methods', *Mershon International Studies Review* 40 (1996): 229–254.

— 'From Strategy to Security: Foundations of Critical Security Studies'. Paper presented at the annual meeting of the International Studies Association (ISA), Chicago, Illinois, February 1995. Photocopy.

LaFeber, Walter. 'Johnson, Vietnam, and Tocqueville'. In *Lyndon Johnson Confronts the World: American Foreign Policy 1963–1968,* ed. Warren I. Cohen and Nancy Bernkopf Tucker (Cambridge: Cambridge University Press, 1994), pp. 41–56.

Laird, Robbin F. 'Soviet Arms Trade with the Non-communist Third World'. In *Soviet Foreign Policy in a Changing World,* ed. Robbin F. Hoffman and Erik P. Laird (New York: Aldine, 1986).

Latham, Michael E. *Modernization as Ideology: American Social Science and "Nation Building" in the Kennedy Era* (Chapel Hill, NC: University of North Carolina Press, 2000).

Leffler, Melvyn. *A Preponderance of Power: National Security, The Truman Administration, and the Cold War* (Stanford, CA: Stanford University Press, 1992).

— 'What is Meant by National Security?' *Journal of American History* (1990): 77, 1: 143–153.

— 'The American Conception of National Security and the Beginnings of the Cold War, 1945–48'. Working Paper, International Security Studies Program, the Wilson Center, Washington, DC. 1983.

Light, Margot. *The Soviet Theory of International Relations* (Brighton: Wheatsheaf, 1988).

MacDonald, Douglas J. 'Communist Bloc Expansion in the Early Cold War: Challenging Realism, Refuting Revisionism', *International Security* 20, 3 (Winter 1995/96): 152–188.

MacFarlane, S. Neil. *Superpower Rivalry and 3rd World Radicalism: The Idea of National Liberation* (Baltimore, MD: The Johns Hopkins University Press, 1985).

Maclear, Michael. *The Ten Thousand Day War: Vietnam: 1945–1975* (New York: Avon, 1981).

McKinlay, R. D., and A. Mughan, *Aid and Arms to the Third World* (London: Frances Pinter, 1984).

MccGwire, Michael. *Perestroika and Soviet National Security* (Washington, DC: The Brookings Institution, 1991).

— *Military Objectives in Soviet Foreign Policy* (Washington, DC: The Brookings Institution, 1987).

McMahon, Robert J. 'Towards Disillusionment and Disengagement in South Asia'. In *Lyndon Johnson Confronts the World: American Foreign Policy 1963–1968*, ed. Warren I. Cohen and Nancy Bernkopf Tucker (Cambridge: Cambridge University Press, 1994), pp. 135–172.

McNamara, Robert. *The Essence of Security: Reflections in Office* (New York: Harper and Row, 1968).

— *In Retrospect* (New York: Random House, 1995).

Melanson, R. A., and D. Mayers *Reevaluating Eisenhower: American Foreign Policy in the 1950s* (Urbana, IL: University of Illinois Press, 1987).

Millikan, Max F. *American Foreign Aid: Strategy For The 1970's* (New York: Foreign Policy Association, 1969).

Morgenthau, Hans. 'Preface to a political theory of foreign aid'. In *Why Foreign Aid?* ed. Robert A. Goldwin (Chicago, IL: Rand McNally, 1963).

Morss, E., and V. Morss. *US Foreign Aid: An Assessment of New and Traditional Development Strategies* (Boulder, CO: Westview Press, 1982).

Mosley, Paul. *Foreign Aid, Its Defense and Reform* (Lexington, KY: University Press of Kentucky, 1987).

Muscat, Robert J. *Thailand and The United States: Development, Security, and Foreign Aid* (New York: Columbia University Press, 1990).

Nelson, Joan M. *Aid, Influence, and Foreign Policy* (New York: Macmillan, 1968).

Neumann, Stephanie. 'Aid, Arms and Superpowers'. *Foreign Affairs*, 66 (1988): 1044–1066.

Newman, John M. *JFK and Vietnam* (New York: Warner Books, 1992).

O'Neill, Robert. 'Western Security Policy towards the Third World'. In *The West and the Third World,* ed. Robert O'Neill and R. J. Vincent (Basingstoke: Macmillan, 1990), pp. 208–223.

Pach, Chester J. *Arming the Free World: The Origins of US Military Assistance Programs 1945–1960* (Chapel Hill, NC: University of North Carolina Press, 1991).

-- 'Military Assistance and American Foreign Policy', in Michael A. Barnhart (ed.), *Congress and United States Foreign Policy: Controlling the Use of Force in the Nuclear Age* (Albany, NY: SUNY Press, 1987).

Packenham, Robert A. *Liberal America and the Third World* (Princeton, NJ: Princeton University Press, 1973).

Paterson, Thomas G. *Meeting the Communist Threat: America's Cold War History* (New York: Oxford University Press, 1988).

Petersen, Howard Charles. *Needed: A New Foreign Aid Policy* (New York: Committee on Economic Development, 1957).

Poe, Steven C. 'Human Rights and Aid Allocation under Ronald Reagan and Jimmy Carter', *American Journal of Political Science* 36, 1 (1992): 147–167.

— 'Human Rights and US Foreign Aid: A Review of Quantitative Studies and Suggestions for Future Research', *Human Rights Quarterly* 12 (1990): 499–512.

Prados, John. *Presidents' Secret Wars* (New York: William Morrow, 1986).

Pye, Lucian W. *Politics, Personality, and Nation Building: Burma's Search for Identity* (New Haven, CT: Yale University Press, 1962).

— 'The Politics of Southeast Asia', in G. Almond and A. Coleman (eds), *The Politics of the Developing Areas* (Princeton, NJ: Princeton University Press, 1960).

Reeves, Julie. *Culture and International Relations: Narratives, natives and tourists* (New York: Routledge, 2004).

Riddell, Roger C. *Foreign Aid Reconsidered* (Baltimore, MD: The Johns Hopkins University Press, 1987).

Rosenau, William. *U.S. Internal Security Assistance to South Vietnam: Insurgency, Subversion and Public Order* (New York: Routledge, 2005).

Rostow, W. W. *Eisenhower, Kennedy and Foreign Aid* (Austin, TX: University of Texas Press, 1985).

— *The Diffusion of Power: An Essay in Recent History* (New York: Macmillan, 1972).

— *Politics and the Stages of Growth* (Cambridge: Cambridge University Press, 1971).

— *The Stages of Economic Growth* (Cambridge: Cambridge University Press, 1960).

Rubinstein, Alvin Z. *Soviet Policy toward Turkey, Iran and Afghanistan, the Dynamics of Influence,* (Westport, CT: Praeger Publishers,1982).

— *Red Star on the Nile: The Soviet–Egyptian Influence Relationship since the June War* (Princeton, NJ: Princeton University Press, 1977).

Schlesinger, Arthur M. *A Thousand Days: John F. Kennedy in the White House* (Boston, MA: Houghton Mifflin, 1965).

Schoenbaum, Thomas J. *Waging Peace and War: Dean Rusk in the Truman, Kennedy and Johnson Years* (New York and London: Simon and Schuster, 1988).

Schwarz, Benjamin C. *American Counterinsurgency Doctrine and El Salvador: The Frustrations of Reform and the Illusions of Nation Building* (Santa Monica, CA: RAND Corporation, 1991).

Sestanovich, Stephen. 'The Third World in Soviet Foreign Policy, 1955–1985'. In *The Soviet Union and the Third World: The Last Three Decades,* ed. A. Korbonski and F. Fukuyama (Ithaca, NY: Cornell University Press, 1987), pp. 1–23.

Shafer, D. *Deadly Paradigms: The Failure of US Counterinsurgency Policy* (Leicester:

Leicester University Press, 1988).

Sheth, D. L. 'Nation-Building in Multi-Ethnic Societies: The Experience of South Asia'. *Alternatives* 14 (1989): 379–388.

Shils, Edward. 'The Military in the Political Development of New States', in John J. Johnson (ed.), *The Role of the Military in Underdeveloped Countries* (Princeton, NJ: Princeton Univerity Press, 1962).

Simpson, Bradley R. *Economists with Guns: Authoritarian Development and U.S.–Indonesian Relations, 1960–1968* (Stanford, CA: Stanford University Press, 2008).

Smart, Lyman F., ed. *Proceedings: Regional Conference on Institution Building* (Logan, UT: Utah State University, 1970).

Smith, Tony. *America's Mission: The United States and the Worldwide Struggle for Democracy in the Twentieth Century* (Princeton, NJ: Princeton University Press, 1994).

Smolansky, O. M., and B. M. Smolansky. *The USSR and Iraq: The Soviet Quest for Influence* (Durham and London: Duke University Press, 1991).

Stauffer, Robert Burton. *Nation-Building in a Global Economy: The Role of the Multinational Corporation* (Beverly Hills, CA: Sage Publications, 1973).

Taylor, Maxwell. *Uncertain Trumpet* (New York: Harper & Bros., 1959).

Tomasevsky, Katarina. *Development Aid and Human Rights* (New York: St. Martin's Press, 1989).

Tucker, Nancy Bernkopf. 'Threats, Opportunities, and Frustrations in East Asia'. In *Lyndon Johnson Confronts the World: American Foreign Policy 1963–1968*, ed. Warren I. Cohen and Nancy Bernkopf Tucker (Cambridge: Cambridge University Press, 1994), pp. 99–134.

UNESCO, Office of the Regional Adviser for Social Sciences in Asia and the Pacific. *Dynamics of National-Building* (Bangkok: UNESCO Regional Office for Education in Asia and the Pacific, 1983).

Valkenier, Elizabeth K. *The Soviet Union and the Third World: An Economic Bind* (New York: Praeger, 1983).

Van den Ham, A. P. 'Development cooperation and Human Rights: Indonesian-Dutch Aid Controversy'. *Asian Survey*, 33, 5 (1993), 531–539.

Welch, W. *American Images of Soviet Foreign Policy* (New Haven: Yale University Press, 1970).

Westad, Odd Arne. *The Global Cold War: Third World Interventions and the Making of Our Times* (Cambridge: Cambridge University Press, 2005).

Wolpin, Miles D. *America Insecure: Arms Transfers, Global Interventionism, and the Erosion of National Security* (Jefferson, NC: McFarland & Co., 1991).

Wood, Robert Everett. *From Marshall Plan to Debt Crisis: Foreign Aid and Development Choices in the World Economy* (Berkeley, CA: University of California Press, 1986).

Wurfel, David. *Filipino Politics: Development and Decay* (Ithaca, NY: Cornell University Press, 1988).

Yergin, Daniel. *Shattered Peace: The Origins of the Cold War* (New York: Penguin Books, 1990).

Young, Crawford. *The African Colonial State in Comparative Perspective* (New Haven, CT: Yale University Press, 1994).

Zimmerman, Robert F. *Dollars, Diplomacy, and Dependency: Dilemmas of US Economic Aid* (Boulder, CO: Lynne Rienner Publishers, 1993).

Unpublished archival resources

Dwight D. Eisenhower Library Collections

National Security File

White House Office, NSC Staff Papers
  Operations Coordinating Board (OCB) Central File

White House Office, Office of the Staff Secretary (Goodpaster) File

White House Office, Office of the Special Assistant for National Security Affairs (OSANSA) File
  Records
  National Security Council Series (Subject Subseries; Policy Papers Subseries; Briefing Notes Subseries)

Ann Whitman File
  Dulles-Herter Series
  National Security Council Series (Meetings and Memoranda Subseries)

John Foster Dulles File
  White House Memo Series
  Chronological Series
  Subject Series

President's Citizen Advisers on the Mutual Security Program, Records, 1956–57

Draper Committee File

John F. Kennedy Library Collections

National Security File
  Meetings and Memoranda Series
  Departments and Agencies Series
  Country File

Records of the Committee to Strengthen the Security of the Free World (Clay Committee)

Lyndon B. Johnson Library Collections

National Security File
  National Security Council Meeting Series
  Subject Series
  National Intelligence Estimates Series
  Country File

Confidential File
  Subject Series
  Mutual Security File

Administrative Histories

National archives

RG 59 Department of State
RG 273 National Security Council
    Operations Coordinating Board

Interviews

The Hon. Herbert Brownell, former Attorney General, at his New York Office (April 1993).

The Hon. William Bundy, Former Assistant Secretary of State for Far East Affairs, at the US Naval Academy, Annapolis, Maryland (June 1995).

Tran Ngoc Chau, Former South Vietnamese Assemblyman and Ambassador, Coordinator of Revolutionary Development Cadres, at the University of Colorado, Boulder, Colorado (June 1996).

The Hon. William E. Colby, Former Director of the Central Intelligence Agency, by Telephone (November 1995 and December 1995).

Major Steven E. Courtney, Historian, US Special Operations Command, at Reston, Virginia (November 1995).

The Hon. C. Douglas Dillon, Former Assistant Secretary of State for Economic Affairs and Secretary of the Treasury, at his New York office (May 1994).

General Andrew J. Goodpaster, former Special Staff Secretary to President Eisenhower, former NATO Commander, at his Washington, DC Office, April 1993 and by telephone (October 1993).

The Hon. Townsend Hoopes, former Undersecretary of Defence for International Security Affairs, at Bethesda, Maryland (April 1993 and July 1994).

Professor Walt W. Rostow, former Chairman of the Policy Planning Council, Department of State under Kennedy, former Special Assistant for National Security Affairs under Johnson, at his Austin, Texas office (March 1993 and October 1993, and by telephone, January 1994 and March 1996).

Dr Michael Tolle, former Project Officer, CORDS, at the University of Colorado, Boulder, Colorado (June 1996).

Index

EU authorised representative for GPSR:
Easy Access System Europe, Mustamäe tee 50,
10621 Tallinn, Estonia
gpsr.requests@easproject.com

www.ingramcontent.com/pod-product-compliance
Lightning Source LLC
Chambersburg PA
CBHW050607280326
41932CB00016B/2942